The Political Campaign Handbook

The Political Campaign Handbook

Media, Scheduling, and Advance

Arnold Steinberg

Lexington Books
D.C. Heath and Company
Lexington, Massachusetts
Toronto   London

Library of Congress Cataloging in Publication Data

Steinberg, Arnold.
   Political campaign handbook.

   Includes index.
   1. Campaign management—Handbooks, manuals, etc. I. Title.
JF2112.C3S73   329'.01   75-43130
ISBN 0-669-00481-2

Published simultaneously in Canada

Printed in the United States of America

International Standard Book Number: 0-669-00481-2

Library of Congress Catalog Card Number: 75-43130

Contents

List of Figures

List of Exhibits

Preface

This handbook emphasizes the political campaign's principal means of marketing the candidate—media (generating news and purchasing advertising) and scheduling (personal appearances and resulting news coverage). Part I provides an overview of the marketing process and explains the necessity for campaign management, a subject discussed more extensively elsewhere.[a] Part II explains how reaching voters through news and advertising requires a unified media strategy. The chapters stress servicing the news media, especially through media-oriented scheduling, news releases, and news conferences; advertising and direct mail techniques are surveyed briefly. Part III explains how scheduling, as a marketing tool, requires criteria and standards to determine the composition of the candidate's schedule, as well as certain mechanics and techniques. Advance work is considered an extension of scheduling, if activities are advanced by mail and telephone; it is treated as a separate topic if an advance man visits the site before the candidate's visit.

Although media, scheduling, and advance are separate subjects, the effective campaign must integrate them. The aspiring campaign news director or press aide must understand scheduling and advance; similarly, the scheduler or advance man must understand media. The material presented is both simple and advanced, hopefully to provide a valuable reference guide for both novice and sophisticated political operatives. Obviously, any campaign handbook, even one limited to media, scheduling, and advance, must omit extended discussion of many points. This handbook's goal is to discuss the most important and timely topics, with a minimum of repetition. Some overlap is inevitable, and the repetition is intentional—for clarity and emphasis.

Several assumptions are apparent throughout this book. First, media, scheduling, and advance do not operate in a void, but reflect overall campaign management and strategy. Second, they are interdependent. Third, they must consider the real world, including the increasingly apathetic electorate and the diverse, and sometimes erratic, nature of the news media and individual reporters. Fourth, the principles outlined here can apply to different levels of campaigns; only, the mode of implementation changes. Although some material is clearly irrelevant to a limited or local campaign, most of the suggested guidelines can be adapted to any campaign.

The successful campaign news director or tour director (scheduler) can serve the candidate's interest most effectively if he considers the perspec-

---

[a] See Arnold Steinberg, *Political Campaign Management: A Systems Approach* (Lexington, Mass.: Lexington Books, D.C. Heath, 1976).

tive of those outside the campaign. The single most significant problem common to campaign managers, news directors, or tour directors is a failure to perceive that most voters and many reporters are not very interested in politics, let alone the specific campaign. The methodology and techniques presented here are of limited use unless they are applied within that broad perspective. The candidate must have confidence in the news and tour directors, but that confidence is misplaced if their operations reflect the insulated thinking of campaign staff and volunteers.

**Part I
Marketing the Candidate**

Introduction to Part I

The primary concern of Part I is the marketing function common to any political campaign. Marketing utilizes the media to generate news and to purchase advertising time and space. Marketing is also a product of the candidate's schedule and its media orientation. Efficient scheduling requires attentiveness to detail; in major campaigns, advance means that an advance staff visits the scene of events to review preparations in advance of the candidate's visit.

Media, scheduling, and advance are interrelated components of the marketing function. Marketing must be integrated into systematic campaign management, and as discussed in Chapter 1, the principles of such management will apply to any campaign, small or large, with only the means of implementation differing. The methodology of media, scheduling, and advance (Chapter 2) must be understood as a delineation of the marketing function. Effective political campaign management presupposes that the campaign is a marketing organization.

1 Political Campaign Management

Any political campaign organization must cope with the turbulent and changing political environment. This environment is a product of many factors that range from the nature of government and politics to the ethical consensus within society. The political campaign manager must operate within the legal limits defined by relevant legislation. The campaign does not exist in a vacuum; it operates within an environment of local, statewide, perhaps national, and even international trends and events. These *macro-factors*—as well as the *macro-political* factors represented by the structure of political parties, changing characteristics of the population and registered voters (demographics), and shifts in public opinion and political preference—impose constraints and present opportunities at the managerial level. A major component of the political environment is the media, which can be decisive in major campaigns.

The management task is to cope with the political environment.[a] At different levels of campaigning the management task has different practical implications. These implications are reflected in the approach to media, scheduling, and advance.

The Management Task

The objective of most political campaigns is electoral victory. Management achieves victory by adapting the campaign to the political environment. Two divergent but essential forces are at work in the adaptive process: the need to separate or divide the campaign organization into geographical, functional, and structural divisions and the need to unite these divisions into a unified whole. The need to focus particular campaign activity, which is accomplished by specialization of task, is called *differentiation*. The consequent need to unite the campaign's operating divisions, including its various committees and affiliated (or support) groups, which insures consistency and unity of purpose, is called *integration*. Without differentiation, the campaign cannot be efficiently divided into press, scheduling, or

---

[a] Many campaign managers approach each campaign as if it exists independent of the environment. For a more complete discussion of the political environment and its relationship to campaign management, see the author's companion volume, *Political Campaign Management: A Systems Approach* (Lexington, Mass.: Lexington Books, D.C. Heath, 1976).

5

precinct work; or into state, regional, county or local units; or into support groups composed of doctors, veterans, or teachers. Without integration the campaign is nothing more than an uncoordinated, chaotic collection of people and resources.

Managing any organization entails several basic elements—planning, organizing, staffing, directing, and controlling. The management of a political campaign entails unique complications. First, management principles must be implemented within or despite a varying ideological context. Issues, ideas, philosophy, and even dogma can interfere with the management process, but they are a real part of political campaigns. Second, the campaign has a short time span. Goals and subordinate goals must be defined carefully to relate to electoral victory. The slim margin of error is exaggerated only by the compensating miscalculations of the opponent. Third, the campaign organization must utilize both paid staff and volunteer participants. Even in a major presidential campaign, the total (hundreds) of paid staff is a tiny fraction of the campaign's volunteer ranks.

The systems view of political campaign management suggests that the campaign is an open system that affects, and is affected by, the political environment. As an open system that is a product of, and must relate to, the world within which it functions, the political campaign operates within an environmental suprasystem. As a system, the political campaign organization has five subsystems:

1. The *structural* subsystem includes the campaign organizational chart, job descriptions, the authority attached to these positions, and task divisions (finance, scheduling, precinct, and so forth) within the campaign. This subsystem includes the structural means devised to facilitate communication, coordination, and integration.

2. The *psychosocial* subsystem includes the personality, temperament, behavior, and motivation of the candidate, manager, staff, and volunteers. These behavioral factors, which have received insufficient attention in the past, are especially important in modest volunteer-intensive campaigns.

3. The *goals and values* subsystem relates the goals and values of the candidate, manager, staff, and volunteers to the campaign's goals and values and recognizes the need to "fuse" these goals and relate them to those of the electorate.

4. The *technical* subsystem is exemplified by the professional and specialized knowledge required in the campaign. This book is primarily concerned with those techniques, methods, and logistics, as they pertain to media, scheduling, and advance.

5. The *managerial* subsystem is the campaign strategy, as influenced by,

and determinant of, other parts of the campaign. This subsystem coordinates the other subsystems and relates the campaign to the candidate.

It is a misconception to believe that the systematic principles of political campaign management apply only to large-scale, well-financed national campaigns. Each campaign must define and adapt to its own political environment. Mastering the methodology of media, scheduling, and advance will not supplant the need for a plan or strategy unique to each campaign. Competent staff and dedicated volunteers require managerial direction. The most elaborate presidential campaign will disintegrate without a strategy. The local campaign operating on a limited budget can win with the optimum strategy.[b]

Levels of Campaigning

This book proposes and defines three fundamental levels of campaigning. Additional distinctions could be made, but these divisions indicate the truism that any campaign must establish priorities carefully and act to achieve those priorities rationally. The *A Level* campaign is a national campaign to nominate or elect a president or vice president. The *B Level* campaign is a statewide effort to nominate or elect a U.S. senator, governor, or major statewide official. The *C Level* campaign is a local campaign to nominate or elect a candidate for assembly, state senate, board of education, city council, or Congress. These three levels are not discrete, as indicated by *modified* definitions (Exhibit 1-1) that provide a useful overview of the budgetary and staffing implications of different levels of campaigning.

The difference between levels of campaigning is illustrated by studying the number of staff members involved in media, scheduling, and advance. In the smallest campaign, a single individual may be the campaign's spokesperson who not only oversees all contacts with the media but also researches the issues and writes the candidate's speeches and literature. This talented individual could also prepare the campaign's newspaper advertisements. In larger campaigns, research, advertising, and speechwriting are usually not part of the news or press operation. The news or press secretary, as the campaign spokesperson is usually called, concen-

---

[b] The systems view is as much a method of doing things, applied in this book to media, scheduling, and advance, as it is an analytical framework for analyzing and managing political campaigns. Campaign strategy formulated in this context considers not only the short-term, immediate, or isolated impact of a decision, action, or statement by the candidate, but its related and indirect effects on the entire campaign. For further discussion, see Arnold Steinberg, *Political Campaign Management: A Systems Approach* (Lexington, Mass.: Lexington Books, D. C. Heath, 1976).

Exhibit 1-1
Levels of Campaigning

Office Sought	Budget[a]	Staff[b]
Level A (National):		
President or vice president.	Millions or tens of millions of dollars.	100+ at general election level.
Level A (Modified):		
May include large-scale, well-financed campaigns for senator or governor in large states (California and New York, possibly Ohio, Illinois, Pennsylvania, Texas, Florida).	$500,000+ for primary $1,250,000+ for general.[c]	30 to 100.[d]
Level B (Statewide):		
U.S. senator, governor, lt. governor, or other major statewide office.	Hundreds of thousands of dollars; could exceed one million dollars.	10 to 50; average about 20 to 25.[e]
Level B (Modified):		
May include local campaigns for county executive, county supervisor, mayor, or congressman if certain conditions exist.[f]	Can be as expensive as statewide contests.[g]	Can be as fully staffed as statewide contests.
Level C (Local):		
U.S. Congress, state senate or assembly, city council, board of education, or other local office.	Tens of thousands of dollars, usually less than $150,000.	2 to 15; more likely, 4 to 10.

[a]The budget figures apply to each candidate's campaign, not the total of all campaigns for a particular office.

[b]The staff figure includes anyone on the campaign payroll, even if an individual is working "on the road" or in an outlying campaign headquarters.

[c]Certain major statewide contests have greatly exceeded these figures, especially the various New York State campaigns of former Governor Nelson Rockefeller.

[d]The wide variance allows for legal requirements in most states to fund all payroll expenditures from the statewide campaign treasury, although the personnel manage, or are employed by, a local campaign headquarters.

[e]The variance reflects the size of state, deployment of staff as field personnel, or hiring staff in local headquarters. In small states, statewide campaigns that have 40-50 staff members are usually overstaffed.

[f]The condition is that the boundary of the race is contiguous with a media market; for example, a candidate for Supervisor of Los Angeles County (Los Angeles media market) or Nassau or Suffolk Counties (New York City media market). A special case is the smaller media market (1-3 television stations) that is contiguous with 1-4 congressional districts, rather than the many districts contiguous with a major city's media market. Finally, another case is a special election called to fill a vacancy; the local contest receives considerable attention because it is "the only show in town."

[g]An example of cost is an election for Mayor of Los Angeles or New York, or for Los Angeles County Supervisor or Nassau County Executive. These candidates rely on massive budgets and staffs rivaling statewide contests in order to penetrate the numerically large electorate. The big-city media market advertising rates comprise a major portion of the budget.

Exhibit 1-2
Media Tasks and Levels of Campaigning

Media Tasks

1. *Spokesperson*: speak in behalf of candidate and campaign.
2. *Liaison*: contact with all media to handle queries, problems, requests for information and materials (candidate's biography, issue papers, photographs, etc.).
3. *News releases*: create ideas for news releases; write, edit releases; oversee their production (typing, duplication) and delivery (by hand, mail, etc.).
4. *News conferences and visuals*: create ideas for news conferences and visuals (i.e., television-oriented, action events); oversee writing, editing, production, and delivery of related news releases.
5. *Scheduling*: Liaison with scheduling to advise regarding media implications of schedule, assess schedule in terms of publicity value, and help alter schedule to achieve maximum media attention; assure that press gets candidate's complete and accurate schedule promptly and that traveling press is properly serviced.
6. *Traveling with candidate*: provide assistance to candidate in dealing with media; provide drafts of statements and ideas for statements; serve as communications link with campaign headquarters regarding media matters.
7. *Administering news operation*: manage aides, secretaries, clerks; provide for orderly office operation; oversee local campaign committee media activity.
8. *Evaluate and service media*: relate the campaign to appropriate media (e.g., print or electronic, weekly or daily newspapers, radio or television) by making news for each type of media and providing relevant delivery mechanisms (e.g., telephone audio feeds to radio stations).
9. *Strategy and counsel*: propose ideas and counsel candidate and campaign in formulation of strategy and plans to market candidate through media (i.e., issues selected, emphasis, positions taken, frequency and types of statements); handle overall public relations, including tactics (interviews, syndicated columnists, editorials and editorial board meetings, etc.) and guidelines for local campaign committees.
10. *Special projects*: draft and send telegrams to groups (especially when candidate has turned down invitation) and deal with ideas, drafting, writing, and editing of brochures, advertising materials; research for statements and issues papers; speechwriting; media liaison with ethnic radio and press; television debates.

Basic Responsibility	*Special Projects*
Level A (National):	
The ranking person travels with the candidate, is spokesperson, relates to traveling media, and has a key role in strategy and media-oriented scheduling. A large staff, under the direction of the ranking person, deals with other media (publicity) tasks.	Advertising agency oversees advertising; research and speechwriters are separate from press; specialists (consultants and full-time) help with television debates, ethnic media, and other areas.
Level A (Modified):	
No more than ten staff involved in the publicity operation.	Separate advertising agency; at least two research staff members, one full-time writer.
Level B (Statewide):	
Probably 2-6 staff in the publicity operation, including one person who is simply a liaison with the scheduling operation.	Advertising agency retained; research and speechwriting may be combined in a unit (2-4 staff).

Exhibit 1-2 (cont.)

Basic Responsibility	*Special Projects*
Level B (Modified):	
Media operation here or at higher levels emphasizes media-oriented schedule; hence, office management, production of releases, etc. allocated to appropriate staff members.	Major city media markets necessitate advertising agency; research and speechwriting combined.
Level C (Local):	
In most Level C campaigns, the news or press secretary should have at least one assistant to type, aid in production, handle telephone queries, to permit the news staff person to spend some time traveling with the candidate. Although there are no visuals for television, the media operation must meet the servicing demands of local print media, especially weekly newspapers.	With enough advertising, an agency is retained; if insufficient, the campaign must have an in-house capacity; one person may be combination researcher and writer; in a very modest campaign, this person could also handle the entire media function.

trates on making personal contact with local and traveling journalists and administering a larger operation staffed by writers, television and radio specialists, secretaries, typists, and support personnel.[c] (See Exhibit 1-2.)

As each campaign task becomes more complex, the staff assigned to accomplish the task grows to accommodate added specialists. Although campaigns do not differ significantly in what they must do, larger campaigns require more people, each with a narrow focus and specialized responsibility, in order to cope with the relevant political environment. In the properly managed campaign, staff growth results in successive division of functions, tasks and responsibilities, so that each person can get his job done and manage his subordinates. Scheduling and advance, like the media operation or any other aspect of contemporary campaigning, illustrate this principle (Exhibit 1-3).

---

[c] In this book several terms will be used interchangeably. The "press secretary" has long been an accepted description of the spokesperson for the candidate and campaign; this person is almost always the senior person in charge of overall news, public relations, and publicity. Because the term has been interpreted by some to exclude radio and television, many campaigns use more inclusive titles—news secretary, news director, communications director, and the like.

Exhibit 1-3
Scheduling and Advance Tasks and Levels of Campaigning

Scheduling and Advance Tasks

1. *Outside contact*: central contact for all groups extending invitation for candidate, including the candidate's supporters and campaign committees.

2. *Scheduling strategy*: assist in defining criteria to be used in accepting and rejecting invitations, including use of time and media market formulas.

3. *Media oriented scheduling*: emphasize scheduling likely to draw publicity or scheduling specific media entries (e.g., news conferences, interviews, editorial board meetings).

4. *Liaison with press staff*: work closely with news or press secretary to formulate media schedule; schedule specific media entries; handle needs of press, especially traveling press.

5. *Detail scheduling*: research and process all details to assure that candidate's schedule is prompt and that all lodging and travel arrangements are in order for candidate, staff, and press; oversee all relevant correspondence with host groups.

6. *Regrets*: oversee courteous responses to invitations that are rejected as well as letters, telegrams, and messages conveying "regrets"; relate to speakers bureau of surrogates who represent candidate.

7. *Candidate's needs*: simultaneously maximize candidate's exposure time and his private and rest time; relate to his personal and family needs.

8. *Evaluating invitations and making decisions*: provide the campaign manager, scheduling committee, news secretary, and others with detailed evaluation of invitations, in terms of criteria, travel and logistical problems, desired frequency of appearance in area, type of group and audience, etc.

9. *Negotiating and modifying events*: work with groups to agree on a mutually acceptable schedule, especially in terms of the candidate's time, the length of his talk, necessity for, and length of reception, etc.

10. *Creating events*: research events and forums that could offer the candidate a platform, opportunity to meet voters, or needed exposure and then secure invitation; invent events, such as rallies or forums.

Advance Tasks

The presence of an advance staff means that the schedule will be more detailed, and its precise time segments and all logistics will be methodically checked by someone who "advances" the trip (i.e., literally traces the candidate's expected itinerary, route, and movements). The advance man[a] insures that the crowd turnout at every event is maximized in terms of quantity and quality; that the schedule is on time; and that lodging and travel are checked and rechecked.

Scheduling[b]	*Advance*
Level A (National):	
Tour director oversees large scheduling staff of aides, clerks, secretaries; travel desk, use of private plane(s); separate staff sections to coordinate with state committees, plan surrogate speaking programs, etc.	Each event probably advanced by both Secret Service and regular advance person; more than one trip into area before candidate arrives. Advance division is large, headed by chief advance man or director of advance.

Exhibit 1-3 (cont.)

Scheduling[b]	Advance
Level A (Modified):	
Tour or scheduling director oversees staff of 3-6 (not counting advance staff). Individual clerks and secretaries have specific responsibilities within scheduling; only the tour director makes decisions and is on a campaign scheduling committee.	Full-time advance director (probably under scheduling, possibly separate) uses 1-4 full-time advance aides or rotates use of volunteer advance staff.
Level B (Statewide):	
No more than 6 staff members work within scheduling, which may be headed by tour or scheduling director, or scheduling secretary with aides; scheduling may be under a deputy campaign manager. If no advance staff within scheduling operation, there may be only 2 or 3 staff members total.	Advance division usually within scheduling. Stress is on local, volunteer advancing, often based on guidelines and checklists supplied by state headquarters.
Level B (Modified):	
Large budget usually supports several scheduling staff members who often can barely cope with correspondence and volume of requests generated by populous metropolitan area.	Need to generate media and visual coverage often results in use of advance staff to help insure success of event and move candidate quickly through congested areas.
Level C (Local):	
In the extreme case, scheduling secretary is also candidate's personal secretary. Ideally, candidate should have scheduling secretary who has no other responsibilities and who preferably has an aide (who may have other responsibilities). Even at local level, scheduling should emphasize correspondence, written confirmation of events, and attentiveness to detail.	Usually no formal advance; ideally, advance improvised by repeated telephone calls to communicate with hosts, confirm logistics, explore all possible problems. If only one person deals with scheduling, this staff member will probably lack the time for much "telephone advance."

[a]Although an "advance man" can be a woman, the term "advance person" is yet to be accepted.

[b]Someone traveling with the candidate is always in charge of making immediate scheduling decisions that arise in the course of campaigning. In larger campaigns, this person is the *traveling* or *field tour director*; in other campaigns, it may be a ranking or designated candidate's aide; in small campaigns, the person who makes these decisions may also handle news media and other tasks, since the candidate might be accompanied by only one person. The person in charge may be simply the ranking staff member accompanying the candidate.

2 Media, Scheduling, and Advance

Every campaign must communicate effectively with relevant groups of voters. Relevant voters are, or can be, registered to vote for the candidate. Clearly, this implies a much larger universe for a presidential campaign than for a local race. Hence, the strategy to market the candidate and communicate with the voters is necessarily different. As the campaign proceeds from a C Level to a B or A Level, the magnitude of the marketing function is reflected in the size, scope, and specialization of media, scheduling, and advance. At higher levels media is more important, both in terms of generating news, principally through a media oriented schedule, and in terms of purchasing advertising. This book's focus is the methodology of media, scheduling, and advance as part of the marketing function common to any campaign.

The Marketing Function

Any political campaign is a marketing organization whose product is the candidate—that is, his appearance, image, rhetoric, speaking ability, party affiliation, attitudes, habits, and so forth. Even a candidate drawn from the private sector has a "record" that includes, for example, his education, professional achievements, community activities, social contacts, family background, and military service. Each candidate has strong and weak points, and the campaign seeks to exploit the candidate's assets and obscure the liabilities. It may also define and even exaggerate the opposing candidate's deficiencies and avoid discussion of his qualifications.

The campaign manager is a marketing executive seeking to reach relevant groups of voters who are analogous to consumers. The primary method of defining the size of the consumer universe is by spurring voter registration. The manager must relate particular kinds of voters (Exhibit 2-1) to specific demographic attributes. Survey research is the most accurate and reliable method of identifying which groups of voters are most important to reach. Surveys identify the electorate in terms of age, sex, religion, race, national origin, income level, educational background, party registration, and other key characteristics. Surveys measure respondent opinions on issues, recognition and perception of alternative candidates, and voter preference; responses are correlated to important characteristics.

13

Exhibit 2-1
Kinds of Voters

Basis of Individual Voter Preference[a]

1. *Party loyalty*. This voter should be made aware of the candidate's party, and then be the subject of an intensive get-out-the-vote campaign.

2. *Party loyalty and candidate attraction*. This voter was loyal to the party and is still registered in that party, but is, like an increasingly large segment of the electorate, apathetic; hence, the nature and appeal of the candidate must, together with party, be a stimulus.

3. *Ideology*. This voter has a high probability of voter turnout if he perceives the candidate in his own image (either liberal/left wing or conservative/right wing).

4. *Issue(s)*. Based on a single issue or several issues, this voter will support or oppose a candidate, if he is reached on the basis of the predominant issue or issues of concern to him.

5. *Negative*. This voter is so strongly opposed to a candidate, usually an incumbent, that he will support almost any alternative, in some cases, even of another party; but media must be used to show this person that a viable, credible alternative exists; this person may stay at home rather than vote for an alternative candidate who does not have a chance.

6. *Ticket splitter*. This independent voter can vote for one party's candidate for president or governor and another party's candidate for another office; often, the ticket splitter votes for a major candidate whose campaign has had substantial advertising and utilization of television and then votes for candidates of his preferred party for lesser offices; the degree of independence is often indicated by the eclectic approach throughout the ballot.

---

[a]These classifications are neither complete nor discrete. Any campaign must find out which types of voters, in terms of demographic characteristics, fall into these classifications, and the most effective way (e.g., television, direct mail, door-to-door pamphleteering) to reach certain kinds of voters with the information or message most relevant to them. The local level campaign can actually pinpoint types of voters on an individual basis through extensive voter canvassing—telephoning and in person; larger campaigns must make statistical generalizations for these and other classifications. The strategist must ask how much does it cost (in time and money) to reach certain types of voters, and what is the probability that, once reached with an appropriate message or appeal, the voters will (a) opt for the candidate *and* (b) turn out to vote for the candidate on election day.

Although survey research is imperative for Level A and Level B campaigns, as well as many Level C campaigns, modest Level C campaigns can plan strategy without a survey. Unlike the larger campaign, which can target electoral subgroups effectively only by pinpointing priority constituencies, the small campaign can rely more on past voting patterns and behavior, the relative success or failure of prior candidates, and current voting statistics and registration figures. If the electorate is numerically small, relatively homogeneous, and the issues few and easily defined, the manager who is intimately familiar with the area may be able to capitalize on his native background by relying on his judgment, intuition, and the counsel provided by his perceptive associates and personal contacts.

The campaign's marketing function is the process of reaching every voter who should be reached. Every voter cannot be personally reached within the campaign's limited time span; in larger campaigns, the candidate's personal contact with individual voters is statistically insignificant. Conversely, the candidate's individual voter contact can determine the outcome of a very modest Level C campaign. In races with small constituencies, candidates are often so preoccupied with strategic maneuvering and administration of the campaign that they are prevented from concentrating on personal campaigning.

Any campaign must formulate a schedule for its candidate. The principles of scheduling apply to any campaign; only their implementation is different. The number of staff involved in media, scheduling, and advance, as well as their degree of specialization, should reflect the truisms that the higher the level of campaigning, the more important the media (and media-oriented scheduling), and the more important the electronic, rather than printed, media (Exhibit 2-2).

Strategy

The ideal political strategist possesses high native intelligence and the kind of wisdom and shrewdness that reflects campaign experience. The strategist can readily define and evaluate options; by using his resourcefulness and creativity, he can sometimes create additional options. He has the ability to select the optimum course of action quickly, even under the most intense pressure. Yet, some strategists can only conceive and create; they cannot perform detailed work. Sometimes the strategist can act as a catalyst for others, although he is incapable of the methodical work that they do at his behest. Other strategists, because they are products of varied campaign experience, are capable of detailed media or scheduling assignments; they have simply graduated to the higher status of strategist.

No strategy, no matter how brilliant, can succeed unless it is properly implemented by competent staff. Conversely, tactics, procedures, and methodology are of limited use if they are not part of a broad strategic overview, within which they take their rightful subservient role. This handbook of media, scheduling, and advance methodology is like a manual of maneuvers and tactics; this book presents ways of doing things that even if followed scrupulously can be part of a well- or poorly conceived strategy.

The campaign manager is more than an administrator. Like a composer or orchestra conductor, the manager creates and orchestrates a strategy that, like fine music, is ordered and precise. Even its moments of spontaneity and naturalness may reflect planning. As each section of an orchestra, and each musician within the section, has a special role, so each section of the campaign, and each staff member within that section, should contribute uniquely to the campaign goal of electoral victory. When acting

Exhibit 2-2

Marketing through Media and through Scheduling and Advance

Media (News and Advertising)	*Scheduling and Advance*
Level A (National):	
All media are utilized, but television news and television advertising spots dominate marketing. Nearly all news is generated on the campaign trail. Advertising should be allocated on the basis of media markets. Nearly all voters are reached by media, rather than appearances.	Scheduling is primarily media-oriented to generate print media coverage and, more importantly, television news coverage. Advancing stresses crowd turnout and visual (i.e., television) effects of campaigning and the need to accommodate traveling media.
Level A (Modified):	
Electorate is reached principally by generating news and purchasing spot advertising on television stations in media markets throughout the state. Radio and print media advertising should be carefully targeted, rather than all purpose.	Scheduling stresses a media-oriented schedule, but also stresses geographic balance. Advancing stresses minimizing travel time in order to travel as widely and appear as frequently as possible around the state. Individual groups can be important.
Level B (Statewide):	
Television is utilized, but often radio and print media reach voters not reached efficiently or at all by television.	The size of the staff should support an efficient, responsive scheduling operation, with some kind of advance work, so the candidate can move around the state. Individual groups are often important factors, not merely for media value, but for reaching a particular audience.
Level B (Modified):	
The big-city media markets mean the campaign, like statewide efforts, is television oriented, including news and advertising. A variety of other media is pursued aggressively, including transportation, outdoor, weekly newspapers, etc; daily newspapers are important here and at higher levels.	Scheduling emphasizes a minimum number of visual events to generate television coverage. At this level and higher, there is emphasis on news conferences, interviews, meetings with influential publishers and editors. Advance emphasizes tight scheduling, especially making the best of automobile transportation.
Level C (Local):	
Media usually do not include television; perhaps some radio and daily newspapers important if they will cover local race; otherwise, great stress on weeklies, especially for advertising. If race is in a one-party-dominated area or issues are hard to define, identification-type advertising (billboards, bus, signs, etc.) may be effective.	The smaller the campaign, the more people-oriented, rather than media-oriented, the schedule. Advance work is nonexistent in the extreme case, or advance is improvised by telephone verification and follow-up of details. Voters are reached directly by appearances, rather than primarily by media coverage of appearances.

in unison with other staff and volunteers, each participant in the campaign acts meaningfully; by acting alone, the participant is like a musician without an orchestra.

Marketing strategy explains how the campaign can achieve a desired level of identification with the electorate and how it can communicate the candidate's positions on issues to the voters. The electorate's perception of the candidate, not reality, is binding; hence, marketing must always relate to the electorate's perceptions. Marketing strategy in virtually any campaign relies on the candidate's appearances and the media coverage of those appearances, as well as purchased advertising, to reach most voters. Scheduling strategy and media strategy refer to the guidelines established in formulating the candidate's schedule, seeking media coverage, and purchasing particular amounts of space and time to get the candidate's message across to the desired subgroups within the electorate.

Media is the delivery of messages both through communications organizations and by the campaign itself. News, features, columns, interviews, editorials, and the like are part of the news-generating component of campaign marketing. Many identical messages delivered simultaneously through the print and electronic media, billboards, bus and subway advertising, and so forth represent the advertising component of campaign marketing. This book concentrates on newspapers and the electronic or broadcast media[a] (television and radio) rather than on the great variety of additional media available for advertising. Due to the book's space limitations, and also because any major campaign will retain an advertising agency, the emphasis is on generating news rather than purchasing advertising.

Scheduling is the unified process of structuring, administering, planning, and implementing the allocation of the candidate's time. It includes the allocation of the candidate's time into blocks—months, weeks, days, even parts of days—as well as the detailed preparation of the schedule. Media-oriented scheduling means formulating a schedule for maximum media impact. This includes the selection of dates, times, and places for release of statements and particular activities, as well as exploiting opportunities for news conferences, interviews, radio and television tapings, editorial board meetings, and so forth. Advancing is the methodical checking and rechecking of the schedule; it connotes a personal visit by a member of the advance staff to each stop on the schedule. Ideally, the advance person literally advances each step the candidate will be expected to take.

Momentum is the campaign's increasing tempo, reflected in more active, intensive scheduling, greater publicity, accelerated advertising, and

---

[a] The terms electronic or broadcast media are used interchangeably to refer to both television and radio.

more successful fund raising. Because scheduling, advertising, and even generating news are partially controllable, campaign strategy should "pace" scheduling and media activities to graduate a tempo. The campaign must stir a minimum of public interest early, although a significant portion of the electorate will not be interested in the campaign until the final stages. The campaign seeks to generate momentum, but not so fast that it cannot sustain and increase its activity—that is, it does not wish to "peak" too soon.

These concepts are interrelated both as part of the marketing strategy and as complementary parts of the campaign. For example, generating news and purchasing advertising should emphasize the same issues; thus, advertising enhances credibility and retention, and the news coverage enjoys the repetition factor provided by consistent advertising. As advertising increases the candidate's recognition, the advance staff finds it easier to generate large crowds. The advance staff also works to insure a punctual, orderly, and productive schedule that presents a positive image to the traveling journalist and thereby favorably affects his reporting of the campaign. Favorable coverage can spur fund raising, and the increased revenue can support a higher advertising budget. These brief examples illustrate the interdependence of media, scheduling, and advance; generally, a campaign excels in each area, or in none.

**Part II
Media**

Introduction to Part II

Media has two components—news and advertising. The chapters in this section emphasize news rather than advertising, because the former is more closely an internal function of the campaign, and the latter can be contracted to artists, designers, writers, and so forth or entirely to an advertising agency. Chapter 3 distinguishes between media that can be used both for news and advertising and media that can be used only for advertising. This category includes printed matter, direct mail, and other traditional advertising methods. Since some of these methods, especially advertising specialties, are devised within the campaign and do not require media billings (purchase of time and space) that generate commissions for an advertising agency, these methods are usually not budgeted within the advertising component of the campaign budget.

Additional chapters explain the need to service the news media, with specific attention given to campaign policy and fundamental concepts (Chapter 4); creating news releases and types of news releases (Chapter 5); conventional news conferences and visuals (Chapter 6); and a variety of important tasks considered as part of administering the news function (Chapter 7). The final chapter in Part II briefly summarizes advertising and direct mail, both of which, although distinct topics, must be considered along with the news media as part of campaign communications strategy.

3 Media as a Marketing Tool

No campaign can use the media efficiently unless it has a plan to reach a well-defined constituency. Media as a marketing tool presupposes a set of priorities defining the relative importance of subgroups within the electorate. In the sophisticated Level A or Level B campaign, Census Bureau data, historical voting records and patterns, demographics, and current survey research are utilized to profile the voter most likely to support the candidate. This profile is successively modified to describe voters relatively less likely to support the candidate. Media is used as a marketing tool by generating news and purchasing advertising to project a certain image and emphasize particular issues—to reach voters who are most likely to support the candidate if they know who he is or how he stands on issues. Ideally, media should be used to reach those with a higher probability of supporting the candidate before reaching those with a lower probability.

Although the analysis in a Level C campaign may not be as precise, the strategist can still define priority groups of voters. Party registration is an important variable. Area of residence, religion, income level, and other characteristics can also be relevant, depending on the specific race. Sometimes a single variable seems to dominate voting patterns; perhaps with a little effort, the strategist can seek to reach voters who combine two or three characteristics. Once the strategy is formulated, even if based on an extraordinary amount of judgment, intuition, and insight, the manager should make certain that every news conference, brochure, newspaper advertisement, billboard, and any other message conveyed through the news or advertising media is consistent with the campaign strategy.

News and Advertising

Wisdom at the highest levels in the campaign is irrelevant unless the campaign can utilize media effectively. This requires knowledge and understanding of the media, its historical development, customs, traditions, practices, and contemporary nature. Within the campaign organization, it is possible to some degree to delegate advertising responsibilities to an advertising agency, but the task of directly relating the candidate and campaign to the news media is inescapable. Understanding the "news business" means understanding the general technical operation of the nation's daily and weekly newspapers, and its commercial television and commercial radio stations. These categories do not even include the great variety of magazines and ethnic publications; specialized trade, professional, and other journals; educational television and radio stations, and so forth.

Until the 1870s, many daily newspapers were merely organs of party propaganda. Then the growth in the number and circulation of newspapers (16 million by 1900) reflected the nation's economic growth. By 1950 newspaper circulation (54 million) reflected the pervasiveness of the daily newspaper. In terms of political impact, other media also appeared. Theodore H. White has suggested that the magazine reached its peak of political influence in 1940 when *Time, Life, Look* and the *Saturday Evening Post* created Wendell Willkie as the Republican nominee. The importance of radio was symbolized by FDR's fireside chats. Today, radio, like daily newspapers and magazines, is overshadowed by television, whose influence is illustrated by the fact that more than 50,000,000 adult Americans watch one of the network news shows each evening.[a]

The dominance of television hardly applies to the obscure, local campaign that has no hopes of television coverage and could never afford to purchase television advertising. The extreme Level C campaign can aspire to generating a visual story, but it must accept the probability of success as very remote. Even the Level A campaign cannot become obsessed with television, since the other media are useful not only in terms of reaching additional voters and different kinds of voters, but of providing *complementarity*—that is, using diverse media to deliver the same message and thereby achieving repetition and reinforcement, similar to complementarity of news and advertising, in which the voter receives the same campaign message from the news media and from advertising.

Weekly Newspapers

Most weekly newspapers are published on either Wednesday or Thursday; newspapers published two or three times a week can be treated as weeklies or as dailies. Generally, weekly newspapers are advertising oriented; their news coverage emphasizes community activities, including commercial, educational, social, and religious events, rather than politics. They only cover national or state campaigns if there is a local "hook," such as, for example, opening a local campaign headquarters, appointment of a local chairman or coordinator, or the appointment at the national or state level of

[a] See Theodore H. White, *The Making of the President 1960* (New York: Athenum House, 1961; Pocket Books, 1961), p. 107. The interested reader should review all of White's subsequent books on American presidential campaigns because of their particular attention to the role of media.

someone from the area. Typically, campaign coverage is limited to the latter part of the campaign period; in extreme cases, the editor delays any coverage until one or two issues before election and often substitutes an informative profile and photograph for news coverage of campaign events.

Many weeklies do not editorialize on political matters or candidates for fear of offending some readers or advertisers. Often these newspapers are small operations headed by an individual who serves as editor-publisher. Typically, the editor-publisher is grateful for political advertising; even modest campaign advertising can be significant for the small weekly. Such advertising may not lead to an endorsement, but it can secure news coverage. In the extreme case, it may be impossible to secure any news coverage without advertising; the implication is that a modest advertisement placed early to show good faith may inspire the editor to use news releases.

Most weeklies have limited editorial and news staffs; some weeklies have no reporters. Many weeklies either print a news release verbatim or "toss" it. The concise, well-written news release relevant to the weekly's readers has a chance of acceptance; the release that requires editing, cutting, rewriting, and so forth often has no chance of publication. It is frustrating for the competent campaign news director to find that his releases are not published because of the "lowest common denominator" doctrine. Applied to a weekly newspaper, this doctrine rationalizes a policy of running little or no political news on the basis of the deficiencies of the opposition candidate's media operation. The editor, forever fearful of devoting more space to one compaign than to another, devotes little or no space to either. Although one campaign mails or hand delivers relevant, well-written news releases, they are not used because the other campaign sends unacceptable news releases, or none at all.

The readers of weekly newspapers (excepting some significant rural weeklies, especially bi- or tri-weeklies) do not expect much news. They are more interested in advertising; consequently, they may keep the weekly in the home for several days, often throughout the peak shopping period (Thursday through Sunday). Political advertising can be effective if targeted to consumers, housewives, and other special groups. For many Level C campaigns, the weekly newspaper is an excellent advertising vehicle, measured in terms of the quantity and quality of its readership.

Daily Newspapers

Political coverage varies greatly among daily newspapers, and an indication of depth of coverage is whether the newspaper has a full-time political editor or reporter who regularly covers government and politics, not just in election years or during campaigns. The number of political reporters or the willingness of the newspaper to shift other reporters to politics during campaigns also indicates the relative seriousness of the newspaper's commitment to covering politics.

Although few weekly newspapers subscribe to wire or news services, all daily newspapers subscribe to one or more wire or news services. The main wire services are the Associated Press (AP), United Press International (UPI), and Reuters. Newspapers may also be part of chains that include cooperating news services, or they may subscribe to such services if offered to independent newspapers. These services include Gannett News Service (GNS), Copley News Service (CNS), Newhouse Service (NS), and major news services operated by important daily newspapers, including *The New York Times, Washington Star, Chicago Daily News* and *Sun Times*, and the *Los Angeles Times* and *Washington Post*. Many daily newspapers, especially the smaller or suburban dailies, rely on wire and news services and on syndicated columnists (columns that they and other newspapers purchase for a nominal amount from a syndicate) for coverage of national political events. The alert reader can usually spot a wire or news service article, because the symbol is placed at the opening of the article, or occasionally in a credit just below the headline, especially if the writer's name is used (a rarity for wire service stories). Syndicated columns often have the name of the syndicate in small type at the end of the column.

The current trend is toward the survival of a single metropolitan (i.e., citywide) daily newspaper or perhaps two metropolitan newspapers, for each city. In the latter case, one newspaper is published in the morning, the other in the afternoon. Suburban growth has supported additional daily newspapers, some of which are converted weeklies. These newspapers are nonmetropolitan; for some readers, they represent their only daily newspaper, and for other readers, they represent a second daily newspaper, purchased or subscribed to in addition to the metropolitan daily. Although two metropolitan newspapers or even several suburban newspapers may be owned by a single chain or share the same printing plant, editorial and reporting staffs are often independent.

The economics of daily newspaper publishing reflect steadily rising salaries, the continuing influence of a variety of unions, higher cost of newsprint and delivery, and a generally higher cost of doing business. The increased home subscription rates and higher newsstand prices—fifteen cents in most cities and twenty cents in some—lead readers to expect more from their daily newspapers. Daily newspapers are beginning to emphasize local news, especially "people" and "service" articles, at the expense of national and international news. These dailies will rely more on wire and news services for national political news, but are reallocating their overall space allocation in favor of more local coverage. This can mean increased coverage of state and local political campaigns.

Newspapers of the 1970s and 1980s will have electronic newsrooms with unconventional, noiseless, paperless typewriters. As the reporter types the story, it will appear on an electronic screen that can show corrections and changes. The typewriter hooks into a computer memory system that permits the editor to retrieve the story for editing and then permits him to provide typesetting instructions and headlines and finally to see on his screen how the story will look in type. Ideally, the changes in production will not only make it easier for newspapers to run late-breaking stories, but will (unions permitting) result in production economies that would allow greater resources for reporting, possibly including local political news.

The new suburban daily newspapers are successful precisely because they specialize in suburban news. Their news and reporting staffs are larger than weeklies, and they resemble metropolitan dailies, except for their greater reliance on wire and news services. Many metropolitan dailies have daily regional editions—that is, the basic metropolitan daily is modified to include news and advertising for a specific region or part of the greater metropolitan area. In addition, metropolitan dailies also compete with the suburban dailies by publishing a weekly or bi-weekly insert section that features news and advertising for a given region. Newspapers sold or delivered in each region of the newspaper's total market include either the daily modifications, or the weekly or bi-weekly insert, for the particular region. The aggressive campaign media director exploits regional news opportunities offered by suburban dailies and "regionalized" daily newspapers by relating events, activities, speeches, statements, appointments, endorsements, news releases, and so forth to specific regions. Similarly, the advertising program exploits the targeting opportunities in specific regions.

Political news is more vulnerable, in the current era of increasing public apathy and disenchantment toward government, than any other kind of news. Political news is read less than sports, entertainment, or a variety of features. Although campaign advertising is substantial in peak periods, it is less than advertising in the entertainment, consumer/food, or business-finance sections. Moreover, political advertising is generally independent of news coverage; in contrast, the news coverage in entertainment or the food sections attracts and complements advertising. Political activists must understand that many publishers and editors simply do not share their sense of civic mindedness.

Radio Stations

Any radio station with regular newscasts is relevant to the campaign's news operation; the station without news is relevant for advertising only. Radio stations affiliated with the networks (ABC, CBS, NBC, Mutual Broadcasting) or with a group of stations (Group W, Metromedia) generally have larger news operations than other stations. The largest news operations are in stations with an all-news format, especially 24-hour stations; their total news programming requires a large staff of announcers, editors, writers, producers, and field reporters to create ideas for news, search out events, and report what is happening in the media market to minimize the repetition of news reporting.

The station affiliated with a network, group of stations, or news service (e.g., NBC now offers an all-news format) usually has two types of news. The station can pick up a "feed" from the national or regional service, including such services as UPI's audio service for radio stations. The radio station may subscribe or use a certain number of minutes hourly, or a particular hourly newscast supplied by a network; or it may select and edit what it wishes to use, sometimes including national features within its local news programs. Alternatively, the station produces its own ("in-house") news, which is basically a collection of local news, features, sports, and weather. These locally produced newscasts may include national news, but it is based simply on the announcer's reading copy edited from the wire service tickers.

Locally produced newscasts, especially those emphasizing local news rather than wire service copy, are most relevant for Level B and Level C campaigns. In large metropolitan markets, however, it is difficult for many Level C campaigns to receive news coverage, because the station's listening audience is a large media market that includes many local districts, sometimes dozens of congressional, state senate, assembly, and other types of districts. The station will only cover a Level C campaign if (1) its listening audience includes only that district or only a few districts; (2) the election is a special election; or (3) the story is so novel, interesting, and audio (sound) oriented that it can be justified. Also, radio stations in metropolitan markets may cover Level C local politics outside the political season, because there is no other political news to compete with the story or they need "filler" for a slow news day.

Radio advertising has the advantage of sound; daily and weekly newspapers are a more passive medium. The reader can avoid an advertisement by turning the printed page; the listener finds it more difficult (but not impossible) to "tune out" the more intrusive radio spot. Like the print media, radio advertising can be used to reach both general audiences and targeted groups. The campaign must choose carefully to select the best radio stations and times of day to reach certain types of listeners. In small towns, radio station news coverage may be linked to campaign advertising, but in larger cities is is usually not a factor. Although rural radio stations can often reach groups more efficiently than other media (e.g., radio stations reaching farmers), all radio stations can be effectively utilized if the listeners are analyzed in terms of their musical tastes, age demographics, and so forth. |Radio spot announcements can be invaluable in generating political rally attendance.| "Traffic time" spots during the peak listening periods for commuters can reach tens of thousands or even hundreds of thousands of listeners and are especially suited for get-out-the-vote efforts during the last week of the campaign.

Television Stations

Current data indicate that 97 percent of American homes have one or more television sets; 41 percent have two or more sets; 64 percent have a color television set. The average household spends more than 6 hours *each day* in front of the television set. Although the 97 percent figure is peaking, the percent of Americans owning two or more sets or a color television set continues to increase. Just as these figures reflect television's importance as an advertising medium for candidates, other statistics indicate television's pervasiveness as a news source. Television news is the primary source of news for more than 60 percent of Americans, and the sole source of news for more than 30 percent.[b]

Statistics do not indicate that people are better informed by television, only that the electorate relies mainly on television for information about government and politics. Television is the most important news and advertising medium for all Level A campaigns and for most Level B campaigns. Television is of limited relevance to most Level C campaigns, unless special conditions exist (e.g., media market boundaries are congruent with one or a few districts; there is a special election). In terms of news, the television station in a metropolitan area cannot cover the multitude of local races, each of which interest only a small portion of its viewers. The exception is the extraordinarily dramatic, visual story. In terms of advertising, television spots are far too expensive for most Level C campaigns, and most of the viewers reached cannot vote for the candidate because they live in one of the many other districts in the media market.

Any campaign coverage must confront the ambiguous federal regulations governing the broadcast media. No one has ever understood the "equal-time" and "fairness" doctrines, which are in a constant state of reinterpretation. The fairness doctrine is usually applied to newscasts and refers to balancing the presentation of different points of views as well as to affording comparable coverage of competitive candidates. The fairness doctrine refers to overall coverage over a period of time; it does not require that each candidate receive precisely the same number of seconds during

---

[b] The Nielsen statistics are the primary, but not sole, source for information on television ownership and viewing habits. Weekly television viewing actually dropped in late 1975, allegedly due to an unappealing new television season. Surveys differ on the precise percentage of Americans who rely primarily or solely on television news as their source of news; some data indicate true figures may be in the mid-60 and mid-30 percent ranges, respectively.

each newscast. The equal-time doctrine is usually applied to interview programs and debates and has been interpreted in the past to mean that a television station, unless exempted by Congress, the Federal Communications Commission (FCC), or voluntarily by all the relevant candidates, cannot interview one candidate without interviewing all candidates for the position; it cannot televise debates of the two or three major candidates, but must afford equal time to all candidates.

Once the political publicist understands that the historic purpose of the FCC has been to restrict entry into the media markets (i.e., to thwart new stations, networks, and innovative types of programming), he can make the best of a difficult situation. He should understand that the practical effect of such government intrusion into the political marketplace of ideas is the television version of the *lowest common denominator* doctrine. Scheming or timid program directors, news directors, or assignment editors invoke the mysteries of the equal-time and fairness doctrines to argue against prime-time debates (which cost advertising dollars) and serious news coverage of campaigns (which cost overtime and may hurt ratings). Often, television executives and radio executives, who are also governed by the FCC, cover all primary or general election campaigns for an office on the basis of the most incompetent campaign. They are so fearful of accusations of bias, or are so secretly reluctant to cover politics, that the campaign generating the least news becomes the standard.

Television news, like all news, is business, but its commercial implications are more ominous because of the pervasiveness of the medium. Television news directors are guided by public apathy toward government and politics. Because they are more concerned with entertaining than informing, political news coverage is given low priority, especially in times other than the weeks before election day. Television news programs are commercially important because (a) they produce considerable advertising revenue, and (b) they "lead in" to the network news and network prime time (with high commercial advertising rates). Station managers want their news to have high ratings so they can charge more for advertising for television news and for the prime-time programs; news viewers hopefully will remain tuned to the station's prime-time shows. If government and political news turns away viewers, such news will be deemphasized.

Magazines

Magazines are usually irrelevant, in terms of news and advertising, for Level C campaigns, except for magazines designed for local readerships (e.g., *New York, Los Angeles, Washingtonian*) or magazines with regional editions to permit local advertising at economical rates. Advertising in a magazine's regional or metropolitan edition can be a cost-efficient method of reaching a small portion of the magazine's national readership.

Level A and Level B campaigns should be interested in the impact of favorable or unfavorable magazine news coverage, especially in *Time, Newsweek*, and *U.S. News*. The political journals of opinion—*Human Events, Nation, National Review, New Republic*, and so forth—provide valuable coverage for generating volunteer workers and ideological financial support. Major magazine coverage in personality, nonpolitical articles in large circulation magazines like *People* or *Parade* can also be helpful. Magazine articles are also important for two other reasons: (1) they can influence other journalists, present and potential financial supporters, and political partisans, and (2) they can be used, in reprint form, to rally support or raise funds.

Magazine advertising usually has the advantage of more complete demographic profiles of readers than newspaper advertising. Magazine advertising is sometimes a cost-efficient way to reach certain kinds of people, especially trend leaders, opinion molders, community activists, and others who are more likely to be politically active and to vote in elections. Magazine advertising also offers superior layout and printing possibilities, and the advertising "lives" for a longer period than the daily newspaper, which is discarded in a day or two. However, the daily newspaper does offer an advertising vehicle resembling a magazine in the form of the supplement—an expensive tabloid inserted within the newspaper.

Additional Media

Every campaign must identify additional media uniquely capable of reaching its particular constituency in quantitative and qualitative terms. The alert media strategist always asks: "How many readers, listeners, or viewers?" and "What kinds of readers, listeners, or viewers?"

The United States has a vast number of journals and magazines that reach many kinds of readers. These include trade, professional, union, corporate, business, and financial magazines. Many publications are "house organs" published by corporations and sent to employees, stockholders, or other groups; union newspapers or magazines are sent to union mailing lists. Professional organizations and trade groups, varying from the Chamber of Commerce or National Association of Manufacturers to a seemingly endless variety of occupational associations, publish timely newsletters, newspapers, or magazines. These publications vary from national or regional to state, local, and even district. News and advertising opportunities should not be overlooked in publications of religious, social, fraternal, veterans, and patriotic groups.

The strategist should identify whether the publication reaches a national, state, or other type of list. These publications also are usually published less frequently than other media, sometimes only quarterly, and their deadlines require long "lead times" before a story, feature, or advertisement is published. If these media present insurmountable problems, the strategist should look beyond publications and examine opportunities presented by ethnic television and radio stations or specialty programming as a supplement to the campaign's ethnic or other targeted media efforts.

Advertising

This section briefly reviews media that can be used only for advertising and not also for news. Since such advertising is usually perceived by the electorate as purchased by the campaign, it has less credibility than news. Although this book's emphasis is on the mass media, which can be used for both news and advertising, the media strategist must understand the relationship of traditional advertising media to news/advertising media, especially as a method of reinforcement, i.e., complementarity.

Printed Matter

Printed materials, although considered media in many advertising textbooks, are not usually included in the campaign advertising budget. They are budgeted separately—as part of printed materials, mailing programs, or special purpose efforts—and can include brochures, issues papers, tabloid newspapers, biographical sketches of the candidate, calling cards used by the candidate, reprints of favorable news articles, and so forth. These printed materials come in all shapes, formats, sizes, and colors and can be designed for hand distribution or for mailing, either within an appropriate covering envelope or as a "self-mailer" with space for addressing and a printed box for bulk postage.

Brochures are typically printed on standard (8½" × 11") or legal size (8½" × 14") paper. A two-panel brochure indicates the paper is folded once; a three panel brochure is folded twice, as a business letter would be folded to fit into a business envelope. Larger size brochures are avoided to conserve paper or to use standard size paper or presses. However, many campaigns have effectively used larger fold out brochures. It should be emphasized that the number of panels refers to a single side of paper; hence, a six-panel brochure, folded five times, actually has a total of twelve panels available. Most brochures are printed to conserve resources, either by using a single color, often black, on white paper, or any single color on contrasting colored paper. Two or three colors or full color (to permit color photographs) adds significantly to printing costs. The most aesthetic brochure is irrelevant unless its theme, issues, and format reflect the campaign strategy.

The most common error in any printed campaign materials is too much copy and too few or no photographs. Any partisan who writes, edits, or produces printed campaign materials may be unable to relate to the intended recipient. The result is either pedantic rhetoric, often polemics in small type with little white space and few photographs to draw interest and break the copy. Unless the intended audience is known to prefer detailed analysis and will read the literature no matter how overbearing its layout (and such an audience is rare), the media strategist must emphasize printed material that will be *read*, not discarded.

Unless printed material is specifically designed to rally partisans, raise funds, or inspire party loyalty, it should be carefully designed and written to appeal to target groups essential for the candidate's victory. The principles of copywriting cannot be reviewed here, but the novice would do well to retain a professional copywriter with *political* experience. Printed matter can be very important in Level C campaigns, and poor presentations can be more than an expensive exercise in futility; emphasis of the wrong issues, or too many issues, can be counterproductive. In sum, the campaign must use competent copywriters, editors, layout and graphics artists, typesetters, and printers. It is important that the perspective of creative and competent professionals be sought, not the insulated views of partisan acquaintances.

Any printed matter, whether it is a brochure, flier, or newsletter, is irrelevant unless the campaign has a distribution plan. Printed matter may be distributed (1) at the headquarters; (2) by the candidate during door-to-door appearances or campaign visits to shopping centers and other public places; (3) by aides or volunteers who accompany the candidate at appearances, especially at speaking commitments; (4) by volunteers who visit shopping centers, subway stations, bus terminals, or other public thoroughfares; (5) by precinct workers who go door to door in their area; and (6) by cooperating organizations, groups, or adjunct committees that are supporting the candidate.

Direct Mail

This is the single most effective method of distributing printed campaign materials. Although fund-raising mailings are a separate category, all mailings should seek volunteers *and* funds, as much for image as for practical results. The most important direct mail list is the campaign's own "house" list of those closest to the candidate, his past and present supporters, loyalists, and partisans. Other lists can be purchased, rented, or borrowed from county clerks, registrars of voters, party organizations and volunteer clubs, and direct mail companies and list brokers. The mailing operation can utilize labels (usually computer produced) and a professional mailing house, or volunteers can help put out the mailing.

The resourceful manager seeks a vast variety of specialized lists that correspond to the kinds of groups previously mentioned—religious, fraternal, service, social, ethnic, professional, and so forth. Mailings should be tailored to the recipients, rather than be all-purpose and hopefully relevant to everyone. The issues mentioned in a mailing, or the signatory to an endorsement letter, should be relevant to the recipients of that mailing. The ideal campaign direct mail program is really many mailing programs, each modified and designed to appeal best to certain target groups corresponding to the given mailing list.

It would be impossible to enumerate all the variations of direct mail. Most direct mail is either impersonal (mass printed) or personal. The latter includes use of automatic typewriters that "personalize" addresses, salutations, and even include the recipient's name within the body of the letter. Other personal mailings include endorsement letters or postcards sent by campaign supporters to their own lists of friends, relatives, neighbors, fellow workers or churchgoers, or other peer groups. Reference has already been made to self-mailers versus mailings within envelopes. Usually an envelope has no more than two inserts, perhaps a brochure and letter; sometimes a combination response card/business reply envelope is enclosed. Other kinds of mailings include endorsement letters, which can be individually or group signed and which may or may not have long letterheads; questionnaires; simulated telegrams; slate mailings (usually a postcard with a slate of candidates) to be taken to the polling place; and tabloid newspapers.

Major considerations in direct mail include (1) the method of postage—that is, first class or bulk rate; (2) use of commemorative stamps versus a postage meter; (3) acquiring the relevant postal permit; (4) use of business reply envelopes to encourage responses; and (5) the graphic design of the mailing "package" to encourage recipients to open it rather than discard it immediately and to continue reading it once they start.

Outdoor Advertising

Although billboards achieve little more than name recognition, they can to a limited degree enhance image or achieve some issue orientation, perhaps with a single issue. Billboards are low priority for Level A or Level B campaigns, which should rely principally on television, radio, and newspapers. Many statewide candidates insist on billboards because they remember an era when billboards were more important, or because their opponents have them. Billboards are most effective in rural areas where they can efficiently reach voters less susceptible to other media. Billboards are also useful in many Level C campaigns since they can achieve name recognition as well as party identification in situations where the latter is an asset. In some districts, billboards have helped Level C candidates win a primary election.

Billboards require the printing of sheets (usually to cover a standard area of 104 inches by 234 inches) and a monthly rental of billboard space. Larger billboards, elaborate three-dimensional signs, or multivision signs (with vertical, rotating three-sided louvers) are usually prohibitively expensive for the campaign. Since the printing cost of billboards is a given regardless of the short-term (usually one or two months) rental of space, billboards are relatively inflexible, especially considering the need to contract for space and order the printing of sheets well in advance of the rental period. Delays in putting up the campaign's billboard sheets cost valuable time; it is little consolation that the sheets remain in place after election, until the space is rented again.

Billboard rental costs are based on the number of people likely to see the billboard. A typical advertising package is rated for its "showing": a *100* showing means the advertising agency or billboard company estimates that 100 percent of the buying (i.e., voting) public will see the message during a thirty-day period. In a Level C campaign, strategic placement of billboards on busy thoroughfares throughout the district can connote a viable campaign and imply districtwide support.

Other forms of outdoor advertising include placing signs in store windows, pasting sheets (called "snipe sheets") on building site enclosures, and placing lawn signs in front of houses. These outdoor positioning alternatives usually imply persuading campaign supporters, whether storeowners or residents, to display the signs and examining legal complications for displaying signs elsewhere. Usually, such outdoor advertising is low priority for Level A and most Level B campaigns, but can be quite useful for Level C campaigns, which should exploit every opportunity to place posters or yard signs. Such outdoor advertising can consolidate support and imply momentum by creating a bandwagon effect. One cost-effective method of outdoor advertising for all campaigns is budgeting a little more for headquarters rent in order to find a location that has heavy automobile and pedestrian traffic and then positioning large, professional signs overlooking the campaign headquarters.

Outdoor advertising requires *professional* assistance to insure that the graphics are appropriate and consistent. Slogans, typography, and graphics for all outdoor advertising should be consistent with other campaign literature. Although outdoor advertising can offer an advantage of being seen by many voters within a short time span, this advantage is only relevant if the lettering is simple and straight, bright, and in sharp contrast to the sign. In addition, more expensive ink and billboards with night lights that facilitate night viewing can help maximize the billboard's effectiveness. Above all, any outdoor advertising should have only a few words; the candidate's name should always be in the largest letters. It is usually inadvisable to use photographs in outdoor advertising.

Outdoor advertising is becoming increasingly unpopular in campaigning because a disinterested public finds such advertising more aesthetically displeasing than informative. Unless outdoor advertising offers special benefits in reaching voters who truly cannot be reached by other media, the campaign strategist should be guided by the fact that many voters are turned off by such "pollution." Not only are yard signs and telephone pole signs offensive to many voters, but they may violate local laws or zoning codes. Outdoor advertising always runs the risk of zealous youthful supporters putting signs or posters somewhere without the owner's permission. Telephone pole signs, snipe sheets (on building sites), and similar advertising can have negative effects on those voters who know that these signs are often not removed after election day.

Transportation Advertising

This category primarily includes buses, trolleys, subways, commuter trains, taxis, and automobiles. "Car cards" are found in the overhead racks and in other interior locations of public transportation vehicles; larger cards can be purchased for use on the outside (front, side, rear) of vehicles, or within bus, subway, or railroad stations. The two basic elements in such advertising involve the printing of the cards or sheets and the rental of the space. For Level C campaigns, in which such advertising is more relevant, special consideration should be given to insuring that the vehicles actually travel within the candidate's district. Transportation advertising can be useful for Level B and even Level A campaigning, if it is carefully targeted to reach specific urban or rural groups. For example, a candidate for office in New York State can reach specific ethnic groups by advertising at certain subway stations or on certain subway trains in New York City.

The classic example of transportation advertising is the bumpersticker or bumperstrip, usually placed on the front bumper, or rear, or both. Unless professional counsel is retained, campaign novices are likely to make the common mistakes of choosing the wrong sizes, poor colors or inks, inappropriate lettering, or putting too many words on the bumperstrip (usually the candidate's name and office is sufficient). Campaign veterans know that selecting a sticker with the proper adhesive can determine whether the sticker is removed easily after the campaign is over. Bargain stickers may save a few pennies, but they will not be used if supporters believe they will not come off easily. Bargain stickers may also have ink that fades in sunlight! The rise in public apathy and the urge for individual privacy have drastically curtailed the use of bumperstrips. Campaigns use them because they are a tradition, but only a tiny fraction are actually placed on automobiles; no one ever quite knows how the other 98 percent disappear. Any campaign using bumperstrips should have programs to put the stickers (with the owner's permission) on automobiles.

Putting stickers or signs on any automobile window usually violates some kind of law. The partisan supporter can be given a "car topper"—a mount affixed to the top of the car. Specially designed sheets, bumperstrips, or posters are placed on both sides of the topper. Because these toppers are expensive, they are given only to the most dependable partisans.

Advertising Specialities

This category includes some of the most expensive and wasteful campaign ideas. Only the imagination can limit enumerating every kind of specialty: buttons of all sizes and varieties, matchbooks, calendars, potholders, pens, pencils, paperweights, shopping bags, key chains, earrings, cufflinks, tieclasps, necklaces, and all kinds of bracelets, pendants, and jewelry, rulers, phonograph records, photographs "autographed" by the candidate, books written by the candidate, and so forth. Campaign veterans remember such classics as the Goldwater ruler ("He will lead, not rule") or the red, white, and blue garter used in Ronald Reagan's 1966 gubernatorial campaign (called a "Reagan supporter").

These novelties should only be used if they at least pay for themselves and preferably if they raise funds for the campaign. Scarce funds and time should not be allocated to such wasteful diversions unless they are clearly revenue producing or used selectively as incentive gifts for campaign staff or volunteers. There are two exceptions. First, some novelty items are useful communications tools; for example, the doorknob hanger, which is a piece of paper that hangs around a doorknob and is printed with the candidate's message, or which is in the form of a plastic bag containing literature or a premium gift that can be left on doorknobs by precinct workers. The second exception is the relatively low-cost, practical gift that is inscribed with the candidate's name and is distributed early in a Level C campaign undistinguished by emotive issues. It is possible for voters in such situations to appreciate a practical gift like a potholder, which would thus justify its relatively high cost. Thimbles, sewing kits, fingernail files, and other costly novelties may be appropriate for the local campaign, but they are too expensive for mass distribution in a Level A or Level B campaign. The major campaign concentrates on a minimum quantity of campaign buttons, balloons for major rallies, and other special novelties.

4 Servicing the News Media

Servicing the news media means creating news so journalists have a job to do and then assisting them to do their job. The campaign cannot generate news unless it understands news, and it cannot help journalists cover news unless it knows their needs. The campaign that is not newsworthy is not worth covering, and the campaign staff that is unresponsive or uncooperative makes the campaign too difficult to cover. Although the campaign should try to be newsworthy enough to make coverage imperative for the news media, the campaign should also accept the premise that it needs the news media more than the news media needs the campaign.

News media strategy evaluates the relevance of different types of media and specific media outlets to the campaign, and it generates news according to the criteria and needs of the relevant media. The campaign's policy is conducive to news coverage if it reflects an open, positive attitude toward the media and a detailed knowledge of how the news business works.

Strategy

No news media strategy can evolve in the absence of an overall campaign strategy. This strategy suggests how many voters must be reached in terms of differentiating among demographic groups and in terms of voters who need to (a) know who the candidate is (identification and party); (b) perceive what he is like (image); and (c) identify or associate the candidate with positions on certain issues (issue orientation). News media strategy is confined to generating news, features, editorials, news conferences, interviews, and so forth, but it must be part of a coordinated media strategy that considers both news and advertising media.

Orchestration

Orchestration of the news media strategy implements the decisions made at the outset of the campaign. These decisions relate to evaluating the candidate's strengths and weaknesses in terms of projecting an image, selecting a theme, and choosing several issues. Orchestration reflects the realization that before the electorate can be reached, the news media must be reached.

39

The campaign must establish the candidate as a viable, credible, and authentic entity with the most important media (particular publications, television or radio stations) and leading journalists. Then the campaign can utilize the trend-setting media and individual journalists to help propagandize those media outlets and individual journalists who follow, rather than lead, a trend.

Orchestrating the news media strategy can only mirror the overall campaign strategy, which should have been carefully formulated. If the campaign strategy is subject to erratic shifts and is hopelessly contrived and modified to conform to the second guessing of every volunteer chairman, the news media strategy will suffer. If the campaign theme and selection of issues were imprudently decided, the news media strategy cannot overcome the deficiency, it can only make the best of it. In other words, the candidate's theme and issues must be relevant to the electorate, because the news media is roughly interested in the same issues that concern most voters. Circulation, readership, listenership, and viewership reflect whether the news media is reporting on subjects of interest to its reader/listener/viewer consumers.

Pacing. Once issues are chosen, the strategist orchestrates the news media campaign by pinpointing the number of times each issue needs to be emphasized to achieve the desired publicity. For example, if drug abuse is an important campaign issue, how many times should the candidate hold a news conference, make a speech, or participate in a television-oriented visual on drug abuse? The strategist for a Level C campaign understands that the principle is the same: finding creative, original, and new ways to dramatize the same issue or issues to get repeated publicity in relevant media. Repetition of issues is necessary to raise public consciousness and aid voter recollection; issue orientation is very difficult to achieve in the average voter's mind. Many candidates are satisfied with identification, but issue orientation achieves identification and something more—it relates the candidate to issues, perhaps even certain positions on issues, in terms of electorate perception. Repetition does not mean saying the same thing over and over again; it means receiving publicity on the same issues repeatedly by raising a key issue or issues in *different* newsworthy contexts.

Pacing the campaign requires planning and controlling both the overall news exposure of the candidate—in terms of his statements, news conferences, interviews, and media-oriented schedule—and the number of news exposures in print or electronic media on particular subjects or issues. The first concerns *momentum*; the second concerns the issue *mix*. Proper pacing, as evident in the ensuing discussion on phases, prevents the campaign from peaking too soon, yet guarantees the campaign maximizes early publicity. Specific pacing controls the frequency of the candidate's visits to particular regions of the country, states, cities, or parts of a district, depending on the level of office sought. Two visits to the same area in a short time period may compromise the publicity value of both visits; hence, pacing visits requires coordination with scheduling.

An excellent example is the candidate for statewide office who visits two or three cities the same day. The extra travel time seems inefficient from a scheduling perspective, but is wise from the publicity point of view. This pacing assumes that the most favorable ratio of publicity generated to time spent in a media market is achieved by brief rather than prolonged visits. The well constructed visual will achieve the desired television coverage and net acceptable radio and newspaper coverage; additional time spent in the city will result in added coverage, but not enough to justify spending more time. Visiting another city the same day can net another publicity "splash" in that city's local media.

Pacing for any campaign means spreading out the number of announcements, endorsements, news conferences, statements, speeches, issue positions, and so forth to make the campaign appear to have momentum and to assure that this momentum is upward. This means that an inventory of speeches, statements, issue positions, and the like must be translated into specific announcements or speeches on particular dates in certain cities or before selected groups or audiences. Pacing means the campaign makes news on its terms by selecting its issues, timing, audience and having some control over the quantity of coverage it receives. For example, too much publicity on the wrong issue can have a negative effect. Too little publicity on an important issue or endorsement can compromise the campaign strategy.

The important relationship between orchestrating media strategy and pacing of stories was illustrated by the early stages of Ronald Reagan's campaign against Gerald Ford. In September, 1975, Reagan erred in proposing an ill conceived $90 billion dollar cut in federal spending. The plan could not be defended in simple terms. During late 1975 and throughout the first part of 1976, Reagan repeatedly encountered intensive questioning by reporters probing the economic program. Because the campaign lacked an overall strategy, within which a media strategy would allow for pacing of major stories, the Reagan campaign generated little news of a substantive or issue nature. Thus, reporters had little new to report, and they were needlessly tempted to return, again and again, to Reagan's controversial budget program.

In contrast, if the Reagan campaign had researched and developed issue positions during late 1975, *before* the candidate began his frenetic campaign schedule, the campaign strategists and news director could have planned numerous news releases, announcements, speeches, position papers, reports of campaign task forces, and other issue oriented *news*. The campaign would have orchestrated and paced news on *its* terms, rather than allow a void encouraging reporters to fill the substantive news gap with more criticism of the $90 billion plan. In sum, the campaign would have been less likely to be on the defensive.

Phases. Every campaign should have phases of development that are internal planning devices that may not be explicitly stated or evident to the public. In the *preliminary* phase of news media development, the strategy is formulated, mailing lists are put together, media research is conducted, key media contacts are made, and editorial board meetings along with other introductory meetings are held. All the planning for the campaign is finalized, so that when it is formally launched, the news operation is ready to go.

The preliminary phase resembles, and may overlap, the *introductory* or *identification* phase, which is the beginning stage of getting the candidate's name out. Identification may also mean increasing voter recognition not only of the candidate's name, but also his face and appearance as well as his party. The third phase is the *issues* phase, which attempts to achieve issue orientation by relating the candidate to certain carefully selected issues. These issues are simultaneously important to the electorate and to the candidate; they are not merely contrived issues selected to suit the latest public opinion poll. The campaign strategy indicates to what extent the candidate must be perceived merely as empathizing with the voters on an issue (sharing their concern) and to what extent he must advance specific proposals to resolve issues. The fourth or *consolidation* phase is designed to reinforce desired perceptions in the electorate, relate recognition to identification and issue orientation, "take care of loose ends" by making extra effort where strategic goals are not being met, and mount a get-out-the-vote drive.

These phases are not discrete but necessarily overlap. In addition, some geographic areas or groups of voters may be part of one phase, while voters in another area or of another demographic group may be in a second phase. This is especially true in terms of the winner of a primary election who has allocated considerable time to his first priority of securing a base of support within his party before going after the support of independents and members of the opposition party. It is conceivable for the candidate to be consolidating support within his base before he is even widely known among the electorate as a whole.

The news media policy reflects the graduated development of the campaign over time. Within each phase, strategy calls for the candidate to achieve a desired level of publicity on certain issues or for saying certain things. The phases defined here are not inflexible; perhaps they can be divided or other phases inserted for a particular campaign. For example, the news media strategy of a campaign may reflect its overall strategy of discrediting the opponent early in the campaign to establish a negative image of him solidly in voters' minds at the outset; then while the opponent is still recovering, the candidate can concentrate on building his own image, stressing issues, and otherwise "picking up the pieces" of the opponent's campaign.

Major Stories. The news media strategy calls for clear delineation of important news stories. These major stories, varying from an important speech, issue position, dramatic proposal, or attention-getting endorsement, are planned in advance. This does not mean that unplanned major stories do not occur. For example, the reaction of the candidate to a news development may itself be a major news story. Orchestrating major stories means making certain they receive the substantial publicity the campaign desires—that is, releasing the news when and where the campaign wants.

Orchestrating major stories means releasing them during slow news periods, or at least not at times when the news is dominated by other events. Sometimes the campaign cannot control circumstances, as when major nonpolitical occurrences happen without warning and obscure political news. More often the campaign can control the tempo of its news, and it can call attention to a major story by not releasing competitive stories during the same day or time period. For example, an important news release should probably not arrive simultaneously with a routine news release. Similarly, releasing a major story—for example, making an important speech with dramatic proposals—must be consistent with media deadlines. If the speech will occur after the deadlines of relevant media, whether the deadline be a network television deadline for a Level A campaign or a weekly newspaper deadline for a Level C campaign, the media strategists must find a way to beat the deadline. This is usually done before the event by permitting an interview or releasing a text that is to be used concurrent with, or shortly following, the actual event.

Another example illustrating the need to orchestrate major stories is avoiding preempted or dated stories. Preempted stories are simply statements, speeches, news releases, and so forth that would have been major stories if the word had not "leaked" to the media. The best example is the prospective candidate whose major news conference to announce his candidacy receives nominal media attention because he let his decision "slip out" in an interview a few days before. The dated story is one that is no longer news; if released the wrong day, it receives a fraction of the coverage it should have received. However, since the information is out, it is dated and no longer considered news. For example, weekends are slow news days and can be exploited, but major announcements can be buried if the campaign deals with editors or reporters on the night or weekend shift or selects inexperienced journalists to write the story. Once the story appears in print or is aired on radio or television, even though it may be inadequate or receive insufficient "play," it is unlikely to be revived because it is dated.

Surrogates. Orchestrating news media strategy calls for exploiting publicity opportunities offered by friendly individuals and organizations. For example, suppose a union was planning to endorse a candidate and the announcement was judged newsworthy by the campaign. It would make more sense, generally, for the union, rather than the campaign, to hold the news conference. First, this strategy indicates the union wants to get the news out and is proud of its actions. Second, the union has the responsibility for the news conference. (Obviously, the campaign must make certain the union is able to call a news conference and knows how to get the media to attend.) Third, the campaign is not the supplicant asking the media to cover another of its events; the union is requesting coverage.

Surrogates can be individuals or organizations endorsing the candidate; for example, ad hoc, adjunct, or supporting committees affiliated directly or indirectly with the campaign committee, or unrelated organizations making statements or taking positions that are favorable to either the candidate or the stance he has taken on an issue or that are unfavorable to the opposition candidate. In the Level A campaign, but also in other campaigns, surrogates can be elected officials or community leaders who accept speaking commitments in behalf of the candidate. The campaign should work to get maximum publicity for such surrogates, just as it would publicize such surrogates even closer to the candidate as his wife, family, or close relatives.

Another example will illustrate how news media orchestration can utilize surrogates. Suppose a statewide candidate's travel schedule would keep him out of a major city for nearly a week, although campaign strategy called for his appearance in that city at least twice a week. During this time period, the campaign manager could be enlisted to make a major, newsworthy statement so that the campaign could get some publicity in this media market during the candidate's absence.

Strategic Tips

Each campaign must appraise the media realistically. The Level C campaign should seek television coverage only if it can present a powerfully visual story. Although television coverage of local races is rare, the Level C strategist's realistic attitude is not defeatist to the point of foreclosing exploitation of a potential visual. Level A and Level B campaigns should emphasize television, but not to the exclusion of the print media. No campaign can afford to alienate media by a snobbish preference for certain types of coverage. News media strategy for any campaign rarely if ever suggests sole reliance on a single medium; each medium must be exploited to the maximum, because each reaches some voters who cannot be reached by other media. Voters receiving the same message from various types of news media will benefit not only from repetition, but from the reinforcement uniquely provided by the media mix.[a]

Within any medium, particular media outlets (e.g., television stations, weekly newspapers) can be shown to be more effective in reaching certain target groups. Advertising data, survey research, input from volunteer leaders, judgment, and intuition help the media strategist to assign priorities. Some outlets may be more responsive than others because of personal relationships or friendships with the candidate, campaign manager, or campaign news director, or generally because of favorable bias. Since any media outlet is only an aggregate of individual journalists, personal contact and biases affect the media outlet's relationship with the campaign. These personal factors can be as important as the media outlet's inherent ability to reach certain kinds of voters.

The news media strategist is also concerned with specific news programs, interview programs, syndicated columnists, editorial sections of the newspaper, and so forth. The strategy seeks to maximize exposure within each segment of the media outlet. This means television and radio news, talk shows, interview programs, the newspaper's front page, its editorial page, syndicated columnists, society news, and the like. Just as influential media outlets and individual journalists are targeted early for cultivation so they can in turn influence other media outlets and journalists, each component of a media outlet is also targeted for special attention. In the early stages of the campaign, favorable syndicated columns, lengthy photo-interview spreads, or a friendly magazine piece may set the tone for the quantity and quality of subsequent media coverage. Throughout the campaign, targeting efforts at all components of each medium reinforces the overall effort; for example, society page coverage of a campaign fund-raising party will help stimulate front-page news coverage of the candidate's statements.

Listed below are ten strategic tips relevant to relating the campaign to the news media:

1. Each type of media is concerned with *its* constituency. Television and radio are interested in news that concerns viewers/listeners throughout

---

[a] Media diversity relates to both news and advertising. Certain media, either through news or advertising, or both, can reach particular kinds of voters or demographic groups better than others. Advertising agency data, plus the cross-tabulations provided by survey research analysis of reading, listening, and viewing habits of voters who respond a certain way to questions, help in planning news *and* advertising media strategy.

the media market. Daily newspapers are interested in stories that concern their metropolitan or suburban readership, and weekly newspapers are concerned with a more limited readership.

2. Each type of media prefers stories it can best cover. Television prefers visual and picture stories, radio prefers audio stories; print media are concerned with more substantive stories, although they appreciate being apprised of opportunities for interesting photographs. Remember that electronic media editors want something more than a reporter explaining what is happening; in television, the audience should see it; in radio, the audience should hear it.

3. Each type of media defines *immediacy* differently. The weekly newspaper has a weekly news cycle, compared to the daily newspaper's daily news cycle. Television is one day or less, and radio is even more immediate. The closer the campaign's news to the deadline of the type of media or specific media outlet, the more immediacy the news has.

4. News is defined on a relative, not absolute basis. A nonpolitical visual story may win out in television coverage over a less visually attractive political story. A seemingly newsworthy political story that "breaks" on a heavy news day may be "buried" in the coverage of momentous nonpolitical news. Routine political news may receive substantial coverage on a slow news day.

5. Since media outlets have pride and provincialism, editors will pursue or follow-up stories initially broken in their own outlets. Their news policies may also be affected by editorial priorities—that is, editors are more inclined to cover subjects or issues deemed important on the editorial pages. Jealousy can also prevent an editor from following up a story that a rival media outlet first broke.

6. Journalists are competitive, insecure, and, as a whole, unoriginal. *Time* and *Newsweek* influence each other; so do *The Washington Post* and *The New York Times*. Strategy should play competitive media against each other by making the campaign so newsworthy that competitive media, media outlets and individual journalists will try to outdo each other in covering the campaign.

7. The precampaign period, especially the summer months, should be utilized for personally meeting relevant media personnel, *before* the hectic pace of the campaign. Ideally, the campaign news director should meet media personnel before seeking their help in covering a story.

8. The campaign should adapt its schedule to the most relevant media. Level A and Level B campaigns should be morning-oriented for visuals, wire services, and coverage throughout the day. Level C cam-

paigns should be oriented toward weekly newspaper publishing deadlines and toward providing some events for the daily newspapers that can be induced to cover the campaign.

9. The campaign should generate news when the candidate is doing nothing. Even when the candidate has a rest day, the campaign headquarters should make news by issuing statements in his name, using surrogates, or otherwise exploiting the media's constant need for news.

10. Weekends are slow news periods, and the campaign should make a special effort to advise media of the candidate's weekend appearances for possible tapings or even live television and radio programs. The campaign should establish a working relationship with night and weekend editors to provide them with news during off periods, including statements prepared for weekend release.

Making News

The political campaign that cannot make news does not deserve coverage. Contrary to civics textbooks, the news media does not exist to help the democratic process. News is a business that succeeds or fails depending on whether it fulfills the public's desire for information. If the campaign does not generate news, the media looks to the opposition, or looks outside politics altogether.

Defining News. News must be current, immediate, and topical—as defined by the type of media and specific media outlet. For example, the morning news conference may be newsworthy for the afternoon newspaper, but might receive less coverage in the next day's morning newspaper. News must be of interest and concern to the readers or listeners of the specific media outlets. Newspaper editors and television and radio news directors know what their readers, viewers, or listeners want to know; their circulation or ratings depend on how well they judge their constituency.

Public opinion surveys indicate what is on the public's mind and what, therefore, concerns editors. The candidate must do more than address himself to these issues, he must do so in a newsworthy way. The news media strategist selects the places and times that are likely to be most newsworthy for release of particular statements by the candidate. The campaign maintains an inventory of speeches, issue papers, statements, and so forth that can be readily adapted to news developments to enable the candidate to comment on issues that are in the news that day or hour.

The media strategist understands that the relative newsworthiness of a story determines how the information is given to the media. The visual story deserves television coverage; it should not be relegated to a news release, although news releases may also be distributed. The newsworthy reaction of a candidate to a dramatic development just carried on the wire service ticker should be taped for immediate distribution to radio stations, although a release may also be distributed. The more newsworthy the campaign activity, the less likely that a simple news release will be sufficient. Mailing of news releases has many purposes, but rapid dissemination of news is not one of them; only hand delivery of releases can effectively connote immediacy.

The campaign philosophy should be to exploit every news opportunity without, in effect, "crying wolf too often." If the campaign news director uses all his influence and contacts to push stories of marginal value, what will he do when he has an important story to push? The objective is to exploit the news media without letting journalists feel exploited—that is, to utilize the media without the media feeling "used." An example of aggressive utilization of the media was provided by the many campus demonstrations of the sixties, in which organizers called one news conference to announce the demonstration and another to protest lack of cooperation on the part of the university or city in granting a parade permit. The demonstration resulted in still more publicity; then days later, organizers called a news conference to assess the demonstration or charge police brutality. It took nearly a decade for many journalists to realize they were being used.

Place and Time. Once issues are chosen and their emphasis planned, campaign strategists must select ways of dramatizing these issues. Although the most dramatic and effective ways often present themselves as the campaign progresses, many ways can be chosen in advance. For example, visuals can be planned by relating issues to a relevant environment; for example, the candidate discussing high food prices tours a market and talks with shoppers. If the campaign's research staff knows when the government's inflation statistics will be published and is confident they will show rising prices, the visual can even be planned for that day or the next day. Pursuing the same example, if the government unexpectedly announces a foreign grain purchase that will push up domestic food prices, the campaign must be prepared to capitalize on this development. News is fragile because it can be dated quickly; unless the campaign can immediately and aggressively exploit news developments, it will never achieve the full news potential of its issues.

The place at which the candidate makes a speech, issues a statement, or acts in a particular way may be newsworthy or help make the story newsworthy. For example, a candidate opposed to forced bussing to achieve racial balance would probably receive more publicity for his issue paper on bussing if he called a news conference in a city embroiled in a bussing controversy. Similarly, the candidate prepared to make a major speech on labor issues might choose a labor convention or union forum.

Visual events are designed to stimulate television coverage precisely because of the "backdrop" they provide for the cameras. Although the good print media story is not necessarily a good visual story, the visual is usually also a good print story. Media-oriented scheduling emphasizes dramatic, photogenic localities—shopping centers, conventions, street rallies, walking tours. Ideally, locations are tied to issues; for example, visiting a drug rehabilitation center and then issuing a statement on drug abuse, or riding a train or subway to discuss transportation problems. When a visual locale is combined with immediacy, the news effects are overpowering. For example, assume a candidate has proposed mandatory prison sentences for individuals using a firearm in the commission of a crime. Imagine the visual if the candidate stated or restated this position at the scene of an armed robbery and homicide committed the prior day by two men on probation.

Incumbent/Challenger. Any incumbent can use the prominence and stature of his office to generate news before the campaign begins. The taxpayer-funded staff, office, telephones, mailings, travel allowance, and so forth are perquisites that help the incumbent communicate with the electorate and the media. Publicity opportunities include introducing legislation, conducting hearings, announcing government projects or grants, visiting government facilities, or making various types of fact-finding tours. The aggressive incumbent secures publicity when he is thinking about introducing legislation, when it is introduced, and then when the hearings are scheduled, when it is reported out of committee, when debate occurs, when it is passed, and finally when it is signed.

Since the incumbent has the initiative, the challenger must look for publicity opportunities before the campaign begins. As a declared candidate, the challenger may be subject to fairness, equal time, or analogous, informal print media policies. Moreover, the public is usually more skeptical of the pronouncements and actions of a declared candidate than of the aspiring, undeclared challenger who is able to use nonpartisan forums to speak on ostensibly nonpolitical subjects. The local groups should act in a surrogate capacity to generate publicity, so the aspiring candidate does not appear to be the supplicant.

Any incumbent who does not fully exploit the publicity value of the office makes the reelection task more difficult. Incumbency has disadvantages, including having established a record that can be attacked. Hence, its primary advantages—power, legitimacy, government perquisities— should be utilized, especially to generate publicity related to the incumbent's official responsibilities, rather than his reelection campaign.

Policy

The campaign policy toward the news media must be twofold. First, the attitude must be positive; the candidate and news director should be accessible, open, and honest as well as personable, cordial, and cooperative. Second, the policy must be service oriented—that is, its objective is to make coverage of the campaign as easy as possible for each journalist.

Campaign versus News Media

The relationship between campaign and news media should stress cooperation rather than the competition engendered by adversaries. The campaign with a positive attitude, service-oriented policy, and steady flow of news will find the news media receptive to reporting the campaign. The campaign with a negative attitude, inept servicing, and a scarcity of news will find itself subject to critical reporting—that is, for the little news coverage it merits.

The campaign should have only one spokesperson other than the candidate. Even the campaign manager should defer to this spokesperson— usually called a press secretary, news secretary, press aide, or communications or news director. Ideally, this person should have experience as a working journalist, but many former journalists may be unsuitable for the campaign job. Many journalists have never had staffs working for them, or they are loners who have worked on an assignment-to-assignment basis rather than within the framework of a thematic appeal dictated by strategy. Clearly, any member of the working press hired for the campaign should be someone respected and liked within the profession.

The spokesperson handles all news media contacts, except for those he delegates to others; for example permitting subordinates to handle schedule queries, mail the candidate's biographies and photographs, and so forth. This individual is responsible for all news releases mailed by the campaign, including local news releases. Since the spokesperson cannot read every local news release if the campaign is Level A or Level B, he must establish guidelines governing the production, content, style, and limitations of local releases.

The spokesperson must have the full confidence of the candidate. The candidate and spokesperson must have rapport—their "chemistry" must be right. The spokesperson should have the authority to speak for the candidate, and the news media must understand that this authority is unambiguous. Similarly, the news media should have no doubts that the spokesperson understands the campaign's strategy and plans, is aware of what the candidate and campaign are doing, and has easy access to the candidate, campaign manager, and staff.

Suspicion, distrust, and hostility can become self-fulfilling prophecies. The news director should have an amiable, even-tempered personality, and he should not seek confrontations with the news media. Some of the most successful press secretaries have been emotional and hot tempered, but they are the exception, not the rule. The news director should be poker faced, not easily excited, and able to feel at ease and project confidence, even under the most penetrating, intense questioning. Although his prime responsibility is to the candidate, the news director should be perceived by the news media as their *advocate*—that is, a person who is interested in generating relevant news stories, arranging interviews, helping journalists with deadlines and scheduling problems, and so forth.

The news director or spokesperson should be perceived as open and candid; responsiveness need not compromise discretion. The competent spokesperson can answer questions succinctly and honestly, without misleading or lying to journalists. Responses such as "I am not in a position to help you there," "I don't know, but I will find out and call you back," or "I just can't comment" are preferred to misleading or false statements. Obviously, there is uncertainty about credibility and competence if the spokesperson is always answering questions with something like, "I can neither confirm nor deny that." The news director who understands the relationship between the campaign and the news media knows it is the reporter's *job* to be aggressive, persistent, and pushy, just as it is sometimes the spokesperson's job to respond politely, tactfully, and responsively—to a point. The competent spokesperson resolves in his mind, in the moment he ponders before answering a question, precisely how far he will go in responding. He speculates internally on the number and nature of possible follow-up questions, and his answer should not raise additional questions (unless the spokesperson wants those questions raised).

The news director/spokesperson functions best if the candidate is respected and liked by the news media. The articulate candidate can receive more publicity before being "overexposed"; the inarticulate, insensitive, or uninformed candidate can exceed his tolerance level in a short interview. This candidate can project poorly, "misspeak," or make serious errors unless his exposure to the news media is rationed. Because the competent news director has studied the strengths and weaknesses of the candidate, the news media strategy emphasizes the strengths and downplays the weaknesses. The news director is always careful to insure that his role as liaison and ombudsman for the news media, especially his clearing and auditing of interviews with the candidate, are not interpreted as manipulative or as exerting an undue amount of control over the candidate.

Guidelines. The spokesperson is not a candidate for office; hence, he should not seek publicity for himself, but for the candidate. The spokesperson should be low key and low profile; he should not be constantly quoted by name, although he should be willing to be quoted by name, if a reporter insists. The spokesperson should not engage in the type of extended dialogues with reporters that may result in stories centering around the spokesperson's views. Unless care is taken, most of the guidelines in Exhibit 4-1 can be abused even by seasoned professionals.

The news director should not be overzealous. He should thank an editor or reporter for lengthy or special coverage, but he should not express gratitude for routine coverage. Thank you letters from the candidate or news director can be very helpful. He should be available to the news media, but he should not be a nuisance or pest (*journalists* are permitted to be nuisances or pests). Finally, the news director should remember that most reporters have no special interest in making the campaign spokesperson look good; nor do they wish to make him look bad, but they will if his incompetence makes them look bad. If they miss a deadline or include erroneous facts, statistics, or other data in their stories because the news director is incompetent, the news director will suffer, and so will the campaign.

Bias. If the candidate and news director are open and cooperative, reporters will overlook an occasional error by the candidate or campaign. If the campaign's attitude is negative and its servicing of the media poor, journalists will tend to seize on the candidate's every slip of the tongue. Traveling media are especially eager to maintain a cordial relationship, but antagonistic or inept campaigns make it easy for some reporters to "cut-up" the candidate or campaign. For example, sloppy advance work permits reporters to write about a "half-empty" banquet hall or photographers to show empty seats in frontline tables.

The campaign with a positive attitude, proper servicing, and competent advancing will find itself and its staff described in stories as professional, efficient, and "politically savvy." Even if the campaign is not explicitly praised, stories will portray the candidate and campaign more positively. Incompetent media servicing insures that the campaign will be explicitly described as novice, inefficient, or "amateurish." Even if the campaign is not so characterized explicitly, the reporters' contempt will permeate the coverage of the campaign.

Bias cannot be evaluated unless the news media is properly serviced; otherwise, how much of the problem is attributable to incompetence and how much to bias?[b] Nor can bias be judged on the basis of coverage of a

---

[b] Understanding of news concepts is also important. For example, suppose a partisan supporter objects that a newspaper story on the candidate's news conference placed too much emphasis on the wrong subject, which was also the lead and headline of the story. Closer examination reveals that bias is not the reason; the candidate was improperly briefed and did not understand that the lead is based on what is most newsworthy about the news conference, and his imprudent response to a question overshadowed the opening statement (and reason for the news conference).

single story, because too many variables can affect the size or mood of a story. Bias is always the first rationale advanced by local partisans for poor coverage. Many Level A and Level B campaigns place too much importance on local supporters' preoccupation with bias. Not only do many local political activists have a negative attitude and poor servicing policy, but they are chronic complainers. In contrast, the campaign should only complain in the extreme case, especially if the complaint is made to the television or radio station manager with a copy to the FCC, or the complaint is sent directly to the FCC. Intimidation can be an excellent tool for individuals and groups outside the political campaign situation, but it can actually worsen coverage for a candidate.[c]

Sometimes presidential campaigns assign a staff member to tape all of the candidate's remarks, both as a means of self-defense if he is misquoted, and as a convenience to the news media.

Servicing

Servicing the news media is a natural consequence of a positive attitude toward journalism and reporters. The campaign news director should understand that reporters are pressured to produce a minimum output of interesting and topical stories, with audio impact for radio and visual impact for television. The campaign news director who understands the strengths, weaknesses, preferences, and peculiarities of journalists can best produce news for the deadlines of various media. The news director must persuade the candidate of the overriding importance of news coverage and explain the specific requirements and deadlines of alternative media, individual media outlets, and journalists. The news director's persuasion, explanation, and periodic reinforcement spur the candidate to be generous with his time, as well as cooperative and responsive with the news media.

Media Personnel. Many reporters are in the "news business" to earn a living, not for a higher or more noble purpose. This is especially true in the electronic media, notably television; many reporters covering candidates in metropolitan media markets have little interest in current or political events, and some barely read the daily newspapers. Some broadcast reporters may attend a news conference without any prior research or preparation, their questions are often sophomoric, and they may even be unable to define the story's lead. These problems have been aggravated by the FCC's "affirmative action" emphasis to encourage or *force* television and radio stations to hire reporters on the basis of racial, ethnic, or sexual

---

[c] For an excellent discussion of techniques of network television news bias, see Bruce Herschensohn, *The Gods of Antenna* (New Rochelle, N.Y.: Arlington House, 1976).

Exhibit 4-1
Guidelines for the News Director/Spokesperson

1. Treat different types of media, media outlets, and individual journalists fairly. Avoid giving special privileges, extra lead time on stories, confidential information, and so forth to favored journalists. Fairness sometimes means *unequal* treatment: print and electronic media must be treated differently to be treated fairly—in terms of their unique needs. Remember that what is perceived as favoritism will make many enemies for each friend made.

2. Answer questions and return telephone calls promptly. Don't be evasive; don't lie; don't stall. If the news director cannot return a telephone call, a subordinate should; the reporter may be on a deadline, or the subordinate may be able to answer a routine query (e.g., on the candidate's schedule).[a]

3. Keep commitments. Never make a commitment to provide information, return a telephone call, get a reporter a seat on the campaign plane, and so forth unless you can keep the commitment.

4. Let the reporter write the story. Don't give gratuitous advice or ask to see the story as it is written or before it is sent. If rapport between news media and campaign exists, the journalist may seek counsel regarding what the lead of the story should be; be responsive, not patronizing; suggestions should be gentle, not overbearing. Don't be pushy as to offend; don't criticize style.

5. Push the campaign's news stories. Don't encourage reporters to use different leads or get sidetracked, unless the revised story can conceivably benefit the campaign or the reporter is prominent, assertive, and has superior news judgment; the story will be written anyway. Encourage the reporter to use the campaign's preferred "angle"; don't be led astray into supporting speculation for a reporter's novel angle that could hurt the candidate.[b]

6. Use discretion. The spokesperson should not be forever talkative, or he may succeed in getting publicity, but the *wrong* kind. When in doubt, stop talking.

7. Act like a colleague or peer. Don't act superior. Empathize with reporter's problems, especially those who earn poor salaries or are away from their families. But don't become so close that the candidate or campaign is compromised. Beware of the alcohol problems prominent in the news profession.

8. Turn the other cheek. Insist on corrections or retractions only if the error is monumental. Don't complain to a reporter's superiors about mistakes unless they are repeated, frequent, or damaging. Don't go to a superior before discussing the problem with the reporter. In a good campaign, complaints should be rare or nonexistent.

9. Start with a clean slate. Don't write off allegedly antagonistic or hostile media outlets or individual journalists, but give them a new chance.

10. Be humble. Don't hesitate to ask editors and journalists how they can be helped, what their deadlines and precise requirements are, what their preferences for news release formats and styles are, and so forth.

---

[a]Many campaigns institute a formal system to log telephone calls. Each time a reporter or editor calls, the time, name of the caller, media outlet, subject of call, and person taking the message are entered in the daily log. When the call is returned and the matter handled, its disposition is noted in the log, including time the call was returned or matter handled and by whom. The log can be reviewed throughout the day and at the end of the day to insure follow-up.

[b]The spokesperson should not accept a damaging assumption within a reporter's question. For example, "Do you think the President's trip to campaign for Smith will help him?" or "Will Mr. Smith's position on the public works legislation further cut his support among union

members?'' Another example is the "Do you deny that . . .?" form of questions. In the first example, the reporter may ask the question to determine if the President has already agreed to a campaign appearance as yet unannounced; or, if a hypothetical question, to put the campaign in a position of speculating that a possible trip might hurt the campaign. In the second example, either a "yes" or "no" response accepts the assumption that Smith's support among union members has *already* been cut. In the final example, the spokesperson, by denying a charge, no matter how ludicrous, is put in the position of dignifying it. The lead or headline can be, "Smith Denies . . . ." based on the spokesperson's denial. In many cases, these questions are best answered by either explicitly rejecting the assumption or instead, of answering yes or no, making a short, affirmative statement of position. For example, "The campaign has not yet decided whether individuals from outside the state will be campaigning for Mr. Smith, let alone who or when. Just as soon as any firm commitments are made, you will know." For example, "Mr. Smith's position on the public works legislation is entirely consistent with his campaign platform of cutting federal spending. He believes this platform is in the best interest of all Americans, including union members." Finally, responding to the "deny" type question, the spokesperson often simply makes a flat statement such as, "Mr. Smith believes that . . . ." or "Mr. Smith's position, which he has reiterated throughout the campaign, is that . . . ."

These points apply also to the candidate who must answer questions at news conferences or in interviews. Many questions are of the "When did you stop beating your wife variety?" There is an explicit or implicit assumption that cannot and must not be accepted by the candidate. The correct response is *not*, "Last Tuesday." Nor is it, "I do not beat my wife," since this could result in the headline, "Smith Denies Wife Beating Charge." Notice that this headline, and the news story on which it is based, may never mention who (if anyone) ever made the charge. The correct response, pursuing this simple, classic example, is "I believe very strongly in the institution of marriage. Perhaps my viewpoint reflects the happiness that my wife, Mary, and I have shared for the last twenty five years. We love each other deeply. No marriage is perfect, but ours comes as close as anyone's." Essentially, many news conference questions and answers are *political* versions of this example. Finally, if there were still a follow up question, "Mr. Smith, do you or don't you beat your wife?" the reply would be something like, "Of course I answered it. The answer is obvious and inescapable from what I have just said."

In conclusion, the candidate or spokesperson should be alert for questions posed in such a way that either a "yes" or "no" answer presents problems. Although there are seemingly only these two alternative answers, it is possible, as shown, to answer the question on the candidate's or spokesman's own terms.

quotas. In the print media, political news coverage is complicated by the fact that the journalistic profession, outside of the major newspapers and the largest media markets, is not financially rewarding. Many reporters who cover government and politics for smaller dailies or for weeklies experience high turnover, partly due to relatively low-pay scales.

For a variety of reasons, including the media's exposure of Watergate, enrollment in journalism schools is growing rapidly. This influx of potential reporters into a job market growing less rapidly than journalism enrollment may encourage reporters to stay where they are, because alternative jobs are scarce. Already some wire service offices have stopped hiring, and the result is that reporters who cover political stories are relatively more seasoned. The candidate's news conference should not be a training ground for the novice reporter; this has been the case too often in the past.[d]

The news director and staff should emphasize personal contact with as many individual publishers, editors, and reporters as possible. The news director should visit newspapers and television and radio stations before the campaign begins, and he should maintain telephone contact—even when he does not need a favor. The humble news director who regards his job as a continuing learning experience, reflecting constant changes in American journalism, is better able to become friends with working journalists; such friendship enhances the professional relationship between campaign and media. The news director should take the initiative to make appointments with media personnel—at times convenient to the workday and deadlines of the individual journalist. The initial meeting is a get-acquainted session for the campaign news director to introduce himself and to indicate clearly both the campaign's positive attitude toward the news media and its interest in proper servicing. This is the time to discuss practical matters—such as finding out who the relevant staff members at the media outlet are (and meeting as many of them as possible); querying editors regarding deadlines and busy days of the week or times of the day; and determining policies toward news releases (e.g., format, length, convenient delivery method), news conferences (e.g., ability of the news media outlet to cover news conferences and their criteria for newsworthiness), feature stories (e.g., on candidate's wife, family, local volunteer leaders), and so forth.

The nation's most experienced and respected political reporters are generally not preoccupied with their self-importance. Strangely enough, the reporters climbing the ladder to the top, especially the novice who is looking for another Watergate, are impressed with their own power and importance. The talented campaign news director is able to humor these journalists by making them feel as important as they wish to feel.

Weekly Newspapers. If the newspapers make endorsements or if the campaign is in a local district involving a few weeklies, the news director

---

[d] The U.S. Department of Labor estimates that there will be four new journalism graduates for each job opening. Although the number continues to increase (for example, a 16.5 percent increase between 1974 and 1975), job openings will probably not increase. Newspapers are holding jobs constant or in some cases retrenching. One reason is the increased costs of publishing, especially labor and newsprint (which increased from $165 a ton in 1973 to $250 a ton in 1976). Increased competition for relatively few openings will keep salaries low, except for the major publications with unusually high salaries. For example, a reporter at *The Los Angeles Times* earns about $30,000 within eight years; a reporter at *The New York Times* earns $22,672 after only two years; a reporter at *The Washington Post* earns $24,700 after four years. However, the small and medium size newspapers have much lower salaries. (*Christian Science Monitor*, Nov. 25, 1975; *Wall Street Journal*, Jan. 19, 1976).

(probably called press secretary) should meet the publisher. One person may be publisher and editor; if not, meet the editor who makes news policy. Larger weeklies may have a city, news, or managing editor or a reporter who specializes in civic affairs, local government, and local elections. This reporter may cover Chamber of Commerce, community and service club activities in off-campaign periods. Weekly newspapers are usually limited operations, and the Level C candidate and press secretary should meet as many personnel as possible. Level A and Level B campaigns should encourage local volunteer leaders to make contact in their own community with weekly newspaper personnel. The candidate for statewide office should have weekly newspaper editors on his statewide mailing lists, and they should be notified of, and invited to, local appearances and news conferences when the candidate visits the area. It is sometimes advisable to schedule a luncheon exclusively for local weekly newspaper publishers and editors. Often weeklies are part of a chain, with a single publisher and several editors and reporters, or a single publisher-editor for the entire chain, with a couple of reporters who service all the weeklies that comprise the chain.

Because weeklies have small staffs, they usually do not cover campaign events and news conferences. Therefore, the campaign should take the initiative in supplying the relevant person at the weekly with news releases, photographs, and captions. Ideally, these releases should be hand delivered by individuals known to the local editor rather than mailed "blind." Since weekly newspapers are often distributed free to maintain circulation figures and justify advertising rates, this preoccupation leads to flexible deadlines for advertising, but inflexible, early deadlines for news. It should be reiterated that the news release should arrive before the newspaper's deadline (usually Monday or Tuesday, but sometimes sooner, for publication Wednesday or Thursday), and the release should require little or no editing.

Daily Newspapers. The publisher and editorial board decide editorial policy. Newspapers that are part of chains may have autonomous authority— that is, local editors decide local endorsements. The candidate and news director should meet the publisher, editor or executive editor, associate editors, editorial page editor, and editorial page writers; these individuals help shape editorial policy. Other key contacts (who may or may not be on an editorial board) include the news or managing editor as well as the metropolitan and city editors; these individuals help decide how much space is allocated to political news and the individual reporter's assignments. Also, the attitude of editors may have some effect on the reporter's attitudes.

The metropolitan or city editor usually oversees news policy. Larger newspapers have several managing or desk editors working different shifts. It is prudent to make initial contact with all the relevant personnel, learn their names, and add them to the campaign mailing list. It is important to learn which editors decide how many staff, how much overtime, travel, and expense budget is to be allocated to political coverage, and which editors decide which reporters will cover the campaign. Major metropolitan newspapers will usually rotate reporters among Level A and Level B campaigns to minimize the effect of a reporter's bias on any one campaign. Editors also don't want reporters to be unduly influenced, favorably or unfavorably, by any campaign. Mailing the campaign schedule to editors as well as reporters facilitates this rotating process.

Other personnel the campaign may encounter include: (1) the *assignment* or *roving reporter*, who has no specialty and is getting diverse experience on different parts of a daily newspaper that can afford few specialists; (2) the *correspondent*, who reports from abroad, Washington, D.C., the state capitol, a domestic bureau, or the suburbs; (3) the *beat reporter*, who is based at the city hall, the courthouse, the jail, or the like; and (4) the *political editor* or *reporter* who specializes in government, politics, and campaigns. Another important personnel group includes copyeditors and the desk and rewrite staff, who take reports over the telephone from a reporter, often by using a tape recorder, correct for grammar, syntax, and factual errors, and then rewrite and edit the story to fit space requirements.

Radio Stations. If there is a chairman of the board or president, this person is analogous to the newspaper publisher; the vice president and general manager is usually the chief operating officer. Both individuals may utilize an editorial board to decide on endorsements, which, like the endorsements of newspapers or television stations, are far less important than the quantity and quality of news coverage.

The station's news director usually decides how much of the station's time will be devoted to political news. In larger stations, assistant news directors and assignment editors help determine reporting priorities, workloads, and specific assignments for reporters. The 24-hour all news stations have shifts, with a ranking editor on each shift who edits or writes copy and who may assign reporters in the field. At smaller stations, an individual may be both reporter and on-the-air announcer, in contrast to larger stations that distinguish between announcers and reporters. Smaller stations may use news releases if they are very short and do not require substantial rewriting or editing to conform to "audio style." The larger, more competitive stations use news releases mainly for background or to stimulate story ideas. These releases project the campaign's image and may stimulate interest, but they do not serve radio's need for *immediate* news, unless the release is hand delivered. Even then, it is preferable for the news to be in audio form—a tape, telephone interview, or the actuality itself (the radio reporter covering the candidate's event or news conference).

Although reporters in larger radio stations have little influence over their story assignments, they affect the coverage by selecting what to tape, what questions to ask, and what commentary to add. This discretionary power is especially important in coverage telephoned to the station by the reporter at a campaign event; the report is "live" or shortly after the event. If the reporter brings the tape back to the station, he may do his own editing—thus affecting what is actually aired. The shift editor, or the news director at a small station, usually decides how much time to allocate to the story; hence the campaign should maintain personal contact with the station's news director, assignment and shift editors, and field reporters. Radio is like television in an important respect: once the station sends someone to cover a story, it will probably be used in some form because the station already invested time in covering it.

The news director should determine early the radio station's policy regarding the acceptability of taped statements by the candidate. Will they be used? How long should they be—20, 25, 30, 40 seconds? Should there be two alternate lengths? How topical should they be (e.g., an excerpt from a speech or news conference statement scheduled for that day)? What are the technical requirements of the tape? Will the radio station personnel accept taped statements by telephone? What are the guidelines?

The news director should work out appropriate mechanisms to accommodate all the radio stations in the district or state. The Level A and Level B campaign requires elaborate, impersonal mechanisms; the Level C campaign can accommodate most stations on an individual basis. In both cases, campaigns should beware of selling stories already covered in the print media.

The station's program director, who usually oversees all programming or all programming except news, can help the campaign exploit interview programs, talk programs, and possible radio debates. The campaign should also make contact with the producers and hosts of relevant station programs; in small stations, the host may also be the producer. Through personal contact and continuous follow-up, the campaign can maximize in-person appearances as well as "call-in" interviews. Major stations in large media markets may also have a public affairs or community affairs director who can become involved in programming political coverage, including issues programs, debates, and political educational efforts.

Television Stations. The vice president and general manager is usually the senior decision maker at a network affiliated station; an independent station may have a president or chairman who is above him. The news director negotiates a budget to cover all news operations, within which political news can be a small part. The larger the station, the more administrative tasks the news director has, and the more influential the assignment editor. Major stations have associate, deputy, or assistant assignment editors who help determine which stories to cover and which reporters to assign to those stories. These assignment editors have life-and-death power over political news; in large media markets, they administer as many as a dozen camera crews, and they can order a reporter to cover or not cover a story. Television field reporters cannot even eat lunch without the concurrence of the assignment editor.[e]

Except in small stations, most anchormen and anchorwomen simply read the news; they do not write it or decide how much time to give to each story. The news producers typically have the ultimate decision on which stories make it on the air (most that have been previously covered are aired) and how much time each story and reporter will get. Producers may also permit occasional live interviews with the candidate who can visit the studio during the newscast. The field reporter is important because, like the radio reporter, he affects the tone of coverage and is likely to participate in editing the film of the campaign event or news conference. This reporter is usually given a limited amount of time, stated in minutes and seconds, and is expected to present the most vivid, interesting footage of the candidate or event, with a minimum of commentary or with comments as the viewer sees footage (''voice over silent film'').

The campaign should establish personal contact with the television station's interview and talk show producers, talent coordinators, and hosts regarding appearances by the candidates, television debates, and special telecasts. If the station has a public affairs, community affairs, or editorial director, this contact should also be cultivated.

Magazines. It is important to realize that although *Time* and *Newsweek* correspondents file lengthy dispatches, only a few appear in print and only a tiny fraction of the copy is actually published. The copy is heavily edited, severely rewritten—often under tight deadlines. The resulting stories written by each magazine's ''nation'' staff may barely resemble the original correspondent's dispatch, although *Newsweek* is trying to improve the process and has at least adopted a policy, since 1975, of listing the names of the correspondents and New York City editor/writer to indicate some accountability. *U.S. News & World Report* generally covers political campaigns by permitting its field reporter to write the final story.

The Level A and Level B campaigns should become acquainted with the bureau chiefs and correspondents of these magazines and any other relevant magazines. Level B campaigns are often wise to treat out-of-state

---

[e] Some network affiliate stations in New York and Los Angeles have as many as eighteen crews, counting the mini-camera or helicopter crews.

dailies as magazines. For example, *The Wall Street Journal*, *The New York Times*, *The Washington Post*, *Christian Science Monitor*, and other major dailies and news services may maintain bureaus, correspondents, or "stringers" (occasional correspondents who are paid only when articles are used) in the state capitol and principal cities in the state. These contacts should be cultivated and should receive campaign mailings, so they are primed to cover the campaign if requested by their editors. Perhaps the campaign can even spur coverage if the news director sells the local bureau chief or correspondent on the national news value of the campaign.

Other Media. Each campaign must assess the importance of the wide variety of other media—ethnic, union, corporate and house organ, and so forth—and the importance of making and cultivating individual contacts. No statewide campaign can afford not to make key contacts early with the wire service bureau chiefs, political writers, and field reporters whose coverage can penetrate daily newspapers throughout the state.

Media Concepts. This survey of political journalism and personnel contacts would be incomplete without a brief review of important definitions or concepts.

Deadline. Any deadline imposes subordinate deadlines; for example, typesetting, editing, fact verification, writing, film editing, and film developing. Know the practical implications of any deadline.

Lead. The most important part of the news story; it is alternatively the opening paragraph or the headline, which is based on the opening paragraph. In the electronic media, it is either the precommercial introduction ("Next we'll hear about . . .") or teaser, or it is the opening line of the reporter. The campaign should push stories for which it can define the lead or several possible leads (all favorable).

Reaction Statement. This is the candidate's reaction to a major news development. The efficient campaign minimizes the time between a news development (e.g., when the item crosses the wire ticker) and the candidate's reaction—that is, the issuance, taping, or filming of his statement. Reaction statements should seem assertive and definitive, not negative or defensive. Although promptly issued, they should not be rash or poorly worded. They may be brief and succinct, but they say something, and they are quotable ("good copy"). The well-run campaign issues many reaction statements to exploit publicity opportunities, but these are in addition to, not instead of, its planned publicity initiatives. The reaction statement is always consistent with campaign strategy, and it should be a net plus for the campaign.

On-the-Record. Anything the candidate or spokesperson says or does is unequivocally authorized for publication or airing unless (a) stated otherwise in advance; (b) the journalist accepts the stipulation; and (c) the journalist's word is trustworthy. Journalists do not want to know what they cannot use, unless they also receive substantial material they can use.

Off-the-Record. The statement or activity cannot be reported. The journalist is not obligated to honor an off-the-record request made after the action or statement; the understanding must be in advance of the statement. When speaking off-the-record, which should be the exception and not the rule in the campaign, the spokesperson may have to reiterate that the journalist in question not only cannot report the conversation, but he cannot relate it to another journalist for him to report.

Attribution. The source of the quotation may be mentioned, and the source quoted directly. Not-for-attribution permits material to be used, but not attributed to the source.

Background. This usually means not for direct attribution, but otherwise quotable if attributed to a "high source," "reliable source," "source close to the candidate," or an "informed source." *Deep* background usually specifies more ground rules, often only indirect rather than direct quotation, or attribution to a mythical or disguised source. News directors use background conversations to plant story ideas and leads with journalists.

Exclusive. The campaign may give information or a story to a single media outlet or reporter without giving it to anyone else. This calculated risk could make enemies and cause rival outlets or journalists to become jealous and hostile. If exclusives are rotated among competitors by giving stories to the most interested or relevant media or journalists each time, the campaign news director can successfully exploit this policy.

Advance. Like an exclusive, an advance (i.e., giving a story to one media outlet or reporter before giving it to others) involves favoritism. The advance can reward the aggressive, hard-working journalist persistently pursuing a story; it can also establish rapport with a journalist, who now "owes" the campaign. Like an exclusive, this policy is best used by experienced news directors.

Feature. Unlike "straight" news, the feature is less current and immediate, but still topical and of general concern. It usually has a human interest angle and may have some appeal to readers, listeners, or viewers not normally interested in politics.

Editing. Electronic and print media both have decision makers who actually decide what or how much is aired or printed. If the campaign is dissatisfied with the final output, it should determine whether the reporter or the editor is the culprit.

5 The News Release

The news release is the necessary, but not solely sufficient, condition for a campaign news operation. The higher the level of office sought, the less important the news release, because news is made on the "campaign trail." Regardless of the type of campaign, news releases are only relevant if they concern *news*. The value of news releases is significantly enhanced if the recipient has had personal contact with the candidate and his news director and if the delivery of the news release is not solely a function of the postal service.

Two additional overriding considerations relate to the effect of the news release. First, its topic and substance must reflect campaign strategy. Second, its newsworthiness must reflect the recipient's news judgment— that is, its importance, timeliness, topical concern, and so forth are judged by an editor in terms of the publication's constituency and the amount of space available.

The primary function of the news release is to communicate news that can be aired or printed. Most news releases result in print media coverage, because radio prefers audio stories and television prefers visual stories. Some news releases are shortened and rewritten in broadcast style to increase the likelihood of use by radio stations.[a] The primary function of the news release should not obscure an important related function. News releases provide background information for reference and files, use in editorial endorsements, and use by reporters who may subsequently be assigned to cover the campaign. Moreover, they indicate activity and can project a positive image of the campaign by conveying professionalism. Putting key journalists on mailing list for releases may not generate stories, but it may stir interest that can lead to stories days, weeks, or months later.

Format and Style

Various public relations firms and publicists vary format and style, but certain rules and uniformity must be observed to insure that the news

---

[a] News releases written for radio are to be used on the air, rather than appear in a newspaper story. Hence, these news releases are written in conversational, even nonsentence form, with special emphasis on phonetics. The interested reader can purchase current editions of informative style guides published by the two major wire services for one dollar each. These are *The Associated Press Broadcast News Stylebook* (New York: Associated Press, 1975) and *United Press International Broadcast Stylebook* (New York: United Press International, 1975).

release looks like a news release. The busy editor must be able to identify the source of the news release readily, judge its timeliness, and grasp its subject matter at a glance. Even the quickly written reaction statement should be in proper release form, but the news release that is not rushed into production should be flawless, with special attention to avoiding errors in grammar, diction, spelling, or typing.

Structure and Appearance

Any news release should have several basic parts: the printed stationery heading; release instructions; campaign contact; headline; possibly dateline; and text. It should be neat, clear, and legible, with particular attention given to the finished product (i.e., the duplicated copies). In addition to the types of errors mentioned above, common errors include omitting sentences or paragraphs in typing a final draft, omitting or transposing digits, using the wrong days or dates in release instructions or within the text, errors in punctuation, and omitting quotation marks.

Stationery. White paper, preferably of standard size (8½″ × 11″), should be used. Since most news releases should not exceed a single page, some campaigns also stock legal size (8½″ × 14″) paper to use as an alternative— that is, to avoid a second page. Legal size paper can also be used for speech excerpts and texts. Obviously, only one side of the paper should be used.

An important digression concerns the use of "covering" releases. Generally, any news release of more than two pages should have a covering release. This version, which is limited to one page (and preferably less than the full page), refers to the accompanying, longer material (e.g., a speech text). Thus, the busy editor can quickly scan the covering release to note the lead and basic information, and he has the option of reading the longer release to get more copy or for background.

The printed heading of the stationery should be distinctive, yet easily read. The logos (typography) should be attention getting and totally consistent with the logos used on all campaign materials—other stationery, envelopes, business cards, signs, billboards, brochures, and newspaper advertising. The printed heading should be a color other than black; more than one color is helpful, but the colors should be the official campaign colors. Within the heading, the word "news" or "news release" should be prominent; for example, "Smith Campaign News" or "News From Smith for Congress." The printed heading must include the name of the campaign, its full address (including zip code) in smaller type, and the telephone number (including area code). Never put any part of the heading along the side or at the bottom of the stationery, although a required disclaimer line showing the name of the printer may be printed at the bottom.

The standard (#10) business envelope should have the address in the customary upper lefthand corner, with consistent typography and colors. In the lower lefthand corner, the words NEWS RELEASE in all capital, block letters may be printed. Campaign schedules, or corrections to the schedule, should be mailed in envelopes with the words IMPORTANT: SCHEDULE ENCLOSED printed or rubber-stamped in the lower lefthand corner, instead of the words NEWS RELEASE. In Level A and Level B campaigns, the schedule is usually the most important kind of news release.

Ideally, multipage releases, such as speech texts, speech excerpts, related news releases, and campaign schedules should be mailed in manila envelopes (usually $9'' \times 12''$) if the enclosures are more than ten pages. The manila envelope should resemble the format of the business envelope. If photographs are sent, cardboard backing should be inserted, and the words FRAGILE: PHOTOGRAPH ENCLOSED or DO NOT BEND: PHOTOGRAPH or something similar should be rubber-stamped on the envelope. Multipage releases should always be stapled in the upper left hand corner.

Release Instructions. The preferred position is the upper left hand corner of the stationery, usually double or triple spaced below the printed heading and beginning flush with the lefthand typewritten margin. Most releases should use the words FOR IMMEDIATE RELEASE in all capital letters. This indicates the information can and should be utilized as soon as received. More cumbersome is FOR RELEASE UPON RECEIPT, which connotes that the release is received by different media outlets or editors at different times. In the past, a date was listed below either of these instructions. However, if the release is current and the campaign's distribution system efficient, listing a date can be redundant and confusing. The date is more likely to prevent rather than encourage publication, especially if the release arrives after the date, or even on the same date, if the editor believes competitors received the release earlier that day. Never use a date in the release instructions if it will *discourage* publication, as can happen if the release arrives after the date.

Dated Release. If the news release concerns an event yet to occur and the release will arrive by mail or other means before the event, the release instructions will be dated; for example, FOR RELEASE: MONDAY, OCT. 20. Including the year is usually unnecessary, but including the day of the week avoids confusion. Conscientious editors and reporters honor dated release instructions, but they may ignore them or discard the release if the instructions are foolish or amateurish. The instructions should facilitate, not inhibit, use of the news release.

In the example, the release instructions indicate the information can be disseminated anytime after midnight, Sunday, October 19. This means that a 24-hour all news radio station could use the information in news broadcasts aired anytime after midnight. A daily newspaper could utilize the information for any newspapers distributed on Monday; this may be interpreted to delay usage for the *preview* edition of the Monday newspaper, if that edition is sold at newsstands on Sunday evening. Dated release instructions do not prohibit researching or writing the story before the release time, nor do they prohibit editing, typesetting, or layout. The television or radio station can film or tape before the release time. The sole consideration is actual publication or airing of the news.

Timed Release. In sophisticated, fast-moving campaigns, release instructions can be very precise. For example, FOR RELEASE: MONDAY, OCT. 20 PMs indicates that publication or airing Monday afternoon or evening is acceptable. The important guideline is whether instructions encourage or inhibit coverage. In Level A and Level B campaigns, journalists expect precise release instructions; for example, FOR RELEASE: TUESDAY, OCT. 21—10 A.M. These instructions might apply to a news release based on a news conference scheduled for that time; publication or airing of the statement before the news conference might limit publicity, relative to the news conference's potential. As a practical case, consider an afternoon newspaper whose first street edition is out at about 11 a.m.; only subsequent editions could cover the news conference, because it occurs around deadline time for its first edition. However, the campaign can give the night editor the release the prior evening. The editor, a desk or rewrite staffer, or a reporter can write the story in the past tense, as if they covered the news conference, and the story can appear in the first edition. If the newspaper sends someone to cover the news conference, later editions can have an updated story or even a photograph.

Other variations include such phrases as HOLD FOR: or ADVANCE FOR:, which are followed by the day, date, and time. When these releases are used by wire services, they may repeat the release instructions on the wire or vary them slightly to reflect their own style. These instructions enable the wire service to run a story before it can be released, with directions for holding the material for publication or airing or for indicating the material is an advance for subsequent publication or airing. A more categorical variation, for example, EMBARGOED UNTIL WEDNESDAY, OCT. 22—2 P.M., is usually reserved for important announcements, especially White House, Pentagon, and other sensitive news sources. In such cases, it is not unusual for the wire service to prepare copy but not even run it on the ticker until the specified time.

Advisory or Background. If information in a news release is primarily helpful, rather than for publication—for example, a change in the candidate's schedule—the word ADVISORY may be used instead of FOR IMMEDIATE RELEASE. In this case, or when BACKGROUND or BACKGROUND INFORMATION is substituted, the information can still be published or aired, but the implication is that the news release is mainly intended to provide information to help the reporter do his job.

Special Instructions. The campaign may issue certain news releases for particular media. Weekly newspapers might receive a release with any of the following instructions: FOR RELEASE WEEK OF MONDAY, OCT. 26 or SPECIAL TO WEEKLY NEWSPAPERS: WEEK OF MONDAY, OCT. 26 or SPECIAL TO WEEKLY NEWSPAPERS: RELEASE WEDNESDAY, OCT. 28. If all the weekly newspapers are published on Wednesday, the last instruction might be the most appropriate. These instructions are especially relevant to the campaign that does not mail all news releases to weeklies, but mails one important release each week. The rationale is that an editor willing to use one story each week will use a good release but will not take the time to select one release from a dozen, let alone write a composite story drawn from several releases.

The broadcast style news release, which is in capsule form and written as if the words are to be spoken, might have special instructions to indicate its intended use; for example, FOR IMMEDIATE RELEASE TO RADIO STATIONS should indicate that radio stations, and no other media outlets, are receiving the release, just as the examples above imply weekly newspapers are the exclusive recipient.

In a Level C campaign, it is possible to modify a news release to fit the individual requirements of each weekly newspaper, perhaps by substituting names, phrases, or a paragraph, or by adjusting overall length. The added effort may guarantee publication. In these cases the news release instructions can also vary. For example, SPECIAL TO THE ELM CITY GAZETTE can be used with or without more specific instructions; FOR IMMEDIATE RELEASE TO THE ELM CITY GAZETTE is also acceptable.

News releases based on news conferences, statements, reaction statements, or actualities may arouse interest at radio stations but only inspire nominal coverage because the information is not audio oriented. Sometimes the radio station may not use the release at all because it is competing against a less newsworthy, but audio-oriented story. Sometimes, campaigns place a typewritten instruction, double spaced, just under the regular release instructions (or, alternatively, under the name of the contact person); for example, AUDIO RELEASE AVAILABLE: 212-725-7277 or AUDIO TAPE FEED AVAILABLE: 212-725-7277 or STATEMENT ACTUALITY AVAILABLE: 800-666-3000 are all acceptable (the last telephone number is toll free).

Another special instruction sometimes placed just below the normal release instruction explains enclosures or attachments. For example, NOTE: COMPLETE SPEECH TEXT ATTACHED indicates to the recipient that the entire text of the candidate's speech is attached or enclosed, although the brief release mentions only the most newsworthy portions.

Additional References. If the headline or text of the story mentions any days or dates that can be confused with the release day, date, or time, the writer should consider parenthetical insertions of the day or date; for example, *Monday (July 8)* or *July 8 (Monday)* within the headline or text may prevent confusion, although only the day or the date, not both, will probably be used in publication or airing, or simply *today* or *yesterday*. Whenever *today* or *yesterday* are used in the release headline or text and can be confused with release instructions, parenthetical clarification should also be considered; for example, *today (July 8)* or *yesterday (July 7)*.

The tense of the verbs in the release is a function of the release instructions (day, date, time) and dateline, if one is used (see below). Announcements and schedules can be future tense; releases written after the event can be past tense. However, releases written before the event with release instructions delaying publication or airing until the event, are written in the past tense (e.g., "Smith said today" or "Smith said this morning").

Contact Person. In the top righthand corner of the news release, typewritten below the printed heading, approximately symmetrical with the release instructions, is the name of the contact person. Alternative formats include: CONTACT: John Smith; PRESS CONTACT: John Smith; PLEASE CONTACT: John Smith; MEDIA CONTACT: John Smith; FOR FURTHER INFORMATION. PLEASE CONTACT: John Smith; or FOR ADDITIONAL INFORMATION, PLEASE CONTACT: John Smith. If the campaign's telephone number is not prominently featured in the printed stationery heading (letterhead), it should be in parentheses after the contact's name.

The contact person listed is always the news director, press secretary, or whoever is the campaign's senior spokesperson. Sometimes a second name is added because this person actually wrote the release or is more conversant with its contents. Never add a second name unless that person is known to the media and acceptable as an alternate spokesperson (e.g., the deputy press secretary). It is inadvisable to list more than two persons; occasionally a second or third person is listed as a specific kind of contact. For example, LOCAL CONTACT: John Smith or ELM CITY CONTACT: John Smith followed by Smith's local telephone number provides a local contact for Elm City media, if the subject of the news release concerns events or people in the Elm City area.

Another variation would be to provide a contact for radio stations. Examples would include: AUDIO CONTACT; RADIO STATION CONTACT; AUDIO TAPE AVAILABLE; or similar words, followed by a colon and the name and telephone number of the contact.

Telephone. If the news release lists only one name, then whenever anyone calls the campaign headquarters and asks for the contact, the mention of the name should indicate the call is media oriented. The single name is a code word, a convenient mechanism for reporters and editors who are not always in a position to remember more than one name. They become accustomed to the news director's name, perhaps one or two other names if they are actively covering the campaign, and they may ask for these names regardless of the names listed on the release. The campaign's telephone system should provide for immediate routing of such calls to the proper person, with the following guidelines: (1) the media contact telephone number should be answered beyond regular campaign business hours; (2) the telephone should not ring more than a few times before being answered; (3) the person answering the telephone should be courteous, professional, and responsive and, above all, able to refer the caller quickly to the right person, especially if the news director is traveling.

The news release should list only one telephone number, and it should be a rotary line (actually several lines, with automatic rerouting of calls to whichever line is open). In large campaigns, the news operation should have its own telephone system so that the editor or reporter does not waste time going through a switchboard. In any campaign, the most important reporters who regularly cover the campaign will insist on, and should be given, direct access lines to speed communications. In the large campaign, the news director and staff should be reachable through the switchboard, special news operation telephones (rotary system), and direct lines. Callers should never be asked to call a second number within the headquarters to reach the contact person.

Many Level A and Level B campaigns have "800" toll free numbers, especially for use by radio stations in securing audio feeds. In some cases, an 800 line can be automated to provide the audio feed and then disconnect. If the line is not automated, the customary guidelines apply.

The telephone number given out for any contact person should always be rechecked before the release is distributed. The line should not be left unattended, especially in the period immediately following distribution of the release. The line should not be busy and it should never be answered by someone who cannot convey a professional image. For many callers, the person answering the telephone may be the first or only personal contact with the campaign. When campaign events occur in the evening or on weekends, or in larger campaigns involving major travel for journalists, the telephone line must be attended from about 8 a.m. until late in the evening, perhaps 8 or 10 p.m. If necessary, direct telephone lines, an answering service, or special night lines can be used. Journalists covering Level A campaigns with fast-moving travel schedules are often given the news director's home telephone number.

Queries. An editor or reporter may need to verify facts, numbers, or quotations in the news release. Questions may arise as to the use of a word or phrase, or a reference to prior positions of the candidate or his opponent.

Controversial releases may require telephone confirmation that they are authentic. The caller may inquire about substantiation or proof of a serious charge, or he may request background information. Often, the caller wants to know the significance of the news release: "How does it relate to campaign strategy—does it modify, toughen, or soften strategy, or is it a new strategy?" Since news releases may arouse interest in the campaign without inspiring an immediate story, the caller may be seeking more information about the campaign. News releases may inspire requests for interviews with the candidate or to travel with the candidate.

Other queries relate to obtaining past news releases, media information kits (background of the candidate), photographs, the candidate's biography, issues papers, speech texts, and so forth. These requests may be routine, but many telephone calls are made under deadlines. Even calls not made under tight deadlines can be very important, such as invitations to editorial board meetings, television or radio program interviews, and the like. News releases announcing campaign events, the candidate's appearance, or entire schedules will stimulate calls regarding dates, places, and times. Editors or reporters may call to determine more information (e.g., expected crowd size, topic of speech) to help them decide whether to cover or attend the event or whom to send. When these queries relate to the candidate's schedule, the news operation should act as the journalist's ombudsman, rather than shift the query to someone in the scheduling operation.

Preparing the Release

Proper newswriting reflects professionalism and makes the journalist's job easier. Writing the release includes the headline and dateline, the text, and the use of newswriting style (see Figure 5-1).

Headline and Dateline. Commercial public relations firms sometimes omit a headline, because headlines are discarded or rewritten by headline writers. Nevertheless, the campaign news release should always have a headline so the recipient can instantly note its topic and decide whether to toss it or continue reading. News releases without headlines may be tossed; with a headline, the news release can be routed to the proper person.

The headline should be typed, upper- and lower-case letters; centered vertically between the release instructions/contact person lines and the text; and centered horizontally. The headline should be one line, unless it will be too long for the normal margins or if dividing it into two lines makes it clearer. The headline should be attention getting and "snappy," but it should be truthful and reflect the topic of the news release. It should not exceed eight or ten words; preferably, it should be in sentence form, with a

FOR RELEASE:
Thursday, Sept. 14
--10:30 A.M.

FOR ADDITIONAL INFORMATION,
PLEASE CONTACT:
Harry Jones
Mike Kelly (audiotape)

SMITH WOULD OUTLAW GOVERNMENT PRICE FIXING
--CANDIDATE SCORES INFLATIONARY POLICIES FAVORING BIG BUSINESS--

Los Angeles, Sept. 14--

Harry T. Smith, Republican candidate for United States Senator, today
proposed that Congress outlaw price fixing by the federal government. Addressing
the opening session of the California Consumer League statewide convention at
the Biltmore Hotel, Smith said his first priority as Senator would be to end
what he termed "inflationary policies favoring big business."

"I intend to introduce comprehensive legislation to ban any price fixing
by Washington bureaucrats," Smith told the assembled delegates in his keynote
address this morning. "The Department of Agriculture is keeping food prices
high, and the government's regulatory commissions maintain high prices in
trucking, freight, airline travel, and many other fields. These policies favor
the entrenched big business interests by preventing competition and lower prices.
They are an insult to the American consumer."

Smith, who has made deregulation a major plank of his Senate campaign,
said his economic study task force is already at work preparing legislation
to provide for a gradual, phased end to price supports and price floors.
According to his plan, no department, agency, bureau or commission of the
federal government could prevent any firm from lowering its prices or
prevent a new competitor from entering the field.

9.12.76sj
(FULL SPEECH TEXT ATTACHED.)

Note: This illustration shows the body of a simple, covering news release. It should be typed
on distinctive news release stationery with an appropriate heading (e.g., SMITH CAMPAIGN
NEWS) and information, especially the telephone number.

Figure 5-1. Sample News Release.

present-tense verb and without unessential articles and conjunctions.
However, announcements may use the future tense or an infinitive, "Jones
Will Visit Elm City" or "Jones To Address Kiwanis." Often, a tentative
headline is written before the draft of the release, because the writer knows

the desired message; then the headline is modified and rewritten to perfection after the release text is finalized.

The headline is always based upon the first paragraph of the news release, because this lead should summarize the story. If the news release has a subsidiary point besides its major point, a subhead may be typed, single spaced, just below the headline; for example,

SMITH CALLS FOR FEDERAL TAX AND SPENDING CUTS
Republican Candidate Issues 10-point Economic Program

indicates that the tax and spending cuts are the main story, but the candidate's ten-point economic program is a subsidiary story.

The dateline is used mainly in Level A and Level B campaigns, which include considerable travel by the candidate. The dateline can show location, time, immediacy, and news relevance. It is analogous to the opening of a wire service, news service, or correspondent's dispatch to indicate the origin and date the copy was written. The origin and date of stories from abroad are always listed. However, datelines are omitted in news stories about events within a newspaper's circulation area and are not often used for other domestic cities.

Datelines on the campaign news release are typed either on the line immediately above the first line of the text, or typed as the opening of the text, followed by two hyphens and then the lead paragraph; for example, Los Angeles, Oct. 30--. In either case, the dateline begins flush left with the margin and should be underlined. These datelines should be used to call attention to the place and date of an event, especially if the candidate is traveling, or if the release is distributed in advance of an event, speech, or news conference. Once the dateline is used, the text can refer to "here" instead of the city, or to "today" instead of the date, although parenthetical clarification is sometimes added (but rarely used in the published news story, except to explain different time zones).

Text. The news release text is typed double spaced, although it is acceptable to type the last few lines single spaced to prevent the copy running into an additional page. Double-spaced copy is easier to skim, read, and edit; it leaves room to rearrange copy and place editing and typesetting symbols. Single-spaced releases will probably be tossed. Occasionally lengthy speech texts or excerpts are single spaced, but only when they are provided more for background, rather than for use in their entirety, and when the covering news release is double spaced.

The text should begin about one-third down the length of the paper, but it may be higher to fit on the page. The text, like other typewritten parts of the release, should be neatly typed, preferably on an electric typewriter, and duplicated on Xerox, IBM, or other high quality *dry* copier. If mimeographing is used, special attention should be given to typing high quality stencils (always on an electric typewriter), neatly correcting all stencil errors, and maintaining the machine in good working order. Any campaign should have more than one person who can operate the duplicating equipment and at least two pieces of duplicating equipment.

Elite typing (12 spaces to an inch) is preferable to pica (10 spaces). Left and right margins should both be about an inch, although the left margin may be one and one-half inches to permit editorial/typesetting instructions to be written or allow for the effect of stapling a multipage release. Paragraph indentations should be uniform—at least five, no more than ten spaces. Ideally, words should not be hyphenated at the end of a line, and paragraphs should not be split between pages. These rules, designed to avoid confusion as to syllables or to permit different typesetters to set different pages, are flexible. For example, the paragraph rule could result in too much white space at the bottom (there should be at least one inch).

If the news release is more than one page, the word — MORE— is typed, double spaced and centered, below the last line of copy on every page except the last. This insures that the reader or typesetter knows there is more copy. Succeeding pages are usually on plain white paper or "continuation" sheets with a small heading printed in the upper lefthand corner; for example,

SMITH FOR CONGRESS
PAGE:

If plain white paper, rather than printed stationery, is used, similar copy is typewritten five lines from the top. In the format above, one or two words may be typed in after the name of the campaign to indicate the subject of the news release; this is called a "slug" or "slug line" analogous to the slug of type set at the top of a galley to indicate that the typesetting is part of a particular story. The page number, single spaced, just below the continuation line, is usually repeated three times as shown below.

SMITH CAMPAIGN: Taxation
—2—2—2—

The end of a news release is clearly indicated by typing END or 30 or ###, double spaced and centered, below the last line of copy. The campaign can also use its own symbol if consistent; for example, *10.28.76jk* indicates the news release was typed on October 28, 1976 by a typist whose initials are jk.

Newswriting Style. Although the news release should reflect favorably on the candidate and campaign, the normal news release should be written like a news story. Unless it is simply speech excerpts or an entire speech text, and so titled, the news release expresses opinion only within attributed quotations. The release text should be written simply, clearly, and crisply. Its sentences and words, especially verbs and adjectives, should be short and understandable; avoid jargon and slang. Grammatical construction should be uncomplicated, and there should be no errors in spelling or diction. Above all, the release should be well written, accurate, and factual.

The aspiring campaign news writer has ready access to a dictionary, thesaurus, reference book of misspelled words, and appropriate style guides. The writer wants to produce a release that, space considerations permitting, could be published verbatim by a newspaper. If editors are conditioned to expect professional releases from the campaign, they will have a positive view of the campaign. The busy editor will know that any campaign news release has something to say and requires little editing. The quality news release makes it easier for the editor and reporter to do their job and hence makes for better media relations.[b]

Lead. The lead is the opening sentence or two sentences of the news release. Since most paragraphs in the news release should not exceed three sentences, the first paragraph is the lead. A journalism text lists different types of leads, but the classic lead, which answers the "5W's and H" is most relevant to political journalism. The lead should answer all or most of the following questions: Who? What? When? Where? Why? How?

Who is involved in the story?

What is happening?

When is it taking place?

Where is it taking place?

Why is it happening?

How did it happen?

In political news releases, the first four or five questions are usually the most important. The first question usually concerns the candidate, who should be identified in exactly the same way throughout the campaign (e.g., "Richard J. Smith, candidate for Congress in the 26th District" or "Dick Smith, Republican candidate for Congress"). The lead always begins with the answer to the most important question placed near the beginning of the sentence; this usually means, but not always, that the candidate's name begins the lead. It should be noted that if a dateline is used this answers the "when" and "where" questions, although the lead may refer to "today" and "here."

[b] The classic primer is the readable guide prepared by William Strunk, Jr., and E.B. White, *The Elements of Style*, 2nd ed. (New York: The Macmillan Co., 1972). In addition, each wire service publishes guides that are available for about one dollar each—*The Associated Press Stylebook* (New York: Associated Press, 1975) and the *United Press International Newswire Stylebook* (New York: United Press International, 1975).

The lead conveys the essence of the news release. It presents the campaign's viewpoint or editorial judgment as to what the story's angle or twist should be. It is the campaign's preference for what should determine the headline, since headline writers base their headline on the lead of a story. The lead should be written and rewritten until word count is minimized. Use two sentences only if one sentence will not do. Remember that the answer to any one of the questions may determine the news value of the release, and the answers are always articulated in terms of the news value of the relevant media. For example, the news release prepared for weekly newspapers regarding the campaign's appointment of a local volunteer chairperson in their area would spotlight the "who." Above all, the lead should be brief, specific, factual, and clear (watch pronouns, places, days, dates, and so forth); the verb selected should be the most strongly descriptive verb possible.

Inverted Pyramid. Traditional newswriting style is termed the inverted pyramid because each succeeding paragraph is less important than the one above it. The theory is that an editor pressed by space considerations can cut the *typewritten* story from the end; if the story is *typeset*, the necessary number of lines also can be cut from the end. This process works quite well if succeeding paragraphs provide more elaboration on the 5W's and H, rather than answer them for the first time. The inverted pyramid writing concept is so important that the release should be written, rewritten, checked, and double checked to insure that no paragraph or sentence farther down the text is more important than a paragraph or sentence above it. Miscellaneous facts should always be at the bottom.

A quotation, like any other sentence or paragraph of the news release, should naturally flow from what precedes it and into what follows it. The quotation, which is the best place to insert opinion, should be the second paragraph, possibly the third. Usually quotations are limited to one paragraph; if more than one, the quote marks are always omitted at the end of each paragraph except the last, but are always included at the beginning of each continuing paragraph.

"The best way to use a quotation is in two parts," the writer said. "The second part is as shown here."

Types of Releases

The political campaign should plan many news releases by maintaining a *futures file* that includes any idea that could be written into a news release. This file should include all options that might be available to the candidate days, weeks, even months ahead—for example, taking positions on issues, making speeches or announcements—and it should also include possible events with news potential—for example, committee formations, appointments of volunteer leaders, endorsements by prominent citizens. The futures file should be reevaluated daily to determine when specific news release options should be pursued for maximum news impact.

The futures file insures that the campaign produces a steady flow of news releases. The minimum flow is augmented by opportunistic news releases that exploit news developments, especially by reporting the candidate's reaction to them. The futures file may contain many news release ideas that can be held in readiness for the most propitious time, a criterion based on news developments and the candidate's travel and appearance schedule. The futures file may simply note that particular events require news releases; the release and substance of the wording may be best determined near the time of issuance. The lead of each news release is based both on the reading of the scheduling division's file on the event or on the candidate's speech text and the current news environment. The futures file is also termed a *hold file* to indicate that it may include an inventory of news releases scheduled for distribution at various times before, during, or after an event; each release has a different lead.

The candidate's announcement of candidacy, filing for office, formation of campaign committee, appointment of volunteer leaders or campaign manager are examples of possible news releases or news conferences. Many events that justify a news conference for a Level A or Level B campaign justify only a news release for a local campaign; conversely, precisely the opposite can be true—depending on the event or subject. News conferences are often accompanied by news releases, but the reverse is not necessarily true, especially for the local campaign that rarely calls news conferences and uses the news release as its basic communications vehicle, especially to reach weekly newspapers.

The distinction between planned news releases, which may originate in the futures file, and opportunistic news releases, which are issued on short notice to exploit news developments, is not always precise. Many of the most effective news releases that seem opportunistic can be issued so quickly only because they are adaptations of planned news releases. For example, the campaign with a full inventory of possible news release texts on issues can rapidly edit and adapt a text to news happening that day; the more comprehensive the futures file, the more rapidly the campaign can issue news releases on current events while they are still current, for the simple reason that most of the news release is already written.

Since the futures file may indicate dates for which news releases should be issued for particular events, these dates must be reviewed continually to determine the deadlines they impose. Any news release target date imposes deadlines on staff members involved in the writing and editing of the release, as well as technical deadlines peculiar to the campaign's delivery system—mail, hand delivery, and so forth. For example, the news release based on a major speech cannot be prepared until the speech text is written.

Events

Any campaign event—fund-raising dinner, rally, headquarters opening—is a potential news release. Releases issued before an event can arouse public interest and stimulate attendance. If there is any reasonable chance a pre-event news release can be printed or aired, it should be issued. A single fund-raising dinner can be the subject of several news releases that first announce the dinner, then the selection of the dinner chairman and committee, selection of the site, the name(s) of the guest speaker(s), and so on. Several releases should be issued for a campaign event if each news release has a different lead with news potential for the local media, and if the releases are distributed at reasonable intervals of time. The guideline governing leads also applies to post-event news releases that announce the amount of funds raised at a dinner or report what the banquet speaker said. However, post-event releases should usually be issued as soon as possible so that information about the event is still news.

Since news in a major campaign should be generated while the candidate campaigns, news releases are often prepared and dated in advance of events. The news release reports what has not yet happened but refers to it in the present or past tense; the release is datelined the day of the event. It is mailed or distributed before the event (or ready for distribution at the event) to enable the busy editor or reporter to write an article before the event and a possible deadline. The alternative, preparing and distributing the news release after the event, is usually impractical, because its contents are no longer news.

Speeches. The news director examines the draft of any speech text closely to determine the most exciting, newsworthy portions. If the speech lacks a quotable section, or offers conflicting leads of a lower priority to the campaign than the most desired lead, the news director may recommend redrafting portions of the text. Even a dull speech can generate news if one or two paragraphs are rewritten or inserted to draw media attention. Indeed, the candidate's basic speech that is delivered daily can be covered by the news media repeatedly if the speech text is adjusted slightly each day. Modification of the speech is like fine tuning an automobile: too many changes make for uneven and inconsistent performance. The objective is to insert paragraphs of local or particular interest to each new group, and to make the text relevant, topical, and immediate—in terms of the day's news events. This objective may require adding or dropping a section or relating a current news development as an illustration or example to part of the text. Almost any speech text can be modified to produce a new lead each day, so that reporters can feel they are reporting something that has not previously been said (and reported).[c]

The advance text of the candidate's speech is given to reporters both to make their jobs easier and to insure accurate reporting of the text. (See the guidelines for speech news releases in Exhibit 5-1.) Distributing an advance text well before the speech permits the traveling journalist to complete and file (i.e., submit for publication) the story before the speech and his possible deadline. The journalist can then relax during the speech; some reporters have been known to even avoid attending altogether. The advance text is especially valuable for television and radio personnel; it enables them to determine precisely which portions of the speech they wish to film (letting them cue camera operators) or tape record. The advance text is an absolute necessity for the reporter whose deadline is after the speech's scheduled delivery time, and for the wire or news service that wants to distribute an advance (*hold for release*) story to its subscribers.

Issues. Whenever possible, the candidate's issue positions should be related to events (speeches, news conferences, visuals, headquarters opening ceremonies, and so forth) on the campaign schedule, so the date and place can help make the story news. One exception may be issues papers that are deliberately released during slow news days, especially on weekends, or when the candidate is not campaigning. These news releases, or those based on relating issues to events, should be scheduled at intervals throughout the campaign. The campaign should not hastily use its entire inventory of research data and issue positions, nor can such material, the foundation for news releases or news conferences, lie dormant. Issues news releases, like the scheduled events to which they are often linked, should be paced to assure the campaign's upward momentum.

Support. Any support for the candidate has potential as a news release, news conference, or visual. Publicity may announce the formation of local campaign committees or adjunct groups (Doctors for . . . , Veterans for . . . , and so forth) or the appointment of volunteer and adjunct committee leaders. The campaign seeking to establish a viable image may even publicize the formation and membership of its committee. The news director must continually review the list of possible individual and group endorsements, local and adjunct committee formations, and any demonstra-

---

[c] The term speech connotes formality and a length of twenty or thirty minutes, perhaps longer. If the candidate speaks briefly at an event or reception, the talk may be called "remarks," which implies the candidate spoke for a few minutes, perhaps ten or fifteen minutes at most. The news release text or excerpts may refer to remarks.

Exhibit 5-1
Guidelines for Speech News Releases

1. While many candidates who speak extemporaneously or who habitually depart from a prepared text feel uncomfortable with a prepared text, the news director should explain to the candidate the need for having *something* to give to the media, preferably in advance.

2. An entire speech, speech excerpts, or a brief news release may be issued. If the entire speech or lengthy excerpts are issued, a covering news release is usually issued. Any release notes the place, group, date and time of the speech.

3. The advance text may include an introductory note; for example, "Occasionally Mr. Smith departs from the prepared text to speak extemporaneously but will stand by this text." This answers the candidate's insecurity and the reporter's need for a text; however, departures from the text should be stylistic and insignificant, they should never involve potential news leads (unless by design).

4. The candidate who opposes an advance text, or who will not accept an advance text by deadline (allowing for the typing of the text and news release) should be persuaded to agree to exceprts. Regardless of the candidate's departures from his notes or prepared remarks, he must incorporate the excerpts that have been issued.

5. Excerpts should emphasize the lead or leads that the campaign considers important; thus they are strategically, not randomly, chosen. Excerpts have the benefit of brevity. Elipsis show missing words from a sentence; preferably, whole sentences should be excerpted. Three asterisks centered in the middle of a blank line show that excerpted paragraphs are not consecutive in the speech.

6. The covering news release emphasizes what the campaign considers to be the lead; hence the release should be issued with a text and probably with excerpts also. If neither speech text nor excerpts are used, a release should be issued to provide the setting and context of the speech and should include at least a few quotable sentences that the campaign desires as the lead *and* that the candidate will definitely incorporate when he delivers the speech.

7. The candidate who departs significantly from an advance text or who omits excerpts can jeopardize the desired lead (by impetuously introducing a new lead in delivery); the candidate may also impair the campaign's relationship with the news media, especially journalists who wrote an advance story based on the advance text or excerpts.

8. Advance texts and excerpts clearly titled do not need quotation marks within the news release, if the entire release is quoted material.

9. Excerpts do not give away the entire text of a speech; the campaign may wish to guard an entire text if distribution will compromise *future* coverage of the same or a similar speech.

10. Once an advance or prepared text is distributed, alert reporters may compare the delivery with the handout; departures in delivery may be the subject of a news story, and significant departures can become the lead. ("Smith departed from his prepared text to lash out at his opponent's position on . . ." or "Although Smith's prepared text included a reference to . . ., Smith in his delivery omitted . . .").

tions of support for the candidate to determine whether a news conference, or merely a news release, is warranted. Then the news director determines the place and time for a news conference or schedules an appropriate time for distributing a news release. Only the news director knows how a possible news conference or news release can fit within the campaign's overall news program and its scheduled flow of publicity.

The individual or group making an endorsement can be encouraged to issue a news release on their stationery. Indeed, many adjunct committees are formed by the campaign to have additional outlets for publicity. If a group clearly outside the campaign organization—for example, a labor union or permanent (rather than ad hoc) ethnic group—intends to endorse the candidate, the campaign should provide informal technical assistance, which may include drafting a release or statement, briefing members of the group, and even supplying a media list. The objective of the group mailing a release or making telephone calls to the media for a news conference is for it, and not the campaign, to be the supplicant seeking news.

Other Releases

Electronic media news releases are appropriate video or audio delivery systems (Chapter 7). Most of the other news releases, including some noted below, have been previously discussed.

Incumbent. These releases, on official government stationery and usually printed at public expense, are supposed to concern actions and statements of an incumbent that relate to his official responsibilities. Federal officials usually use the franking privilege to mail these releases. The incumbent's entire record and current activities, in terms of legislation, proposals, committee membership, hearings, tours of public facilities, government grants and contracts, constituent problems and concerns, and so forth provide opportunities for releases.

Reaction. Reaction releases, produced quickly to publicize the candidate's reaction to major news developments, should not be confused with reactionary or negative statements. The reaction release includes a positive, negative, or mixed reaction by the candidate to news developments that can be related to the campaign. The reaction statement is either newsworthy solely because of what it says, or because it is issued so quickly following, or virtually concurrent with, the news development that it can be used within the major print or electronic media news story. The reaction statement should be issued only if it can help the campaign; even a statement with neutral effect can enhance candidate identification. Sometimes a reaction statement is issued on a low-priority subject or story because the news media insists on the statement, and the news director cannot gracefully stall until media interest in a reaction statement subsides.

Negative. It is generally unproductive for the campaign to reply to opposition attacks or criticize editorial endorsements of the opponent. News releases should usually be positive in tone; like the campaign strategy that they should implement, news releases should be determined by a well-conceived plan, rather than issued as a knee-jerk reaction to every utterance or new attack of the opponent. Just as the campaign should determine its own strategy, so it should determine what its news releases should say. If negative statements are deemed strategically desirable, they should probably be in news releases issued by other committees; or the news release should quote a volunteer chairman or the campaign manager, not the candidate.

If campaign strategists worry about being put on the defensive by continued false attacks by the opponent, one way to belittle the attacks is to issue a news release that briefly catalogues (in a way beneficial to the campaign) all the opposition attacks and that very succinctly (in a word, phrase, sentence, or paragraph) answers each attack. This news release can be introduced by a paragraph that explains its necessity, and it can be titled "The Laundry List" or similar phraseology. If this news release is responsive, succinct, and well written, it can represent the campaign's one and only reply. The candidate can always refer to the release, and the campaign can distribute it whenever the charges arise again.

Photo Caption. The photograph caption release is clearly titled PHOTOGRAPH CAPTION at the top. If the date and place of the photograph are important and their mention will increase, rather than decrease, the chance the photograph will be used, the caption should include a dateline. Text should be brief and in sentence form; it should clearly identify individuals. Since the dateline will probably not be printed if the photograph is used, it is often advisable to omit *here* or *today* and refer directly to place and day. Sometimes use of a date can discourage use of a photograph by calling attention to its lack of timeliness. Ideally, a photograph and caption should be mailed immediately after an event; this requires technical coordination to develop the film and make many prints quickly.

The feature photograph, which may not require a date, is not designed for immediacy, but for general interest; using a date could be counterproductive. An example would be a photograph of the candidate and his family. Unless the place and date of the photograph are important and timely, they should not be used, and the photograph and caption should be promoted as a feature story (i.e., for use at any time). In the family photograph, the candidate need not be the center of activity; but in most other photographs, the candidate should be the most prominent. In any photograph, individuals are usually identified from left to right, and children's ages are usually mentioned (e.g., "John, 15, Sally, 12, and . . . ").

Campaign Materials. Most sample campaign materials should be distributed within an information kit, but new brochures and other items developed during the course of the campaign may deserve subsequent attention. Materials that are poorly designed or printed or that reflect unfavorably on the campaign should not be distributed to the media. Materials that are distributed may not require a news release, except as required to explain the material's purpose or intended audience.

Caution should be used in mailing article reprints. Reporters receiving the articles may be jealous, and their editors may wonder why their reporter did not break the story. Reprints of many articles in a montage or newspaper format may avoid spotlighting any individual article, and may convey a sense of momentum to the news media, which may be inspired to cover the campaign even more.

Form Releases

Any Level A or Level B campaign should prepare a publicity manual for local campaign chairmen, publicity chairmen, or aides. This manual should include sample "form" news releases to provide the format and general wording for releases essential to the formation and activities of a local campaign committee. *Sample* releases should include announcement of the committee's formation, naming of a chairman, opening of a headquarters, local endorsements, announcements of various types of committee events, announcements of upcoming visits by the candidate, and so on.

The form releases provide the basic model for the local committee, whose local release can be virtually identical to the form, except for substituting appropriate places, dates, and names in the model text. Form releases guarantee a standard format for all campaign releases; their suggested quotations help insure substantive consistency (e.g., a prominent local citizen endorsing the candidate will be quoted for citing reasons the campaign wishes to publicize). The form release, together with other guidelines and materials in the campaign manual, should make it easy for a local chairman or coordinator to produce a release promptly.[d]

Schedules

The importance of the campaign's regularly issuing comprehensive, accurate schedules cannot be overestimated. The schedule, and the efficiency and timeliness with which it is produced and distributed, projects the campaign image to the news media. It should be intensive, helpful, and thorough. Its substantive content—that is, the number and quality of events on the schedule—should indicate that the campaign is viable, seri-

---

[d] During the 1976 New Hampshire presidential primary, President Ford's campaign organization distributed form or "sample" news releases attacking positions of Mr. Ford's opponent, Ronald Reagan. The releases, termed "rather despicable" by Reagan, included suggested quotations to be issued by local Ford chairmen, with the wording of the release and quotation supplied, but name of the person making the accusation left blank. (*New York Times*, January 30, 1976; *Los Angeles Times*, January 30, 1976; *Washington Post*, January 30, 1976).

FOR IMMEDIATE RELEASE
(Updated Friday, Oct. 15)

FOR ADDITIONAL INFORMATION,
PLEASE CONTACT:
Harry Jones
Mary Keene (campaign plane,
hotel reservations, etc.)

HENRY T. SMITH
REPUBLICAN CANDIDATE FOR UNITED STATES SENATOR
OFFICIAL CAMPAIGN SCHEDULE
MONDAY, OCT. 18 - FRIDAY, OCT. 22

Monday, Oct. 18

7:30 A.M.   Weekly breakfast meeting with campaign leadership (PRIVATE)
             Smith for Senate Headquarters
             5601 Wilshire Boulevard
             Los Angeles
             213-930-0000

8:30-9:30   Mr. Smith will review campaign correspondence in his office.

9:30-10:00   Interview with David Broder, Washington Post

10:00   Tour of campaign headquarters to greet volunteers

10:15   Depart campaign headquarters for Los Angeles Police Academy

NOTE TO MEDIA: Auto transportation available from campaign headquarters to
Police Academy and Burbank Airport. Please advise re: campaign plane reservations.

10:45   Arrive Los Angeles Police Academy
             801 Stadium Way
             CONTACT: George Harris (213-387-0101)

             Mr. Smith will review cadet training, including target practice,
             self defense, tear gas and SWAT training). Mr. Smith will
             issue a "white paper" detailing his views and proposals re:
             new police training methods; the candidate will take questions.

11:45   Depart Police Academy for Burbank Airport (Gate #7)

12:05 P.M.   Arrive Burbank Airport (Gate #7 is at west end of private
             4000 Burbank Boulevard   terminal, adjacent to hangar.)
             CONTACT: Hal Falcon, private terminal mgr. (213-873-0363)

12:15   Campaign plane departs for Bakersfield

                          - MORE -

Note: This illustration shows the body of the first page of a schedule news release for the
period of October 18-22 (five days). It should be typed on distinctive news release stationery
with an appropriate heading (e.g., SMITH NEWS RELEASE) and information, especially the
telephone number. Generally, legal size paper is used.

Figure 5-2. Sample Schedule News Release.

ous, and has momentum. Even the schedule for the local campaign should
indicate a respectable level of activity. Any schedule, to the extent that it
makes a journalist's job easier by indicating what is and will be happening,

Exhibit 5-2
Guidelines for Schedule News Releases

1. The schedule is generally *for immediate release*; sometimes it is *for advisory* or *advisory to media*. Schedule corrections may be issued on an advisory basis.

2. Major scheduling announcements that are deemed newsworthy may be handled by issuing a covering news release, accompanied by a detailed schedule. Occasionally, extremely newsworthy scheduling announcements have restricted release times, but there is usually no reason to delay announcing the candidate has accepted a speaking commitment or will be attending a function (unless local chairmen or the host group is given the prerogative of making the announcement first or of making it on a local basis).

3. Schedule entries should include the exact name and address of a location, including the entrance; each entry should include the telephone number, including area code, of the facility, and any direct line, if it can be published. The entry should include, if possible, the name of a contact on the scene. If this person, or another person, can be reached before the event at another number, the name may be listed separately, or in addition to the first person's name. If the telephone number is for an office or home, but not the scheduled stop, it can follow, in parentheses, after the person's name.[a]

4. The schedule is single spaced within each entry and doubled spaced between entries.

5. Schedules are usually long and therefore duplicated on legal size news release stationery if available.

6. The schedule should detail as many whole days as possible.

7. Occasional gaps in days can be noted by *to be announced* or *to be scheduled*. If details for a specific schedule entry, such as precise entrance or time, are still being processed, the entry can read *details pending* or *details forthcoming*, or the specific deficiency can follow. For example, if the candidate's appearance will be sometime in the late afternoon, *Late Afternoon (Time to follow)* or *3-5 p.m. (Exact time to be determined)* can be noted on the entry date.

8. Never delay sending out an entire schedule because parts are missing. The schedule can persuade an editor that the campaign is worth covering; it may affect decisions regarding how many days it should be covered, by how many reporters, and by whom. The schedule must be distributed as soon as possible.

9. If possible, send out a longer schedule, with the first segment detailed, and the second segment blocked out. For example, a two-week schedule could provide details for the first week and only the names of the cities or towns to be visited, on a daily basis, for the second week. At least the news media will know where they will be.

10. Make certain there is no ambiguity between morning and evening; use *a.m.* and *p.m.* at the beginning of sections of the day or throughout; use 12:00 *Noon* and 12:00 *Midnight* if necessary.

11. Attention should somehow be drawn to days or schedule items of particular concern to recipient media. For example, schedules mailed to media in one county may feature, by red markings, the day or days during which the candidate will be in that county. Alternatively, the schedule may be accompanied by different covering releases, each with a lead for a different area; or the schedule may be accompanied by a uniform covering release that highlights in clearly recognizable form the cities or towns to be visited—within the headline and opening paragraph.

12. At the end of each day the schedule should list where the candidate, entourage, and traveling news media will stay overnight (i.e., name of hotel, precise address, telephone number).

13. The schedule should appear intensive, regardless of the candidate's activities; this may be accomplished by listing *Staff Meeting* or *Staff Time* as a euphemism for the candidate's interaction with staff, rest and relaxation, or unscheduled blocks. The less used *Private Time* is also permissible, but more liable to be abused by aggressive journalists seeking interviews. *Private Meeting* is possible but sometimes raises questions about the nature of and participants in the meeting.

14. No item is even listed on the public schedule (the schedule distributed to the news media) unless reporters can attend. Alternatively, the term *private meeting* is used.

15. No item is ever listed unless the facts, address, telephone number, and so forth, are verified and checked, including proofreading *after* typing the draft. Any contact person listed should know the schedule is public and he is listed as a contact.

16. Any errors on the schedule should be corrected promptly, with special attention to the wire or news services that distribute the schedule; corrected schedules or the correction of errors should usually be distributed to everyone who receives the schedule, unless the schedule corrections, particularly minor ones, are useless information to the full list or to those who will receive mail delivery too late.

17. The schedule should clearly indicate any function at which the candidate will speak. *Speech by Mr. Smith* or *Address by Mr. Smith* indicate a longer presentation than *Remarks by Mr. Smith*. The news director should be prepared to explain to any reporter what the candidate is likely to say during any speech or remarks or to provide an advance text if it is a major speech.

18. The schedule clearly emphasizes instructions and details to reporters regarding transportation or lodging; any editor or reporter reading the schedule wants to understand how the logistics affect him or her.

19. The schedule should be from the point of view of the candidate (i.e., when he attends a reception or other campaign event, not when it officially begins or ends); sometimes it is helpful for other information to be in parentheses; for example, *6:40—Candidate joins reception (in progress from 6:00)*.

20. The schedule usually is of the candidate and anyone (spouse or family) that accompanies the candidate—not of the spouse or family if they campaign separately. Such family members should have their own schedules issued, unless their appearances are infrequent and can be easily noted within the candidate's schedule.

---

[a]The campaign scheduling or tour director and news director, or their aides, must decide the appropriate general or specific policy regarding listing of contacts. Perhaps some individuals cannot interact well with reporters or need to be briefed. Another possibility is that the campaign is so well organized that the principal or central campaign headquarters can act as liaison for any reporter trying to reach the campaign entourage or determine last minute details. In sum, any contact person listed should know he is listed and be briefed on possible calls from reporters. The contact person does not discuss policy or issues, but merely the specific logistics of the schedule entry, e.g., entrance, address, parking, access, etc. Often, the contact person is instructed to avoid crowd projections, since he might project too high an attendance, leading to media characterization of the event as a failure if the projection was excessive. The campaign may decide the best policy is to list the complete address and telephone number of each schedule entry, but avoid mentioning the specific contact.

Needless to say, the campaign's *internal* or *detail* schedule maximizes the information, and lists every possible contact and telephone number. This internal schedule should never be confused with a schedule news release; the former is for restricted distribution within the campaign, the latter for the news media, hence the public.

affects the editor or reporter's attitude; similarly, the efficient schedule, which projects well both because it shows the candidate busy and because it provides prompt and complete information to the journalist, affects the recipient's perception of the campaign and therefore affects reporting.

Most campaign schedules reflect certain guidelines (Exhibit 5-2) to achieve a standard format (Figure 5-2). The schedule is important campaign intelligence for any editor or reporter, and as soon as it is produced, it is usually hand delivered where possible and otherwise mailed to the entire media list. Simultaneously, the schedule is distributed throughout the campaign's traveling entourage, including staff and reporters. The campaign headquarters gives priority to confirming receipt of the schedule at wire services, since they often provide subscribers with the candidate's schedule (faster than the subscribers receive it by mail). Local wires may also use parts of the schedule for their "daybook"—the daily list of events that the news media may wish to cover. State or regional wires may feed the schedule throughout the state; if so, the relevant wire service office requires special attention.

6 The News Conference

There are two kinds of news conferences: the conventional and the visual. In the conventional or traditional news conference, the candidate speaks from a standing position behind a podium, or sitting down behind a table, with or without a small podium. The visual news conference is a dramatic, even theatrical setting oriented to television cameras; it usually involves the candidate doing something—interacting with others—instead of talking or reading a statement. The visual is a kind of news conference because it often involves a statement, either an opening statement before the visual activity or a statement during or following the height of visual activity. Like the news conference, the visual exposes the candidate to questions from the news media, throughout the activity or immediately afterward.[a]

The conventional or visual news conference should be called only if it is strategically useful to the campaign; its subject should concern or relate to a campaign issue. The exception is when the news media demand for a news conference on another issue is so overpowering that the news director feels the campaign can incur worse news coverage by avoiding the news conference than by having it. News conference strategy relates not only to choice of issues, but the number of news conferences, their frequency, and their location in particular states, cities, towns, and media markets. It is also important to relate each news conference subject and its opening statement to an appropriate location or setting; to select the optimum time of day for exposure; and to determine both a customary, or normal, length for the news conference and criteria for when to vary it. These considerations may also reflect the candidate's ability to project well at news conferences, especially his willingness to answer questions on the opening statement and diverse issues as well as his skill in fielding questions under pressure.

Conventional News Conference

It is foolish for the campaign to consider the conventional or news conference format if the candidate will do poorly. Some candidates hurt themselves with more than minimal exposure; they reveal their inability to withstand probing questions. Even the bright, articulate, and even-

[a] The term news conference is preferred to press conference because the latter implies exclusion of broadcast media.

tempered candidate must have a positive attitude toward the media in general and toward news conferences in particular. The candidate should understand the role of the news conference as a means for transmitting information to the electorate; by understanding the rationale for questions, the candidate will be less likely to resent them or show resentment.

The news conference can be planned, as a news release can be planned, or it can, like the news release, be an opportunistic way of exploiting news developments. Both the planned and opportunistic news conference are scheduled for the location and time most conducive to publicity. In the case of many newsworthy reaction statements, the location is almost irrelevant to the speed with which the news conference is called. Both cases require exhaustive effort to notify all news media, with the planned news conference giving more notice and the opportunistic news conference possibly being called on a few minutes notice. Analogous to the news release situation, the news director may maintain a futures file of possible news conferences; for example, news conferences may be planned throughout the candidate's schedule, with at least one news conference for each city, town, or area visited. The place, date, and time may be planned in advance; the subject chosen and opening statement may be opportunistic—that is, selected at the last moment on the basis of current news developments.

The conventional news conference, although less likely to draw television coverage, can stimulate such coverage if the candidate is usually newsworthy, has indicated the subject or opening statement is newsworthy, or is just lucky (for example, a slow news day). The presence of television cameras makes the activity visual, although the format may retain its conventionality.

Rationale

The candidate calls a news conference because he has something to say. The candidate usually issues a prepared opening statement (with copies distributed to reporters in attendance) and then responds to questions not limited to the opening statement. If the candidate has an opening statement, it should be newsworthy; journalists resent covering a nonexistent story.

Often, no opening statement is preferable to a meaningless statement. Opening statements can be gracefully omitted if the news conference is called merely as a forum to answer general questions. The candidate who visits an area once, or infrequently, may call a news conference to afford local media an opportunity to ask questions of concern to their readers, listeners, or viewers. The Level A or Level B candidate who travels to several cities or areas in a single day can hold several such news conferences.

Two questions are relevant in determining whether to hold a news conference without an opening statement. Is there sufficient media interest in the candidate that reporters will attend just for an opportunity to question the candidate? Will the candidate's responses provide news so the local media are not disappointed? If the answer to both questions is yes, the candidate's schedule should emphasize the maximum number of news conferences, even several a day if warranted by the schedule, with one important qualification—the number of news conferences should not compromise the candidate's performance.

Coordination

Any news conference must be coordinated to assure candidate preparation and news media attendance. The ill-prepared candidate or the poorly attended news conference can be disastrous. Low-attendance news conferences cause some reporters to wonder whether they made a mistake in attending; their stories usually describe the news conference as "poorly attended," in contrast to the bandwagon psychology underscoring the well-attended news conference with contagious momentum. Coordination involves the detail research and preparatory work required to relate an issue or position to holding a news conference at a certain place on an appointed time.

Coordination requires preparation to brief the candidate; timely notification of all news media, including persuasive telephone calls, to assure attendance; and attention to logistics, etiquette, and protocol. Coordination requires evaluation throughout the pre-news conference period and reevaluation after the news conference to measure results and improve performance.

Preparation and Briefing. The candidate should understand the purpose of each news conference and whether an opening statement is required. The candidate should understand that the opening statement is the desired lead. Occasionally, the statement is an excuse to call a news conference in which a question on an issue will inevitably arise and permit the candidate to generate a lead with his answer. In such a case, the candidate understands that the statement is the transparent lead; the desired lead will emerge from his newsworthy response to an expected question. Since the statement typically is the lead, it should be written and rewritten until its language is polished and precise. The ideal opening statement offers the competent reporter only one lead, not several; however, it may offer two or three alternative leads if they are all equally desirable. The opening statement serves as the focal point for the candidate's briefing.

Statement. Each word, phrase, and sentence in the opening statement is evaluated in terms of what questions may be provoked. Questionable, troublesome, or ambiguous terminology is usually eliminated, unless the ambiguity is intended and the candidate knows it is there. The statement should be sufficiently newsworthy and exciting that it dominates the initial questions. An exception is when major news developments occur just before the scheduled news conference begins; these fortuitous developments may increase media attendance considerably. The candidate can discard the opening statement completely, read it as prepared, or refer to it but avoid reading it; alternatively, the candidate can, before, instead of, or just after the statement, comment on the overriding news development. If the candidate does not wish to seem overly concerned or preoccupied with the news development, he can simply proceed as planned and wait for the inevitable question or line of questioning. Above all, the candidate must be prepared for intensive questioning on the opening statement. (See the guidelines for an opening statement in Exhibit 6-1.)

Questions and Answers. The briefing includes possible questions both on the subject of the news conference and on other subjects; the experienced campaigner knows such questions are based on news events, especially that day or week's major stories. The questions will also reflect the parochial concerns of local reporters concerned with how international and national policies or news affect their area. Reporters are likely to raise questions about issues covered prominently by their newspaper or radio or television station. The local newspaper's editorials and columns provide valuable clues. Local volunteers can also suggest subjects likely to arise in the question period. The Level A or Level B candidate who holds many news conferences each day or week will find about an 80 percent overlap of questions; the remaining 20 percent reflects local issues or the ascendancy of certain news stories, and both types of questions can be covered in the briefing.

Novice journalists may ask general questions, especially the open-ended variety that lends itself to an expository answer on the candidate's terms. Experienced reporters ask specific questions that challenge the candidate's assertions, probe his point of view, and persist in seeking details and substantiation of points in the opening statement or in a previous answer. Skillful questioners relate part of the opening statement or a prior answer to a *news peg*—an event or story prominent in the day's or week's news. The question might be phrased, "In view of . . . (the news development), do you still feel . . .?" They may ask the candidate to comment on someone else's statement, in view of the candidate's stated position on the same issue. Often it is advisable for the candidate to find a way to avoid answering the question directly; this should be done grace-

Exhibit 6-1
The Opening Statement

1. The parts of the statement most vulnerable to intense questioning are its definition of the problem, assumptions, reasoning process, and recommendations in the form of proposals or programs.
2. The candidate should understand and be prepared to defend the statement's assumptions and the reasoning process used to proceed from defining the problem to making recommendations or proposals.
3. If the statement defines a problem and makes policy recommendations, the candidate should expect questions on the relevance of the recommendations to solving the problem; the problem should be stated in a way that lends itself to solution by the candidate's programs.
4. Problems may arise concerning the statement's assertions, facts, statistics, numbers, and dollar references. Any assertion can be questioned for proof or evidence. "Facts" must be supportable. Statistics or numbers in the statement may not require an explicit source, but questions may arise on their validity, source, or context, and the candidate must be prepared.
5. Numbers, statistics, dollar amounts, or budget figures must be rechecked, including a final check after the news release is typed. The entire text should be checked to insure that the statement read by the candidate is identical with the statement distributed to reporters. Watch for extra or omitted zeros, misplaced commas, or confusing millions with billions; check all mathematical computations.
6. The candidate should be prepared to answer reasonable questions about the possible costs of programs or proposals advocated. The candidate should be able to substantiate assertions that recommendations will save taxpayer funds.
7. Adjectives may make good copy; they can also inspire troublesome questions. Colorful characterizations or expressions should be defensible; the candidate should be briefed to answer questions like, "You referred to . . . as . . . . Now, what did you mean by the word (or phrase) . . .?" If the candidate cannot answer satisfactorily, any retreat from the opening statement may be viewed skeptically, cause unpleasant follow-up questions on other parts of the opening statement, or could change (or become) the lead.
8. The opening statement must always be checked for consistency, in terms of the candidate's prior opening statements, campaign speeches, brochures, and so forth. The candidate should know if the statement in any way contradicts volunteer leaders or prominent supporters.

fully and consistently. For example, a candidate for U.S. senator can conceivably decline commenting on any problem peculiar to local government, or entirely within the province of the state legislature, and explain that his priority and commitment are to the challenging problems to be resolved by the federal government and the Senate. However, this position is neither plausible nor tenable if the candidate does not consistently adhere to it.

The candidate should pause momentarily before answering a question to reconsider what will be said. In this instant, the candidate must define or redefine internally the limits of the answer: How much should or can be said in answer to the question? The brief, responsive answer, rather than the lengthy, meandering, conversational reply, is not only more likely to be used by the broadcast media, but insures partially against digressions into dangerous subjects. The convoluted answer can raise new, undesirable questions. Since any answer becomes part of the candidate's public record, he should be cautious and reluctant to stake out new positions. Imprudent answers, regardless of length, can compromise or alter the most thoughtful and well-planned campaign strategy. (See Exhibit 4-1, especially footnote b.)

To reiterate an important guideline, the candidate should not obscure the opening statement by providing answers that in themselves can become the lead. The emotional, exciting answer may guarantee an animated news conference, but it may open an entire line of questioning far afield from the opening statement. The desired lead may be buried deep within a story based on the question-and-answer period. This is acceptable if the new lead is desirable, but it usually is not. Nothing is more disillusioning than the subsequent television story with the undesirable lead; at the very end of the negative coverage, the announcer says, for example, "Smith's statements on the explosive issue of sex education were made at a news conference announcing his new tax reform proposals."

Local Media. The briefing should include the total number of journalists expected to be present, their distribution among print and broadcast media, and, if possible, identification of specific media outlets and individual reporters likely to be present. The candidate should be aware of the interests and biases of local media, media outlets, and individual reporters. The candidate's briefing should always be constructive and affirmative to increase his awareness and sensitivity. The briefing should make the candidate more confident; it should not be so negative or ominous as to disconcert the candidate. The briefing should include an assessment of the relative importance of local print and electronic media as well as media outlets and individual reporters, in terms of circulation, ratings, and types of readers, listeners, or viewers.

No candidate should ever enter a news conference without having skimmed or read the city's morning newspaper. If the news conference occurs after publication of later editions or of the afternoon newspaper, the briefing should also note relevant articles in these newspapers. If the candidate proceeds by automobile to the news conference, the radio should be tuned to a newscast, especially all news radio. These tips help avoid the embarrassing "I didn't know about . . ." or "I haven't read about" response. The candidate who cannot discipline himself to prepare for the news conference should not be holding one; perhaps he should not be a candidate.

Attendance. If there is time to mail announcements of a news conference, they should be mailed, but mailing is never sufficient. Telephone calls must confirm receipt of the mailing and insure that the news media know the time, place, and subject (if any) of the news conference. The telephone call also queries as to whether any additional information is required or whether the editor or reporter has any questions; the caller also asks whether the event will be covered.

Unless the candidate always generates news or the media is unusually anxious to ask certain questions, the announcement and telephone calls may need to stress the subject of the news conference or the reason for calling it. Telephone calls often must *sell* the news conference to skeptical editors whose reporters cannot be everywhere simultaneously. The calls can seduce the media into attending by saying enough to convince editors to assign a reporter to come, but not enough to give the story away. Some news releases announcing a news conference are so complete that the recipient can write the story from the news release. Generally, the subject can be mentioned, unless its mention would compromise a momentous announcement scheduled for the news conference. It is often advisable to include a paragraph relating the news conference subject to recent news developments, although caution should be used if the news events cited are such an obvious peg for the news conference that the editor or reporter will be insulted ("I don't need someone to tell me the *angle* for this story . . ."). In addition, the news conference should not be so overbilled in mailings and telephone calls that reporters feel victimized; the next news conference could be sparsely covered, and the news director calling a news conference for a major story could become like the little boy who cried wolf too often.

The news release announcement should never obscure the date, time, place, and subject of the news conference. This information may be in the one or two paragraph text, but it *must* be prominently featured in the headline, since these facts are important.

Checking news conference attendance is a continuous process that begins with verification of the news media list. It must be absolutely thorough and accurate, and it should include all types of media in the immediate and surrounding area. If the candidate, campaign, or the news conference topic, is relevant to ethnic or other specialized media, these media outlets and journalists should be included in the notification. Extraordinary effort is made to notify the local wire service, whose calendar, daybook, or budget provides major media outlets in the city with a priority list of events to cover. Telephone verification assures that the wire service reports the correct time, address, and subject.

Campaign staff members should keep an accurate, written record of all media outlets and reporters telephoned; the record includes when they were telephoned, whether they had received the release announcing the news conference (if one was mailed), whether they knew about the news conference and were planning to attend; any questions, remarks, or special requirements. The final attendance projection catalogues media outlets in probabilistic descriptions (e.g., "definite," "most likely to expect to cover," "unsure," "probably not," and "absolutely not cover"). Based on the final tally sheet, the news director determines which assignment editors or reporters he should call personally.

Whenever the telephone callers discover relevant information, it should be communicated to the news director. For example, suppose an overextended wire or news service bureau expresses interest in the candidate or story but indicates that although it will be unable to send someone, it would appreciate an advance copy of the opening statement. The news director can use that information to service the bureau properly; indeed, standard practice may be to send wire services advance copies just before the news conference and to send any media outlet that does not attend the news conference a copy (always hand delivered).

Logistics. The news conference should be in a well-known or easily found location that is central and accessible. Often, the local press club or a major hotel can provide a suitable room. The candidate traveling in a new area should be partially guided by local custom in determining the news conference location. Some cities or towns have a press club, facility, or several hotels that are traditional news conference locations. The press club may also be desirable if the rental fee helps the club treasury and thus generates goodwill. The candidate's headquarters, which has the advantage of backdrop, but the disadvantages of being too partisan and too accessible to campaign supporters and volunteers, is another possible location. The candidate's main headquarters may include a specially designed room with a backdrop for news conferences. This arrangement saves charges for renting facilities, including the high prices charged by hotels for coffee and donuts. The headquarters setting is also propitious for television filming of volunteers engaged in campaign activity.

The news conference should preferably be in a ground floor location or with elevator service. The room should have ample electrical outlets and power supply, ashtrays, hot coffee and tea, and possibly donuts or pastry; soft drinks are also appreciated. If the candidate is uncomfortable standing behind a tall podium, he can sit behind a table, usually covered with a clean, plain-colored cloth. If the candidate is the only person speaking, there should only be one chair. If television cameras or photographers are expected, special attention should be given to the backdrop, which in this case is the area behind the candidate.

In Level A and Level B campaigns, the candidate's traveling entourage usually brings a portable backdrop—a cloth, cardboard, or heavy paper emblem. The candidate's name should be prominently featured; the campaign logos and colors are usually used. The backdrop should show up clearly in photographs or television; it need not include a photograph; if one is used, it should be large, clear, and identifiable. The banner or emblem is part of the larger picture backdrop behind the candidate, preferably solid color drapery in preference to a wall; avoid cluttered wallpaper, lighting fixtures, or a mirror.

The news conference location is *neutral* if it does not compromise the candidate. For example, the candidate who holds a news conference at the local political party headquarters may find that the advantage of a convenient, cheap location is outweighed by the backdrop. Party identification, in terms of the actual location that will be reported in the story or the signs or bumperstrips that will be seen on television, may be a liability; if it is an asset, the location may be desirable. The location might also afford other candidates a chance to "steal the show" from the major candidate who calls the news conference.

An alternative news conference format is a news media breakfast or luncheon, with questions following the meal. If the candidate visits an area just once, or infrequently, and if reporters' schedules and deadlines permit an extended function, this format can be useful. It requires attention to a seating arrangement affording optimum access to the candidate and usually does not have assigned seating. It does involve the added meal cost.

Procedure and Protocol. If the candidate usually makes news and the media operation is efficient in notifying the media, attendance will not be a problem. The need to prepare an appropriate opening statement and brief the candidate are still important considerations. Once the elements are in place, the problems of procedure, etiquette, and protocol usually take care of themselves.

Opening. If news conference arrangements are confirmed in writing, by letter or memorandum, and details are checked approximately a half hour or forty-five minutes before the news conference, the news conference can start smoothly. Particular attention should insure that if the news conference is in a public facility or hotel, the legend or other display sign indicates the time and place of the news conference. Since coffee and possibly other refreshments should be available at least fifteen minutes before the news conference is scheduled to begin, corrective action must be taken quickly to remedy any problem.

If the news director is not with the candidate, he can be present to greet arriving reporters; otherwise, someone else should have the assignment, perhaps another staff member, or a local volunteer who is gracious and noncontroversial. The candidate should not be the first person to arrive at the news conference; generally, he should arrive after most of the journalists, but he should not be late. In a local community visited for the first time, the candidate sometimes enters early to chat with local reporters before the news conference formally begins. If reporters are evidently late, the candidate's entrance may be delayed a few minutes so he can use the time profitably; in such a situation, delay would also avoid the embarrassing impression that the candidate is a supplicant seeking coverage, and that the media does not find the candidacy sufficiently newsworthy that they should arrive promptly.

Unless the opening statement is a dramatic announcement, in which case distribution of the statement may be delayed until just before the candidate speaks, copies are usually available on a table and also distributed to reporters as they enter. The news director always has extra copies in the event the initial supply is insufficient or misplaced. If the news conference is in an area visited infrequently or for the first time, information kits may also be on the table or distributed. If the candidate's opening statement refers to other statements or supporting material or it requires background documentation, these may be available on the table or distributed.

A technique that has become increasingly transparent and frowned upon, but still practiced, is delaying distribution of the opening statement until seconds before the candidate begins, to give the news media as little time as possible to analyze the statement for weaknesses. This technique is most effective for those television reporters who need several minutes of study to come up with a coherent question.

Candidate. The extroverted candidate may take the initiative and introduce himself to each reporter; alternatively, the news director, a local volunteer leader, or a press aide who knows local reporters, may perform the introductions. Once the news director determines that most reporters or television crews are present and ready to begin, he opens the news conference with a very brief introduction: "I'm Ralph Jones, news secretary for John Smith and I'd like to thank all of you for coming. Mr. Smith has a brief statement, which I believe all of you have, and following his statement, will take questions." Another introduction might conclude: ". . . Mr. Smith has no prepared statement but wanted to afford all of you an opportunity to question him on campaign issues and any subjects of special concern here in . . . ."

Once the candidate begins reading the statement, he usually continues until finished. If the statement is more than two pages double spaced, the candidate usually reads only the most important sections, unless requested to read the entire statement by television reporters. The candidate should let reporters know he will not read the entire statement: "Ladies and gentlemen, you have the statement, so I'm not going to read the entire statement, just portions. Then I'll take questions on the whole statement, and anything else on your mind." If no television cameras are present or

television reporters waive reading of the statement, and the news conference is beginning late or reporters are on deadline, the news director may
advise the candidate not to read any of the statement. The candidate may
say, "Since you've all had a chance to read the statement, and we're
running late, I'll dispense with reading it, if that's all right, and we can go
straight into questions." Alternatively, "I understand some of you are
already on deadline, so if there are no objections, I won't read the statement, and we can begin with questions, on the statement or anything else."

Most news conferences in large media markets are so fast moving that
reporters ask questions so rapidly there is practically no time between the
end of an answer and the next question. It is usually unnecessary for the
candidate to recognize reporters to ask a question, as is done in a presidential news conference. There is usually no formal limit on follow-up questions, and the candidate should generally avoid trying to restrict reporters'
questions. The reporter who tries to dominate the news conference will
usually be ruled out of bounds by his colleagues as they interrupt to ask
their own questions.

Participants. Many print media reporters take a dim view of their electronic media colleagues and resist being shoved to the rear by camera
operators jockeying for position. The campaign should permit the reporters
to settle their own quarrels and should not complicate matters by permitting campaign supporters at the news conference. They use valuable space
and seats, often in the front; they make noise and have been known to
applaud the candidate or even boo the "biased" media.

The news director usually stands to the side of the candidate—but
outside photograph or camera range. The news director is low key, not
prominent; he is quiet, attentive, and especially cognizant of the time. He
usually speaks only when called upon by the candidate, which is infrequently, if at all. Only in the rare instance in which a news conference is
called to read a statement and answer questions on a single subject, can the
news director enforce the condition. Occasionally, the news director can
interrupt for a point of information, such as clarifying an error on the
candidate's next appearance in the area or the amount of funds collected;
he should not interrupt the candidate to make a correction that reflects
adversely on the candidate; obviously, he should never contradict the
candidate.

Ending. The news director, not the candidate, ends the news conference.
It is usually scheduled to last a half hour, but may end earlier. The actual
length is often a function of the day or week's news developments, which
may inspire many questions. The news conference that lasts more than
thirty minutes is an imposition on the candidate, whose patience wears thin

during an extended period of questioning. The longer the news conference, the greater the chance the candidate will make an error.

At the outset, the news director should indicate whether the news conference has unusual time limitations or will end in less than thirty minutes. If the news director feels that the news conference will end naturally within the allotted time, his judgment may indicate that nothing should be said at the outset. The news media will empathize with the campaign running late, if the campaign generally has a positive attitude and treats the media fairly. But experienced reporters can perceive when an announcement that a news conference will be brief is merely a dodge to avoid expected questions.

The news director is entitled to end a news conference but should not do so without advance warning. He might interject, five minutes before the desired end, "Ladies and gentlemen, we have about five minutes left" or "Time for just two more questions." His judgment may be that the news conference is about to end naturally; hence, he should keep quiet. Alternatively, he may give the five-minute warning seven or eight minutes before the end. The fast-moving news conference may require a second notice: "Just a couple of minutes left," or "Just one more question, please." The news conference can be ended by the news director, who says simply, "Thank you, ladies and gentlemen."

Most campaign news conferences are ended far less ceremoniously than the presidential news conference, in which the senior wire service reporter traditionally says, "Thank you, Mr. President" to signal the conclusion of the news conference. The most convenient way to end a news conference is to let it end itself, if the news director is reasonably confident it will conclude in the allotted time without any prompting. The likelihood of ending the news conference on time is increased if the campaign schedule issued to the media indicates the candidate must depart the news conference at a specified time.

The news director should not permit the news conference to drag if there are no more questions, or there is a considerable interval of time between questions. If the pace of questioning begins to slow, the news director should consider ending the news conference a few minutes earlier than planned ("Well, if there are no more questions," he can say, pausing for a moment, "thank you very much.") In short, the news director should gracefully conclude the news conference before reporters start leaving.

Joint News Conference. If the candidate holds a news conference with another person or group of individuals, all participants should be briefed, and there should be at least one joint briefing. The participants should not contradict each other publicly; there should be no surprise opening statements or responses to questions. If there are differences, the participants should know about them before the news conference; the differences should be resolved or deemphasized in the ensuing news conference. Agreement should be reached on the purpose of the news conference and the person expected to have center stage and answer all or most questions; this person is usually the candidate. If the campaign called the joint news conference, it is responsible for distributing the statement of each speaker.

The candidate should not participate by default in a joint news conference. This happens if a local volunteer leader or another candidate (usually for lesser office) accompanies the candidate to the podium or table, then sits or stands conspicuously behind the candidate. The presence of someone else not only may distort the photographic or visual impression desired by the campaign, but may inspire reporters to question the intruder directly or to ask him to comment on the candidate's answers. The best way to avoid a surprise joint news conference is for everyone involved to understand his own role and for these roles to be clear both to the news media and everyone on the campaign entourage who is holding the news conference.

Scheduling. The general rule is that the news conference should be scheduled early in the day. This permits the candidate's opening statement and responses to questions to be carried in afternoon newspapers and to be disseminated through wire and news services early enough that many newspapers and radio stations can carry the story. Stories that are carried early in the day on radio may well be carried throughout the day; in contrast, the campaign story that is carried later in the day is aired that many fewer times. Usually, anytime between 9 a.m. and 2 p.m. is possible; 10 a.m. is probably the most popular, closely followed by adjacent times (9:30, 10:30, 11:00). The time chosen should also reflect local tradition and custom, the distance from most news media outlets to the news conference site, and the peculiarities of local traffic. The time chosen also reflects the degree of advance notification to the media—that is, news conferences scheduled at 8:30 or 9:00 in the morning permit little or no time for telephoning the day of the news conference. Similarly, Monday morning news conferences are usually scheduled slightly later, because confirming attendance is more difficult due to the weekend interval between normal work days. The time chosen also is a product of whether reporters can go directly from their home to the news conference, or whether they must report to the news media outlet for assignments and camera crews.

The candidate and campaign should establish a reputation for punctual news conferences. This is no easy task, because the initial temptation is to accommodate the news media, especially the television crews, which always seem to arrive late. Although a time cushion can be built into the schedule to permit early arrivals to have coffee and donuts, the candidate's schedule can be stretched only so far. If television camera crews and their assignment editors know the candidate's schedule is firm and intense and that the news conferences always begin on time or only a few minutes late, their attitude will change. Big-city television reporters are so accustomed to late-starting events that they sometimes compound the problem by being late themselves.

The experienced campaign news director has his staff telephoning television stations until the news conference is about to begin, to find out which television crews, if any, will be late, or to convince an assignment editor there is still time to cover the story. One method often employed to service competing television outlets without delaying the start of the news conference in order to accommodate late arrivals is to permit a time cushion following the news conference. This cushion is built into the campaign's internal schedule to accommodate late-arriving news media staff who seek personal interviews. The television crew arriving midway through, or near the end of a news conference, may wish a short interview with the candidate for two reasons. First, it will be used in place of the opening statement or sections of it; the candidate will simply respond to expository questions ("What did you say in your opening statement?"), but the responses will be edited and used on television without the prompting question. Second, the reporter can ask the two or three questions he would have asked at the news conference.

The news director's policy should be even handed to accommodate all television and radio reporters; if necessary, he may need to ration time. Requests for interviews are usually honored in the order they are received or promised, and the candidate should look to the news director for guidance. If late-arriving news media personnel do not object, they can participate in a mini news conference following the formal news conference; several reporters jointly interview the candidate. The alternative is several consecutive individual interviews; the experienced news director knows that many radio reporters, even including those present for the entire news conference, want to ask one or two questions on an exclusive basis following the news conference. If possible, he will try to accommodate them.

The news director should remain silent during a television or radio interview. When the allotted time is nearly finished, he should use hand gestures, not his voice, to signal one or two more questions, or point to his watch. Interrupting an interview can spoil the tape or film and cause bad feeling among the electronic media reporters. The news director whose policy is known to be forthright and service oriented is in a position to indicate before an interview precisely how long it can last. If the time stipulation is firmly stated *beforehand*, the interview is easier to cut. When the interview absolutely must be terminated, the news director moves his hand in front of his neck, as if he were cutting his neck.

The whole post-news conference interview process is smoother if the news director has determined before and during the news conference which media outlets and reporters request or will request such interviews. Once he knows how many interviews are required and how long each will probably last, he can encourage each reporter to have the camera or tape recorder ready, so there is no delay between the end of the news conference and the first interview; subsequent interviews are also consecutive. The news director usually does not ask the reporter *what* he will ask, but how much time is required, or how many questions will be asked. Accommodating late-arriving broadcast or print media reporters, or those with special requirements (e.g., a reporter was ordered by an editor to ask a particular question but didn't have an opportunity in the news conference) enhances the campaign's image with the news media.

Evaluation. The overriding criteria for evaluating the news conference are the quantity and quality of news coverage. Since attendance is a primary factor, the emphasis is on notifying *all* relevant media, including telephone notification, and on assigning some subjective probability or assessment to their attendance. The persistence in trying to persuade some media outlets or reporters to cover a news conference reflects their relative value in reaching the voters; for example, representation of the city's major daily newspaper may be much more important than representation of all four suburban daily newspapers.

After evaluating the number of reporters and media outlets present, and the *quality* of broadcast and print media represented, the next task is evaluating how the candidate was received. The campaign succeeded in delivering the reporters to the news conference; did the candidate provide a newsworthy opening statement and question-and-answer period? In the final analysis, evaluation is based on what is seen on television, heard on radio,, and written in the newspapers. If the press conference was handled properly and the candidate was well briefed—for example, his response to a question did not overshadow the opening statement and intended lead—the coverage should equal or surpass expectations. (See Exhibit 6-2 for the guidelines for conducting a successful news conference.)

The news director should carefully monitor the candidate's performance in answering questions. Each news director develops his own shorthand method to record the total length of time of the news conference, opening statement, and question-and-answer period as well as the amount of time devoted to different subject areas or issues. The report should also include the total number of questions and the percentage or number on different subjects. For important news conferences or at early stages or turning points in the campaign, the news director should give the candidate

Exhibit 6-2
News Conference Tips

1. Don't try to convert reporters. The objective is to give them information for a story and make news, not convert them.

2. Although the preferred opening statement is two or three minutes, it should rarely, if ever, be longer than five minutes.

3. It is often helpful to summarize (thirty seconds) at the end of the opening statement.

4. Even in the case of a joint news conference, there should not be more than three people in front of a microphone (bridge) or set of microphones.

5. Regardless of the number of campaign news or other staff members present, including even the campaign manager, there should still be only one spokesperson at the news conference.

6. The candidate should never touch the microphones during the news conference.

7. The candidate should never place notes on top of the microphone or place notes between himself and the microphone. The notes should be off to the side, and the candidate should be careful to avoid the noise of shuffling papers next to the microphone.

8. Hand gestures can be helpful if the candidate gestures appropriately and thoughtfully, but he should not pound on the table.

9. It is often desirable to incorporate a reporter's question into an answer, especially if the question can be phrased in a way more favorable to the candidate's position.

10. The candidate should be conscious of his voice level and inflection, especially at the beginning or end of the statement or an answer to a question; uniformity and consistency are usually desirable (unless emphasis is desired).

11. Answering "yes" or "no" or some other snappy response will probably not get coverage (especially television); if avoiding coverage of the response to that question is the objective, the answer may be satisfactory. Otherwise, it may not be sufficiently responsive, especially in terms of standing on its own (i.e., without the necessity of the television or radio reporter having to state the question for the audience).

12. Answers should be brief, especially for any individual interviews with radio station reporters. Lengthy answers may not be used at all, or they may be edited poorly (from the campaign's point of view). The campaign news director must *indoctrinate* the candidate to respond in thirty seconds, occasionally sixty seconds; the objective is the equivalent of a solid paragraph response. If necessary, the candidate should be drilled until he perfects brief, responsive answers.

13. It is preferable for the candidate to pause momentarily to think and frame his reply before answering than to begin with intermittent pauses, stuttering, and numerous qualifying phrases—all of which may make the interview, especially radio interview, either unusable or a poor reflection on the candidate.

14. There is no excuse for the candidate not having a mental inventory of very short responses for *any* question with a reasonable probability of being asked. This is the news director's responsibility.

Note: Exhibit 4-1, especially footnote b.

a typed memorandum summarizing his performance; then the two can discuss the memo. Alternatively, they can orally review the news conference by relying on the news director's evaluation notes (Exhibit 6-3).

Visual News Conference

The visual is a picture story planned and scheduled primarily for television.

Exhibit 6-3
News Conference Evaluation Format

Start: 10:05
Opn. Stmnt: 10:06-10:08 (2 min)[a]
Media outlets and reporters present: . . .
Q&A—10:08 to 10:24 (16 min)—8 questions[b]
  —3 on opening stmnt, 5 on other
  —5 other questions divided 2 on domestic, 3 on foreign policy
Questions:
1. Smith, KNBC re: how will drug proposals really solve problem?[c]
answer 150 seconds—(1) cut supply of heroin, (2) increase rehabilitation facilities, (3) make
  stiff prison sentences mandatory for pushers
NOTE: knock out analogy to suburbs; also statistic on number of addicts was wrong—but
  nobody caught; "coke"
ALSO: reply *too long*—too much moralizing, also too much repeating of stuff in opn. stmnt 2.[d]

---

[a]An example of this news director's shorthand is "Opn. Stmnt" for opening statement; other abbreviations are avoided here for clarity.

[b]In this news conference reporters asked eight questions; three were based on the opening statement, the candidate's program to combat drug abuse, and five on other subjects (two on domestic policy, three on foreign policy).

[c]The notes indicate the candidate's response was 150 seconds, about two and a half minutes, and he made three points. The news director wants an analogy to the suburbs dropped for reasons he will indicate to the candidate; also the candidate quoted a wrong statistic on the number of addicts; no one caught the error, but the candidate cannot take a chance; research will verify the numbers. Also, "coke" indicates an expression, word, or phrase quoted directly from the candidate's answer; in this case, the candidate had spent so much time preparing for the news conference that he used the jargon, coke, instead of the more acceptable term, cocaine. The news director felt the reply was too long, was sidetracked into moralizing, and repeated much of what was said in the opening statement.

[d]The evaluation continues with notes on each of the eight questions asked.

The visit by the candidate to a drug rehabilitation center to discuss drug abuse, a senior citizens center to discuss problems of the elderly, or a grocery market to discuss increased food prices are all unoriginal examples of visuals. Even more effective than the planned visual is the opportunistic visual that, like the opportunistic news conference, exploits news. For example, if the United Nations passes a controversial resolution that a presidential candidate opposes, he can immediately fly to New York to hold a news conference in front of the UN building. The dramatic location (in contrast to the traditional news conference setting) and the story's timeliness makes it a powerful visual.[b] It is opportunistic because the campaign seizes the initiative to exploit the story while it is still news.

The conventional news conference is characterized by a routine setting and little or no action; the candidate speaks and answers questions in a room. The visual involves candidate interaction with people and thereby enables the campaign to compete more effectively with nonpolitical visual

---

[b] Even if the case is compelling that the UN visual will attract widespread publicity, is the idea meritorious? The answer always depends on how the electorate will perceive the visual; in addition to generating publicity, does it enhance the candidate's image or detract from it?

stories preferred by television assignment editors to conventional political stories. Possible visuals include almost any kind of personal campaigning—at factory gates, a shopping center, public rallies. Strong visuals are preceded by advance work to generate large crowds, including young people, as well as music, balloons, and signs boosting the candidate.

The conventional news conference may be covered by television despite its lack of visual orientation, but the visual has a higher probability of television coverage or of *longer* television coverage. Moreover, the good visual does not sacrifice radio or print media coverage, since it attracts these media also. The visual so dominates Level A and Level B campaigns that the candidate is often scheduled in two or more media markets each day, with one visual per market.

Most of the points raised with respect to conventional news conferences also apply to the visual, as well as some of the additional points discussed in the following pages. The visual is sometimes termed a ''photo opportunity'' and, occasionally, so specified in the schedule news release. The term emphasizes that visuals are not only for television but also for still photographers. The news director must decide whether it is necessary and advisable to specify ''photo opportunity'' in the schedule news release; it usually is *not* desirable.

Rationale

Like the conventional news conference, the visual is built around a campaign issue and is conceived to produce a desired lead. The visual is a form of news conference because reporters are likely to ask questions before, during, or after the visual activity, or the candidate may formally hold a news conference following the visual activity. The visual must be relevant to campaign strategy; if it emphasizes the wrong issue, the benefits of increased name and visual identification for the candidate could be outweighed by projecting an image or taking a position that loses votes.

The distinction between the conventional and visual news conference is ambiguous and is primarily a function of the degree of visual orientation. The easiest way to transform a conventional news conference into a visual is by introducing visual aids—charts, diagrams, exhibits, or other props. These props should be large enough for television; graphic materials should use bright colors and large print. If necessary, the candidate should have a pointer to aid his visual demonstration. It is the news director's task to sell this event to television assignment editors as a visual.

The creative news director knows that every issue can be represented visually; the challenge is finding an appropriate setting, especially a location convenient to media outlets and media personnel who are willing to cooperate with the campaign. An important stipulation is that the visual not compromise the candidate's image by making him look undignified. The candidate who dives into a filthy river to dramatize the problem of water pollution may receive significant television coverage, but will viewers accept and vote for this candidate? The answer is no, if voters perceive that the type of person who dives into a filthy river is more a performer or clown than a United States Senator.

Coordination

The location of the visual must be oriented more to the location of television stations than to any other kind of media. Assignment editors are willing to send crews quite far for a good story, but there is a limit. Just as for the conventional news conference, planning must consider past practices of local stations, traffic patterns, and related factors. Logistics and advance work involve a much greater investment of staff time than the conventional news conference, but the result is worth the effort. For example, the candidate who wishes to ride a commuter train while issuing his position about the urban transportation crisis, will be in an unstructured environment, in contrast to the controlled environment of the conventional news conference. Campaign staff must determine which train should be used, what time of day, and so forth and also negotiate any problems with the railroad. The problems of accommodating all the reporters may be more difficult than simply providing chairs for those who would cover the conventional news conference.

The visual is termed "unstructured" not because it is unorganized or unplanned, but because it is supposed to occur in a natural setting. The more unstructured (i.e., natural) the visual, the more appealing for television, but the greater the logistical problems, and the higher the risk. For example, suppose the commuter train visual proceeds smoothly, except that the candidate meets an articulate supporter of his opponent, who happens to be a passenger on the commuter train. The passenger could become the center of the visual, upstage the candidate, and change the desired lead. Truly unstructured visuals are more risky if the candidate cannot adapt quickly to new situations.

Preparation and Briefing. The news director should coach the candidate who is reluctant about staging visuals. Once the candidate understands the importance of television in reaching voters, he will display a more receptive attitude. The candidate must be reasonably enthused; otherwise his lack of interest will be apparent during the visual. The candidate's disposition may reflect his confidence, which is partially a function of the briefing.

For example, consider the familiar example of the candidate who visits a drug rehabilitation center to dramatize his concern for drug abuse. The briefing should cover the general issue of drug abuse, the opening statement, if any, and possible questions; it should also cover such details about the center as its history, accomplishments, funding, and the personnel or former drug addicts the candidate will meet. The candidate should be prepared to justify the visit by relating it to the issue; the candidate is more likely to project sincerity if the visit is truly an enlightening experience.

Many visuals succeed solely on the basis of the candidate's activity and require no statement. However, a statement, whether read orally or merely distributed, gives the visual legitimacy. It also provides valuable background or reference material for television reporters to bring to the studio. The news release on the opening statement should be supplemented with background releases citing facts or statistics to support the candidate's position. The statement should do more than deplore a problem; it should propose constructive action. Thoughtful statements of public policy accompany many visuals, partially to enhance the event's credibility with the broadcast media, but also to give substance and body to the story and thereby encourage print media coverage.

The standards for any statement, opening or otherwise, are higher for a visual than for a conventional news conference. Lengthy, involved statements discourage television coverage; the statement, especially its lead, should be lucid and concise. Since reading the statement often contrasts poorly with the desired visual effect, the candidate should be prepared to speak without referring to the prepared statement. Even when the candidate is reading a statement in a conventional, but visually oriented (i.e., with large charts or other props) news conference, the candidate should maximize eye contact.

Attendance. Higher priority should be given to stations with the most widely watched news programs; these stations are usually the network affiliates, which dwarf the independents in ratings. However, all commercial television stations are important, and the campaign should work persistently to have every station cover it. Attendance depends more on hand delivery of releases and follow-up telephone calls than on mail delivery. Attendance also depends on the time of day, and anytime after about 2 p.m. poses such problems as returning to the studio, developing and editing film, planning and writing for the newscast. The morning is the optimum time; alternatively, very early afternoon.

Most television assignment editors will not commit their station to covering a visual until the minute of decision. The purpose of telephone calls is to make certain they know of the event, provide additional information, answer questions, persuade them that the event will be visual and newsworthy. The assignment editor is fearful of committing the station, since it has a limited number of reporters and crews, and other late-breaking stories could make it impossible to keep the commitment. Although the editor will probably be noncommittal the afternoon of the day prior to the visual, the campaign should still telephone at this time. At least one additional call should be placed early the next morning. These calls should be courteous but persistent. The campaign that provides a good visual story for television is not only doing itself a favor, it is doing the station a favor. The well-run campaign news operation cultivates television assignment editors and establishes a reputation for providing quality visual stories. Once rapport is established, the campaign should have several personal contacts in each television station's newsroom, including, but not limited to, the chief assignment editor.

Logistics. To accommodate the television stations in each media market, the campaign news director must learn how each station operates. How large is their news budget? What are the ratings? What is the station's philosophy about political news? How many reporters does it have? How many camera crews? When do the staggered work shifts begin? (For example, stations with the several crews may begin with one or two crews at 7 or 8 a.m. and add another crew each hour for the next several hours; determining when the most crews are available, or new crews are added, can affect the optimum time for scheduling a visual.)

The perceptive news director learns which reporters are more likely to cover political stories as well as the biases and predispositions of individual reporters. He knows when specific reporters are more likely to work— evenings, weekends, or on particular assignments. This knowledge supplements information about the television station's policy on budgeting, staffing, and overtime, as these factors relate to covering political events.

The best way to find out this information is to read the trade publications of the television industry, the television columns in daily newspapers, and any magazine articles on television news. The news director should also establish contacts at the local press club. Above all, he should humbly seek information from contacts at the television station, as well as from the television reporters who cover campaign events.

Any visual activity is always scheduled *loosely* to permit late-arriving television crews to get some footage or to interview the candidate briefly. The campaign cannot forget that the purpose of the visual is to generate television coverage; crews arriving late should be accommodated even if the schedule runs late. However, if the schedule is properly constructed, a cushion is secretly built into the end of the visual to permit individual television interviews.

Taping. If a conventional or visual news conference is not covered by a station, the campaign should persuade the station to improvise coverage, such as taping the candidate at another location later in the day. If the station has the candidate's schedule, it may already intend to tape or film the candidate at another location. The scene may be less dramatic than the earlier visual, but it gives the station the opportunity to cover the candidate. The candidate should be willing, schedule permitting, to visit the television station to tape an interview for the evening news—whether the station initiates the offer or accepts the campaign's suggestion for such a taping. If the campaign is newsworthy and fast moving, any station that is unable to cover a visual because its reporters or camera crews were overcommitted will suggest alternative ways of covering the candidate's activities that day.

Live Appearance. Many stations may compensate for their absence at a news conference or visual with a live appearance by the candidate, usually on the early (5-7 p.m.) news or, in the case of the independent station, on the 10 p.m. news. The network affiliate station's early two-hour news format is conducive to live guest appearances, because the program is so long.

Mini-Camera. The current trend among local television stations, especially network affiliates, is to convert conventional camera crews to the mini-camera (or mini-cam) that permits live telecasts without mobile units. In order to justify spending on such expensive equipment and to provide greater variety for the two-hour news format, stations will cover some events occurring in the 5-7 p.m. time period. Even some traditional events, such as political banquets or receptions, may be covered by the mini-camera, not because they are visual, but because of their immediacy. This means that the candidate engaged in activities during this time period may be able to secure a couple of minutes of live coverage. Another possibility is interviewing the candidate live (on mini-cam) just after a speaking commitment or major event, if the interview can occur in the 11:00-11:30 time period.

Helicopter. The use of helicopter camera crews or other innovative television reporting techniques should be noted by the aggressive campaign, which can construct visuals specifically designed for the technique. Such visuals are more challenging, but they are uniquely suited to dramatic television reporting.

Evaluation. The line between the creative visual and the circus performance is often difficult to draw, but it exists. Any evaluation of a visual must consider not only how many television stations cover it, and how much time is given, but the context of the story. How did the anchorperson introduce or end the story? What did the reporter say before, after, or in voice over, the story? Was the television reporter's attitude clearly patronizing, skeptical, or critical, or was it respectful and sympathetic?

Since the objective of the visual is television coverage, any statement must be constructed so that if *any* part of it is filmed and used, the footage benefits the campaign. However, the statement should be written to favor a certain lead—that is, the likelihood should be that certain portions will be used. Yet, the statement can be the least important part of the visual story; footage of the candidate seeing and doing things, talking to supporters and voters, is preferable to the candidate's reading a statement or simply responding to the reporter's questions. The more visual the story, the more likely it will emphasize the candidate's lead; the less time for the reporter to offer his own commentary.

The candidate in the midst of a visual should always be conscious of the desired lead. The matter of responding in a low-key manner to provocative reporters' questions is even more critical than the conventional news conference. The impetuous, emotional answer, or the statement of a new campaign position or a newsworthy reaction to major news developments, can overshadow the lead of a visual that required many staff hours to conceive and implement. If the campaign successfully promotes its own lead on the early news, the lead is almost certain to be the same on the late evening news. Most major stories on the earlier news are repeated; if they are edited, the lead usually does not change.

Actuality and Availability

The news conference or visual is sometimes confused with the actuality or availability. An actuality is a news conference, visual, or *any other campaign event*—speech, campaign rally, walking tour—as long as the event can be related to a time and place. An availability indicates that a time and place is set aside on the candidate's schedule to accommodate the news media; the availability lacks the formality of a news conference, and there is no opening statement, but the candidate is definitely available for questions.

Actuality

Any statement or issue position of the candidate is more likely to be publicized if it is related to a specific time and place (i.e., an actuality). The time element provides immediacy, and the place provides a reference point. The actuality provides the *when* and *where* of the lead of any news story; the candidate provides the *who* and his statement is the *what*. The actuality satisfies the news media's need to report an event; thus the candidate's position on an issue or reaction statement is not in a void, but in the context of a speech or remarks delivered to a group of people in an actual location. The news director continually reviews the campaign schedule to find possible actualities—that is, entries with a place or time suitable for a story.

Availability

Novice campaigners will call a news conference even when they have nothing to say. They will either have no opening statement or a statement lacking content. Many reporters are offended if they attend a news conference expecting a newsworthy opening statement and none exists, or if one does, it is bland. The *availability*, unlike the news conference, has no opening statement, is informal, and does not include the persistent notification of the media. It means that at a given time the candidate will be available to meet with the news media to answer questions. The candidate may be occupied in other chores but will be accessible to any reporters who want answers to questions.

For example, if the candidate is scheduled to attend an evening banquet, the news director may hesitate to call a news conference if the candidate has nothing new to say or if attendance will be poor for inherent reasons; for example, overtime compensation problems in the local media discourage coverage of evening events. The news director does not want to call a news conference if the turnout will embarrass the candidate or campaign. Alternatively, he contacts the local media, perhaps delivering by hand an advisory news release to local media outlets, by including the availability in the official candidate schedule issued to the news media or by telephoning local reporters. The advisory, which might also be the basis for an item on the wire service ticker or as part of the candidate's daily schedule printed on the ticker, indicates that the candidate will be available to the news media at a specified time and location. The advisory might simply indicate that the candidate will be attending the reception from 7:15 to 8:00 or 7:30 to 8:00 but will be available to the media, or it might indicate a more precise time, such as 7:15-7:30 or 7:45-8:00. If reporters do not take advantage of the availability, nothing is lost.

Sometimes the availability is more a matter of policy than precise announcement. The alert news director is always looking for ways of helping reporters cover a story, and he is often willing to pull the candidate from a reception or head table to help a reporter who must ask a couple of questions before a deadline or to accommodate a television crew that arrived without notice. The campaign's policy of accessibility should encourage the news media to interview the candidate in order to generate news stories. In addition to the policy, the news director may find that the news release advising the news media of the availability insures that reporters know they are welcome; it might also give a newspaper or broadcast editor the idea of sending someone to ask some questions.

The availability should not be confused with the interview that the candidate gives to a single reporter. The interview is specifically related to a particular reporter; the availability is general access for one or more reporters. The availability may include several reporters questioning the candidate together, or a series of brief, successive interviews. The interview can be a creative way of accommodating local reporters. For example, if a presidential or statewide candidate is making a one-time tour through an area, the news director may schedule a brief interview with a local reporter, who is permitted to ride with the candidate while he is in the local area. At the next campaign stop, the reporter departs, and a new reporter takes his place. In this way, the candidate is exposed for a few minutes to a key local reporter during each part of the itinerary.

7

Administering the News Function

Managing and administering the news operation is essential if it is to do its job of producing news. The news director must also be a manager, especially in the Level A or Level B campaign in which he spends much of his time traveling with the candidate. The news director must structure an office operation and delegate authority so that media lists are updated, news releases are written, edited, typed, reproduced, and mailed, and many liaison functions are performed. The news director must assess the volume of work required and then decide the number and qualifications of staff to be recruited. Even in the local campaign, one person should travel with the candidate. If this person is not the news director or press secretary, but serves as an all around candidate's aide, he must have a basic knowledge of the news media and should serve as the news director's surrogate during campaigning. The small campaign headquarters with a few paid staff members requires at least one person who can handle media telephone inquiries intelligently and prepare a news release mailing.

The difference between the small and the large campaign news operation is primarily the size of the staff and budget. The objectives and responsibilities do not vary significantly; the delegation of authority and the degree of specialization vary considerably.[a] This chapter on the structure and functions of the news operation emphasizes some tasks not discussed earlier, with particular emphasis on the delivery system—that is, how to get the news to the media.

Structure and Functions

Since the schedule of the local campaign is person oriented rather than media oriented, the news director or press secretary spends relatively less time traveling with the candidate and relatively more time in the campaign headquarters to produce news releases and monitor public relations programs. In contrast, the news director of the Level A or Level B campaign usually travels with the candidate, because this type of schedule is media oriented and because reporters may travel with the candidate. The travel-

[a] Exhibits 1-2 and 2-2 summarize and relate media tasks to different levels of campaigning. The term "news operation" is preferred to "press operation" because news encompasses broadcast media.

ing news director requires a lieutenant at the campaign headquarters to serve as a communications link between the traveling and the headquarters news operation. Often, the news director's secretary serves as principal liaison.

The emphasis on news releases should not obviate the need for more personal communication by mail. This may include sending personal letters over the candidate's signature after interviews, editorial board meetings, news conferences, or other encounters with the news media. The candidate should be apprised of such letters if he will be seeing the recipients again. The personal communication program should also include correspondence, signed by the candidate or news director, with editors, station managers, news executives, and working reporters. The campaign not only acknowledges media correspondence promptly by return mail, but it initiates correspondence on a variety of topics. For example, letters might query television and radio station managers or program directors about possible interview or talk programs or the station's policy on television debates. Larger mailings might be processed best by automatic typewriters that produce "personal" form letters.

The campaign headquarters should be prepared for unexpected visits from reporters. Even if a journalist arrives without warning, the headquarters' standard operating plan for receptionists should insure that the reporter is received courteously and graciously. If the Level A or Level B headquarters has a security system, including identification paper badges for guests, the news office should dispatch an escort immediately to make certain the visitor is given a media identification badge. The campaign headquarters should be designed so that the reporter, in order to go from the main entrance to the office of the candidate, campaign manager, or news director, must walk through intense volunteer activity. Anytime a reporter is in the headquarters, he should be escorted by a host who can provide a tour, answer questions, and prevent the reporter from eavesdropping on sensitive activity in the private sections (e.g., finance or scheduling) of the campaign headquarters.

Meeting the Media

Even in presidential and other highly visible campaigns, the news director cannot wait for the media to initiate meetings. Although the campaign may be *the* story to cover once it gets underway and many reporters will be initiating contact with the campaign, the preliminary phase requires the campaign to initiate contact. This is much easier for the local campaign that must relate to a limited media constituency. The candidate and press aide should be able to meet almost every editor or reporter personally. There is no substitute for personal meetings with the news executives who decide how much time or space should be given to politics and to the specific campaign.

The news director should not hesitate to telephone an editor to introduce himself and seek an appointment. However, it is essential that the news director and candidate learn as much as possible about the media outlet and editor before any personal meeting.

Introductory or Editorial Board Meeting. Many publications or stations do not have formal editorial boards that oversee policy or make endorsements and thereby provide a useful context for meeting the candidate. Alternatively, the candidate can meet with a group of editors and reporters informally. The weekly newspaper counterpart of an editorial board meeting may be simply taking the editor-publisher to lunch. The objective is the same—establish *personal* contact with relevant decision makers and reporters at the earliest possible time.

The campaign seeks to meet with the news media at a time convenient to the editors or reporters. The campaign news director may suggest a breakfast, luncheon, or dinner meeting that affords a more relaxed atmosphere. The offer should be made for the convenience of the journalists, not as a patronizing gesture to obligate someone by buying them a meal. Major daily newspapers will often offer to host a small editorial board luncheon for a major candidate.

The purpose of any initial meeting is not to seek an endorsement, but to establish contact, get acquainted, introduce the candidate, and explain his motivation for entering politics or the specific campaign. This meeting should demonstrate that the candidate is sincere and decent and that he is a reasonable and honest person. The meeting permits the news director to explain that the campaign wants to cooperate with the news media and has a positive attitude; that it will be persistent, but not overly pushy. The meeting is not designed to convert the skeptical or partisan reporter, but to lay the foundation for communication, to eliminate hostility, and to challenge the preconceptions of biased media.

The early meetings should be a source of information for the campaign, because editors and reporters can indicate how and why they define news as they do. The editors can explain their precise needs, budget and staffing problems, deadlines, and other servicing parameters. Each news outlet can summarize its priorities. For example, the radio station manager or news director can indicate the station's policy on using recorded actualities delivered by the campaign, or transmitted by telephone, or its interest in interviewing the candidate by telephone.

Personal meetings increase the likelihood that the campaign will be covered or covered extensively or fairly. The rapport between candidate and news director, on the one hand, and publisher and editors, on the other, should have a positive effect on the attitude of the working press. Reporters are more likely to take the campaign seriously if their bosses take it seriously. The editorial policy of the newspaper or broadcast station may even favor the opponent, but the endorsement may not be as strong as it would have been without the meeting or it may be more respectful toward the nonendorsed candidate or avoid negative references to him. The meeting may induce a newspaper or station to switch from planning to endorse the opponent to a no-endorsement policy or even to endorsing the candidate who initiated the meeting.

Meetings should be *on the record* unless the media outlet indicates another preference. The campaign should encourage the media outlet to invite a reporter (to join the publisher or editors) to write a story based on the meeting. The newspaper should be encouraged to have a photographer present; the television station, a film crew; and the radio station, a radio reporter or tape recorder. The reporting staff members may not be present for the entire meeting, but long enough to prepare a personality piece, photo story, visual feature, or even a news story on the candidate. Thus, the meeting accomplishes two goals: introducing the candidate and the campaign and generating news coverage.

Since the meeting may be the candidate's first and only leisurely and conversational exchange with the news decision makers, he must be prepared for it. Its length can vary from just a few minutes with a busy weekly newspaper editor-publisher to two hours for an extended luncheon meeting with the publishing and editorial executives and political reporters of a major daily newspaper. The candidate should be briefed to answer all possible questions relating to his candidacy—for example, motivation, position on issues, financial support, relationship to political party and other candidates, possible endorsements by others, and so forth. The candidate should know the names and background of each person who is to be at the meeting and the individual's position of power and influence within the media outlet. The candidate's briefing should analyze the issues most prominently covered by the media outlet, especially those discussed in its recent editorials.

The campaign should not take friendly media for granted, and it should not write off media committed to the opposition candidate. Publishers, editors, and reporters do not like to be taken for granted; they want to be reminded of their importance. The candidate should usually consolidate support among friendly media before cultivating new media contacts. An important, related factor is the mistake of leaking news stories to uncommitted or hostile media in an effort to change their attitude or neutralize their opposition. This policy of trying to persuade neutral or opposition news media to give fairer coverage or to support the candidate editorially will usually fail to achieve that objective and could also alienate the candidate's original supporters in the news media.

The more prudent (but risky) policy is rewarding friendly news media with occasional favoritism. But the favoritism should not be known or easily confirmed, nor should it be blatant. The campaign should also examine the possibility of providing news releases, background materials, facts, and statistics to friendly editorial writers to encourage favorable editorials.

Wire and News Services. The campaign should establish personal contacts at local bureaus and offices of the major wire and news services. If the wire service cannot cover a story, it should always receive the news release by hand in time to write a current story. The campaign must give priority to hand delivering the candidate's schedule, since AP, UPI, and local services may provide a daily list of events (often called a daybook), judged potentially newsworthy, to subscriber newspapers and broadcast stations. The wires also maintain a variety of special services, including broadcast wires used extensively by radio stations, especially smaller stations that edit the copy slightly and then use it as script for the announcer.

The two principal wire circuits are the "A" and the "B" wire. The A wire provides national stories to subscribers throughout the nation; the B wire serves a region with news of interest to the limited geographical area. The campaign should determine where the state or regional wire originates, since this bureau deserves personal attention. The campaign should also determine the decision makers at each wire service; they usually can be found at the city or metropolitan desk. The night editor can be a valuable contact for advance (i.e., *hold for release*) stories.

The Associated Press is a cooperative; it receives copies of files stories from its member newspapers almost immediately. The UPI must wait until local dailies are on the street, and then can send the story on the wire. In either case, the wires receive newspaper editions just off the press, and most wire service offices are located within daily newspaper offices or nearby. The campaign should establish personal relationships with bureau chiefs, metropolitan and city desk day and night editors, and field reporters to learn as much as possible about the local office and how to get campaign news on the wire.

Liaison

The efficient news operation in any political campaign must interact with other parts of the campaign. The news director oversees liaison; in larger campaigns, he depends on individual staff members to be responsible for liaison with particular parts of the campaign. The news operation maximizes publicity for the candidate by interacting with scheduling, research, and other campaign divisions, as well as local committees, adjunct committees, and outside organizations.

Candidate. The news director must know what the candidate is saying—in speeches, brochures, news conferences, and interviews. The candidate's positions must be consistent, without surprise or erratic shifts in position. The Level A or Level B campaign requires a communications system to link the traveling entourage and the campaign headquarters. The presidential candidate should always be accompanied by at least one aide capable of shorthand, and the campaign news operation should always have at least one stenographer available and at least one other competent secretary in the headquarters able to substitute if necessary. Local headquarters or volunteers may also recruit a volunteer or paid secretary to assist the candidate while he is visiting their area. The candidate's aide should also travel with a telecopier.[b]

The purpose of the secretarial and telecopier system is to provide total liaison between the candidate and campaign headquarters. This system enables the candidate to learn about news developments from the headquarters, as well as to be apprised of other campaign information, including copies of the latest news releases and schedules. The candidate can issue reaction statements based on major news developments, and news releases can be simultaneously distributed by the campaign headquarters. The traveling news director can also dictate a news release draft or send one over the telecopier to the campaign headquarters.

Level A and Level B campaigns should rent a wire service ticker (for installation within the campaign news operation) to provide continuous and timely information to help brief the candidate and to provide ideas for possible reaction statements. The ticker enables the campaign to find out about news developments at about the same time as most radio stations; it also helps monitor the schedule and statements of the opposition candidate. The secretarial and telecopier liaison help make the most use of the ticker.

Finally, the news director may prepare a written or oral daily news briefing, or both, for the candidate. This briefing insures that the candidate is informed of news coverage of the campaign, related issues, and important newsworthy events. The research division may also be involved.

Scheduling. Every change in the candidate's schedule must be relayed from the scheduling division to the campaign news operation; the news

---

[b] The telecopier is a portable copying machine that uses a telephone to send a copy of material to another telecopier that also is hooked into a telephone. The machine sends an exact copy in a matter of minutes; advanced equipment can send many copies consecutively and automatically. The telecopier is manufactured by Xerox and can be rented on a monthly basis.

director or an aide decides whether the campaign should issue a revised schedule or an advisory. The scheduling operation also notifies the news operation, through a liaison person, memoranda, or formal meetings, of newly scheduled commitments, so the news operation can evaluate the publicity potential of each commitment and decide how many news releases, telephone calls, and other initiatives are justified by the event. The news operation should review the candidate's schedule, including each change, in light of changing news developments that provide new publicity opportunities.

The news operation is usually responsible for scheduling all commitments that are directly related to news exposure—for example, news conferences, visuals, interviews with an individual reporter or group of reporters, editorial board meetings, television and radio program interviews, telephone conversations for live airing on talk shows, and so forth. Regardless of the precise role of the news operation in arranging the commitment, no such item is accepted by the scheduling division unless the news division authorizes it. Since most media requests are directed to the news division, its staff must be apprised of the candidate's confidential schedule, including the most recent changes. The news director also must have daily updates on the candidate's schedule to know how much time is available if he wishes to invite a reporter to interview the candidate, suggest an editorial board meeting, or persuade a television program producer to have the candidate as a guest. Continuous communication and liaison is required to prevent the candidate from being scheduled at two places simultaneously.

In major campaigns, liaison is also required with the advance division. The advance staff may discover information about an area to be visited that should be included in the candidate's briefing prior to a news conference. The advance staff may also work with local volunteers to confirm that all local media are notified about the candidate's schedule or news conference. The advance staff oversees the logistics (e.g., hotel and transportation reservations) that affect the traveling media. Thus, the news operation should have one person who links scheduling and advance with news. This person may be the same individual who makes certain that campaign schedules are distributed as soon as possible to the media; this requires securing complete data from scheduling, raising any questions and verifying suspense items, and supervising the preparation of the candidate's official, public campaign schedule.

Research. The news operation cannot function unless it interacts regularly or even daily with the research division. The news operation, which deals exclusively with reporters, must use research to process certain queries about the candidate's positions. In addition, the news director is more likely to contribute ideas for news conferences, visuals, and positions on issues if he has access to the latest information, briefings, summaries, reports, and so forth collected by the research division. Research staff members may work independently, or with local volunteers and advance staff, to examine the local implications of national or statewide issues or positions taken by the candidate. Often, research prepares briefings for the candidate on issues as a whole, rather than specific implications for a campaign tour through an area; or, if research prepares the material, it, like the material secured by the advance staff, is incorporated in the news director's briefing for the candidate.

The campaigner should realize that the research staff, including volunteer researchers, can provide the raw material and data that inspire the most creative publicity ideas; such material can be polished into finished speeches, news conference statements, or reaction statements. It is the research division's task not only to collect material, but to collate it and synthesize it in manageable form for quick access by both the candidate and the news division. This task relates to the previously discussed need for an inventory of campaign positions and statements that can be adapted quickly to daily news developments.

Additional Liaison. The news division must maintain liaison with every division of the campaign, adjunct committees, and local committees. Other divisions of the campaign include finance, youth, volunteers, and any other *horizontal* divisions within the overall structure. Adjunct committees are related to the primary campaign committee but retain distinct identity as they try to organize groups of voters (doctors, lawyers, veterans, and the like) to support the candidate. Local committees are simply the *vertical* divisions of the campaign—proceeding down a hierarchy from the national level to statewide, regional, county, district, and local.[c]

Other Divisions. Each division must be encouraged to take the initiative in suggesting which of its activities have publicity potential. The political division should review the list of potential endorsements. The organization division, perhaps part of the political operation, should review progress in organizing the campaign and appointing leaders. Finance should provide information on fund raising, number of contributors, per capita amounts, fund-raising dinners, and other events. Each of these divisions may have ideas or events that can be publicized. Some of the ideas may require the candidate's presence while others will have news or feature appeal on their own. Whether or not each division initiates ideas, the news director cannot

[c] The efficient news operation cannot be distracted by contacts outside the campaign organization; the campaign's other divisions, adjunct committees, and local committees filter contacts to the news operation. This filtering process means news staff members speak on the telephone or meet personally only with those individuals outside the campaign who genuinely have relevant ideas or information.

wait for each division head to begin communications or to bring events to the news division's attention. No one knows better than the news director which events, personalities, or stories have news or feature value. The news director or a member of his staff must persist in surveying divisions as to their activities.

Adjunct Committees. One reason for the formation of an adjunct committee, such as "Doctors for Smith" or "Veterans for Smith," is for publicity. In addition to raising funds or stimulating support within a particular constituency, the adjunct committee provides an excuse for publicity, news conferences, and visuals. It also provides an automatic relationship to certain issues; for example, Smith can hold a joint news conference with the leaders of "Doctors for Smith" to discuss malpractice insurance or tour a veterans hospital with the leaders of "Veterans for Smith."

If the adjunct committee is entirely authentic and sefl-sufficient, its personnel may be responsible for news media mailings, telephone calls, and personal contacts for its own publicity. Often, the news division will provide professional counsel and ideas, as well as the news media mailing list. Alternatively, the adjunct committee may provide leaders, a list of names, or an audience for the news division to use in creating a publicity event, speaking commitment, news conference, or visual. The adjunct committee also helps bridge the gap between the campaign and sympathetic organizations outside the campaign that may wish to offer assistance or can provide ideas or locations for news conferences, visuals, or newsworthy positions on issues.

Local Committees. Any Level A or Level B campaign should prepare a comprehensive publicity manual incorporating the campaign's news philosophy, positive attitude toward the news media, and explanation of servicing. This manual should include a collection of sample news releases, including the form news releases mentioned earlier. The booklet should stress how local volunteer leaders can maximize publicity in their area, with special emphasis on establishing the committee, opening an office, announcing committee appointments and membership, local endorsements, fund-raising events, volunteer and precinct activity, and any events with publicity potential.

The manual should explain the importance of communication and liaison with the state or national campaign headquarters to assure maximum publicity when the candidate visits the area. Proper liaison insures that volunteers can contribute valuable information on issues and local reporters and that they know how to relate their efforts to the campaign's scheduling, advance, and news staff. The manual should also be accompanied by a complete and detailed local media list that has been compiled by the campaign headquarters. Local volunteers may recommend changes in the list, but the final list, and updated lists, are supplied by the central headquarters.

The purpose of liaison and the manual is to explain to local volunteers how to secure publicity, how to treat the local media, and how to treat the media traveling with the candidate. Often, general liaison and the manual are insufficient; the campaign should conduct a workshop or seminar in the campaign's preparatory phase. The workshop can explain policy and servicing in more detail, and it can consider other news-oriented projects that can be adopted by local groups. An example would be a letters-to-the-editor project. Since supplying suggested texts can result in an embarrassing number of identical letters to newspaper editors, the campaign should supply a list of priority subjects, background material, facts, and statistics that can be used by volunteers who are willing to write letters.

Monitoring Media Coverage

The campaign must realistically appraise its news possibilities and then allocate the candidate's limited time accordingly in order to produce the most favorable news impact. News possibilities are appraised in terms of alternative media, media outlets, and individual journalists. The campaign plans specific news initiatives—interviews, statements, news conferences, visuals, and so forth—and a steady flow of news releases to graduate news exposure as the campaign approaches its peak. The campaign must continually monitor print and broadcast media coverage to evaluate both quantity and quality. Typical questions might include: Is there enough television coverage? What about coverage in specific television media markets? Does the television coverage reflect the campaign's emphasis on particular issues? How much radio news is the campaign securing? Which issues are being covered?

Implementing Goals. Broadcast media coverage is measured by time; print media, by space. The campaign must measure time and space exposure in terms of months, weeks, even days. The Level A or Level B campaign should target precisely the desired number of news conferences and visuals—that is, the number of exposures per media market per time period. For example, a statewide candidate in New York might plan a certain number of visits to each media market (e.g., three visits in September to Buffalo). The time period is important because it provides an important constraint. Each day's schedule should generate wire and news service articles, coverage by major daily newspapers, and broadcast media coverage. Different level campaigns can state goals in more specific terms;

for example, the statewide candidate in a campaign dominated by several major daily newspapers will want an article in each dominant newspaper every day, regardless of where the candidate is campaigning. For instance, the statewide candidate in California will want an article in the *Los Angeles Times* daily, even if he is campaigning in San Francisco. The presidential campaign has a far more ambitious goal: a major story on each of the three network newscasts every evening.

Goals are defined on a daily basis because it is difficult, if not impossible, to compensate for lost days. For example, if the campaign does not have a visual one day, it cannot have two visuals the next day. If the campaign is not covered by a major newspaper one day, it cannot secure two articles in that newspaper the next day. If individual days that are lost cannot be made up, the problem of compensating for inadequate news exposure for a week or longer period is compounded.

The news director should have some idea, at the end of each day, how much news coverage the campaign generated. By the end of the day, and cretainly by the next morning when the campaign's monitoring system has reported additional data, the news director should know roughly how many *exposures* (i.e., the individual news articles, television or radio news reports) the candidate received. The number of exposures emphasizes the importance of news and wire services; for example, a single favorable syndicated column or wire service story could be carried in many newspapers. The daily totals can be considered at the end of the week when the strategy committee reviews the campaign's progress. The weekly evaluation must include quantity and quality measurement; the qualitative assessment should consider related factors, such as placement of article or film coverage within newspaper or broadcast, and whether coverage is consistent with campaign strategy.

The daily evaluation of news media coverage need not be so precise that its compilation is unduly time consuming; an accurate approximation is adequate. The news director must have the self-discipline to measure daily progress. Moreover, quantitative monitoring must be supplemented by qualitative evaluation, uusually emphasizing the need for the candidate to receive news coverage on a few key issues.

Time and Space. The most common method of monitoring press coverage is the commercial clipping service. Although it produces a steady supply of articles that can be reprinted for the campaign leadership, prospective donors, and as a source of information, the service is expensive (about $30 to $50 monthly, plus 18¢ to 25¢ per clipping) and slow (clippings are often mailed several days after publication). The clipping service should be supplemented with a system of volunteers in different areas; each volunteer is responsible for clipping certain newspapers on a daily basis. They can use a telecopier in the local campaign headquarters to transmit important articles quickly.

The news operation should subscribe to or purchase important newspapers, magazines, or other publications. Many cities have professional delivery services or special newsstands for out-of-town publications. The alert news director oversees a monitoring system that checks major news magazines immediately on publication; each edition of the newspaper is purchased on publication, and the morning newspaper, if published in a preview edition, is purchased the prior evening. The news director needs to be aware of any stories or developments on the campaign, candidate, opponent, or on other issues since the candidate or spokesperson may be asked to comment on any of these. Monitoring also gives the news director a feel for how the news media is treating various news stories; the preview edition (prior evening) of the morning newspaper is especially useful for giving an advance indication of stories that will receive "play" in the next day's newspapers. Many television assignment editors will also be guided by the morning newspaper in determining news priorities. The major campaign also closely monitors its wire service news ticker, located in the campaign news operation, and keeps the radio tuned to an all news station.

Before articles are put in the candidate's daily briefing file, the news director reviews all of the articles clipped by staff members or volunteers who scan a variety of newspapers and publications. The candidate needs to know how the campaign is being depicted in the news, since public perceptions are largely a product of the news media. Obviously, the candidate should be especially aware of articles or broadcast commentary of reporters who are traveling with him or who are about to interview him.

Unlike commercial clipping services, broadcast monitoring services can report to the campaign quickly—even the same evening as the television newscast. These services can provide transcripts of television and radio news coverage of both the candidate and his opponent; they can send transcripts by telecopier rather than mail. If such service is unavailable or too expensive, the campaign volunteer organization can search for and designate volunteers in different areas; each volunteer is assigned to monitor specific television news broadcasts. Each volunteer times the coverage given to candidate and opponent, and uses a standard form to summarize the story's lead, reporter's commentary, and footage used. These reports not only provide valuable information, but the data can be used to persuade a station to give the candidate greater coverage. An even more advanced system uses videotape television systems that enable the campaign to videotape relevant portions of different news broadcasts. This system provides the candidate and news director with an opportunity to view television coverage, even if they were occupied in a banquet or other campaign event, or were watching a competing station, while the news was aired.

Television and Radio Appearances

Any major campaign should compile a thorough and updated list of the news, interview, and talk broadcast programs. The statewide candidate should have a goal of appearing on virtually every program at least once. An early appearance may mean the candidate can appear a second or third time; caution should be used if the early appearance will be the sole appearance, since the opposing candidate may benefit from an equal time policy by appearing at a more propitious time. The campaign should also exploit every opportunity for telephone radio interviews, especially from the candidate's hotel suite or other temporary location.

Before appearing on any broadcast program, the candidate should be briefed about the name and type of program, format, audience, and host. The host or interviewer should be briefed about the candidate and acquainted with his positions. Both the program and campaign staff should understand the expected length of the interview. The candidate should have some idea about the issues or questions likely to be raised by the host. If time permits, the broadcast appearance should be promoted by the campaign; the importance of the appearance determines how much promotion is appropriate and whether it should be mentioned in the campaign newsletter, a separate mailing to financial supporters and volunteers, a telephone campaign, newspaper advertising, and so forth.

Programs that are taped or aired on weekends should provide additional publicity opportunities, because weekends are slow news days. The aggressive news director should insure that all media are aware of the candidate's weekend schedule, so their crews can interview the candidate at the entrance of the station, before or after the program. The host station will probably ''lift'' a portion of the program for the evening news, which has much higher ratings than the public affairs program; rival stations will use their own brief interview—done just before or after the program. Monday morning newspapers, which have a scarcity of news, may give the candidate more coverage than the typical weekday edition.

Whenever any broadcast programs are taped for future airing, whether later that day or week, print media journalists are expected to write their stories for subsequent publication—that is, concurrent with, or following, actual airing of the program. Whenever a taping is listed on the candidate's schedule, it specifies that the broadcast is taped, and the date and time of scheduled airing is also shown. The news director should then encourage traveling and other media to accompany the candidate to the broadcast and write a story that the newspaper can hold for a few hours or days.

No major candidate should accept television invitations unless he has access to a television adviser or the news director understands the subtleties of television. This is especially true for television debates; the candidate and news director should be aware of the characteristics of these debates (see Exhibit 7-1).

Election Night

The campaign that prepares for its election night news operation weeks in advance will enhance its professional image with the news media. Since practical decisions by broadcast media must be made far in advance of election night coverage for Level A and Level B campaigns, proper servicing requires early planning. The campaign should issue advisory releases and begin telephone canvassing to determine how many media outlets will cover election night, what their technical requirements will be, and how many personnel (and who) will be coming. A special election night task force, established by the campaign three or four weeks before election day, begins by making plans for security and logistics that include particular attention to screening news media credentials and providing a secure working area in front of the stage as well as another secure area, probably a room adjacent to the ballroom, with typewriters, telephones, and refreshments. The news media arrangements also include determining positions for network and television station crews, examining the possibility of a pool camera that feeds into all stations and is usually in front of center stage and on its own platform, and overseeing liaison with the hotel and telephone company.[d]

Experienced news editors, reporters, and producers know the technical requirements, and they will usually deal directly with the hotel and telephone company. They will pay for their own installation and service charges. The campaign will provide extra telephones, on a nonassigned basis, for reporters whose news media outlets did not order telephones. The campaign will also provide, through the hotel or facility engineer, no more than four microphones: one for the public address system and one backup microphone; one for all television and radio crews and one backup. Broadcasters will accept this arrangement provided it is not violated—that is, no station insists on putting its own microphone at the podium; also, there must be no marking or call letters on any microphones at the podium. The result is that competing station microphones do not interfere with each

---

[d] The actual rental of election night facilities is an early priority; the optimum location is reserved weeks or even months before election night, although the election night task force may not begin operating until perhaps three weeks before the election.

Exhibit 7-1
Characteristics of Television Debates

1. The leading candidate usually finds some excuse to avoid debates; the trailing candidate inevitably pushes for the debates.
2. The candidate who wants a debate must be prepared to press for the debate by beginning early negotiations; the other candidate is likely to stall.
3. The candidate desiring a debate should enlist the news media on his side; his news director should emphasize that the debates will have news value, and the news media should be positioned as advocating the debate.
4. The side pushing for the debate should be prepared for every conceivable stall, including technical arguments and alleged technical conflicts; hence, it should have a flexible position, offer alternative dates, let the stations suggest dates or, even better, have the other side provide a list of acceptable dates; in addition, the other side should provide a list of acceptable technical conditions.
5. All negotiations and meetings should be followed by written confirmation of points discussed or agreements reached.
6. Advocates of the debate should push for on-the-record negotiations, with the news media being kept apprised of progress.
7. Negotiators should know their candidate's strengths and weaknesses; for example, negotiators for the relaxed, confident candidate should push for reaction shots (i.e., permitting the camera to show the expression of one candidate while the other is talking).
8. The leading candidate usually tries to limit the issues discussed or to increase the length of opening statements; he is more likely to favor news media questioning of both candidates than each candidate questioning the other.
9. The candidate behind in the polls wants greater latitude for the discussion, favors shorter opening statements to allow for more rebuttal and questions and answers, and is probably eager to confront the other candidate.
10. If issues are selected, negotiators should push for their candidate's strong issues, the opposition candidate's weak issues.
11. Television debates have very limited audiences; most viewers are already committed to one or the other of the candidates. The debate's benefits are its psychological effects on the opposing candidate and campaign, effect on the tone of overall campaign news coverage, print media stories based on the debates, and, most importantly, "lifts" of segments of the debates excerpted for use on television news programs that have much higher ratings than the debates.
12. Negotiators seeking the debate should push for prime-time airing and for permitting other stations in the media market or in other media markets to use the debate; negotiators who don't want the debate should push for Sunday afternoons and for restricted airing.

other, and the candidate is not obscured by many microphones at the podium.

Although the news director should have a secret contingency plan and suggested remarks if the candidate should lose, his public position is victory. He knows that his job does not end on election day, but includes election night as well as the following weeks; thank you notes and possibly a party for the reporters who covered the candidate will be required. These letters and the party cannot be planned in advance, but election night can be planned carefully. Prior attention to detail will affect news media coverage in the weeks *before* election night, because reporters are impressed with the campaign's professional servicing.

The ideal election night policy, unless special circumstances dictate otherwise, provides that the candidate is inaccessible until his victory or concession statement. This policy will only be accepted by the news media if the campaign has a reputation for firm enforcement of any stated policy and for treating competing reporters alike. Once such a policy is established, there can be no exception for any reporter, photographer, or film crew without causing ill feeling among competing media.

Delivery Systems

No political campaign can afford to rely exclusively on the postal service for delivering news releases. Personal visits and regular telephone calls are far more important. Hand delivery of news releases is much more timely than the mail, and it conveys a sense of importance and priority lacking in the mail. The local campaign that emphasizes weekly newspapers should stress hand delivery of releases by individuals personally acquainted with local editors. The higher level campaigns emphasize hand delivery even more, but not for an entire media list of hundreds or thousands, but for the news media on the most pressing deadlines.

Media and Mailing Lists

The campaign should compile the news media list in the campaign's formative stages. Resource materials include *Editor & Publisher, Broadcasting Yearbook, Ayer's, Working Press of the Nation,* the telephone yellow pages, and lists compiled by political party organizations, other campaigns, and community and service groups. The media list must be thorough, accurate, and updated. It should include all relevant media; for example, the newspaper published outside the congressional district may include many readers living in the district and eligible to vote for the candidate. The list should also include the bureaus, news and wire service offices, specialty, ethnic, and any other types of media that might be interested in the campaign.

Essentially the campaign has three different lists: the media, mailing, and hand delivery lists. The media list includes the names of all relevant publishers, editors, and broadcast news editors as well as reporters. It is usually a card file system, color coded by type of media (e.g., daily newspaper, radio station). The front side of the card includes detailed information and names and titles of key people (see Exhibit 7-2), and the

Exhibit 7-2
Basic Information for Media List

1. Name of media outlet.
2. Type of media outlet (daily or weekly newspaper; television or radio station; magazine; bureau or wire service; specialty; ethnic; and so forth).
3. Descriptive data (morning or evening daily, day of publication for weekly; AM or FM for radio, VHF or UHF for television; station frequency or channel).
4. Precise address, including zip code.
5. Telephone number, including area code; additional telephone numbers for news department; night lines; direct lines for key individuals.
6. City and county in which media outlet is located.[a]
7. Affiliations of media outlet (networks, news and wire services, syndicated columnists or commentators, and so forth).
8. Ownership (especially if part of chain).
9. Circulation figures for newspaper; market share or audience ratings for broadcast media, especially Nielsen; qualitative assessment of audience.
10. Names of key decision makers and reporters.[b]
    (a) Print media examples: chairman, president, publisher, assistant or associate publisher, editor in chief, executive editor, associate editor, assistant editor, managing editor, city editor, editorial page editor, metropolitan editor, political editor, political reporters.
    (b) Broadcast media examples: chairman, president, vice president and general manager, program director, advertising and sales manager, news director, assistant news director, public service or public affairs director, editorial director, assignment editor, assistant assignment editors, announcers and reporters, producers and hosts of interview programs.
11. Technical data for each media outlet (e.g., letterpress or offset printing method for newspapers; taping or film facilities for broadcast media).
12. Special opportunities for campaign (society section of newspaper, interview, public affairs, or talk programs for each broadcast station, and so forth).
13. Advertising data.
14. Miscellaneous information (e.g., television debate negotiations, radio station policy on using audio telephone feeds from campaign, and so forth).

[a]The list should be divisible in various ways; for example, geographically, by county, city, zip code, for use by volunteer leaders or advance staff.
[b]When the media *mailing* list is compiled, it includes many (but not all) of these names.

reverse side shows a chronological record of significant contacts between the particular news media outlet and the campaign, including news conferences attended, interviews, perhaps even telephone calls and important correspondence. The mailing list is not an information system; it extrapolates the names and titles of those individuals in each media outlet who should receive campaign mailings (the media list differentiates between names stored for information purposes and those on the mailing list). The mailing list also includes volunteer campaign chairmen, leaders, coordinators, and others who should be sent campaign mailings that will keep them informed and enable them to feel a sense of participation. The third list is quite limited; it includes only the names of individuals and media outlets that should receive releases by hand.[e]

The media, mailing, and hand delivery lists are updated throughout the campaign; the lists may be expanded to include any reporters who telephone the campaign headquarters, attend a news conference, or write a bylined article about the campaign. In deciding what names on the media list should be placed on the mailing list, the campaign usually errs on the side of too many names. Nevertheless, the wasted postage is a necessary cost of insuring that any editor or journalist who could conceivably be interested in or cover the campaign receives regular mailings. Similarly, many publishers receive mailings because they may ultimately affect editorial decisions, specifically endorsement policy.[f]

Media Information Kit

The basic source of information about the candidate and campaign should be the media information kit. At least one kit should be mailed to each media outlet before the campaign officially begins or in its initial stage. As the campaign continues, the kit may be expanded to include new enclosures, but it probably will not have to be mailed again. The kit should be given to any traveling reporters who join the campaign entourage, any reporter who visits the campaign headquarters, or any reporter who requests background information on the candidate. The kit should be available at news conferences, and the candidate's aide should also have several extra information kits, especially when the candidate attends an editorial or other kind of meeting.

The information kit should be professional in appearance and graphically consistent with the campaign's official colors and logos. Although the enclosures of such kits vary, the typical information kit is a carefully collated collection of standard materials (see Exhibit 7-3).

---

[e] In addition to meticulous attention to assure that the media mailing list includes the correct name (and spelling), title, and media outlet for each recipient, it is often wise to have one blind mailing (e.g., addressed to a newspaper's city editor or television station's assignment room) as added insurance. This practice may also be done for certain media outlets on the hand delivery release.

[f] The most efficient media and mailing list system is data processing, which can be programmed to produce printouts of lists or mailing list labels suitable for local committees, advance staff, or special mailings from the main campaign headquarters. For more discussion see the author's companion volume, *Political Campaign Management: A Systems Approach* (Lexington, Mass.: D.C. Heath, 1976).

Exhibit 7-3
Media Information Kit

The media information kit is usually a distinctive, bulky manila folder with two inside pockets. If the kit is mailed, it is inserted in a matching envelope (9″ by 12″—but probably larger). The news director's business card is usually clipped to the top of the kit. The envelope is usually rubber-stamped *TV Information Kit, Radio Information Kit*, and so forth, depending on the intended recipient; the classification is primarily to create a professional impression. Enclosures can include:

1. *Candidate's official campaign biography*: a thorough, well-researched, and well-written presentation including the candidate's entire history—education, military record, professional accomplishments, interests, hobbies, family, and so forth—with emphasis on the favorable aspects.
2. *Spouse's official campaign biography*: like the candidate's biography, an interesting, factual, and concisely written presentation. (If the spouse does not wish to be too visible, this biography can be incorporated in a family section of the candidate's biography.)
3. *News release announcing candidacy*: official statement explaining candidate's motivation.
4. *Sample campaign materials*: bumperstrips, buttons, basic brochures, and any other attractive campaign items.
5. *Article reprints*: collection of favorable articles about candidate, spouse, family, or the campaign. (These can be reprinted on individual sheets, within a booklet, or as part of a tabloid or large campaign newspaper that is folded to insert into the kit.)
6. *Campaign personnel*: biography of campaign manager if he is prominent; possible sketches of other key campaign personnel, unless individuals are from outside state or district.
7. *Issues papers or news releases*: collection of issues papers, important news releases, or speeches detailing the candidate's position on major issues (which the campaign wishes to emphasize).
8. *Visual aids*: usually the official campaign photograph of the candidate; possibly official family photograph (with caption). (Photographs are always black and white, with identification marked lightly in pencil on rear of photo.)
   (a) Daily newspapers receive 8″ by 10″ photo; also 4″ by 5″ version if budget permits; weekly newspapers receive both a 4″ by 5″ (for two columns) and a 2″ by 2½″ (for one column); offset printed newspapers receive glossy; letterpress printed newspapers receive suitable mat.
   (b) Television stations receive 35mm color slides, with candidate off right (not in center); ideally, two slides are sent, especially if campaign includes different programming seasons or one slide has limited use; additional slides can also be mailed later in the campaign.
9. *Political data*: a map of district, if congressional race; otherwise, possible political data (voting, registration statistics) about state. This information could alternatively be incorporated briefly in the candidate's biography.)
10. *Covering memorandum*: an outline from the news director (which can be dated and addressed to the news media) stating the campaign policy for servicing the media, expressing interest in maximum exposure for the candidate, and also listing and explaining each enclosure. (Unlike other materials, which are placed in either of the inside pockets of the folder, the covering memorandum should be inserted in the center of the folder.)

Mailings

The campaign should be able to mail to its entire media mailing list on short notice. This requires an efficient mailroom operation and may entail volunteer coordination. Even in the local campaign that may have individually typed envelopes, many sets of envelopes can be typed and stored for subsequent mailings. Larger campaigns use addressograph plates or a computer system. If any system of preaddressed envelopes is used, additional envelopes must be prepared to accommodate additions to the mailing list or to serve as substitute envelopes for erroneous names or addresses. The Level A or Level B campaign will find it efficient to purchase, lease, rent, or borrow collating and folding equipment; local campaigns will rely more on volunteers for collating, stapling, folding, and stuffing releases.

The campaign should work closely with the post office to insure that mailings meet postal pickup deadlines. News releases, like other campaign mail, should never be left for mailing at the end of the day, but should be mailed as soon as possible and always in time to make the next post office pickup. For Level A and some Level B campaigns, mailing lists can be separated into geographic sections, so different campaign headquarters duplicate and mail the release to the media outlets closest to those headquarters.

Mailing strategy should reflect strategic news guidelines—that is, a steady flow of news from the campaign *and* a steady flow of news release mailings. Special attention is required for advance news releases that are often mailed to insure receipt before the scheduled event. Mailings are also coordinated to conserve postage costs; news releases can be mailed in the same envelope, but an important news release should not be mailed together with routine news releases. Schedules are rarely, if ever, mailed with other releases. Mailings are always sent first class, and a postage meter should be used.

News release mailings should be tailored to the needs of different media. For example, weekly newspapers should probably receive only one mailing, perhaps two, for each weekly issue, unless they indicate they wish to be treated as daily newspapers. The ideal addressing system (namely, the computer) can segregate the mailing list by type of media, as well as by geographic division—for example, by state, county, group of counties, congressional district, or zip code. Suppose the campaign headquarters prepared a release announcing the candidate's visit to an area (or campaign appointments of volunteer leaders or endorsements of the candidate) that was of concern to local, rather than statewide, media; the system could target the release for news media in selected areas or counties, just as another release might be targeted to specialty or ethnic media.

News releases are mailed not only to secure news coverage based on their contents, but to create the impression the campaign is moving; they stimulate media interest in the campaign, and they provide valuable background information. Reporters traveling with the candidate, or who may cover the candidate in the future, may consult their own media outlet files on the candidate. Many news conference questions, interview questions, and the points and questions raised on broadcast interview and talk shows reflect the subtle indoctrination of the campaign mailings. These mailings predispose reporters to talk about issues of concern to the candidate and campaign. Each news media outlet's file on the candidate is largely, sometimes wholly, a collection of news release mailings (i.e., campaign propaganda).

Unlike opportunistic statements and news conferences that require hand delivered releases and telephone calls, planned news conferences or statements can use advance dated releases. For example, assume a candidate for statewide office in California has selected Thursday, October 6, for a news conference in San Francisdo—a location and date selected for strategic reasons, since the candidate will explain his position on an issue of particular concern to Northern Californians. The release can be mailed statewide early Tuesday morning to arrive on Wednesday; even more precisely, mailed late Tuesday evening for certain delivery on Thursday. The objective is for the news release to arrive by mail throughout the state just before or about the same time the news conference is occurring. Recipients can write a story on the Thursday news conference while it is still news. The campaign has used the mails as its own wire service. If the wire services provide no coverage or partial coverage of the news conference, newspapers can still write a story based on the complete opening statement they received in the mail.

Editors and reporters are impressed with advance dated releases that arrive just before or simultaneous with the event. They know that the campaign must be well planned and coordinated in order to have conceived, prepared, written, edited, finalized, duplicated, and mailed a statement in advance of the news conference. Their opinion of the campaign is enhanced, and their favorable view will be reflected in their policy toward the campaign and in their reporting.

Mailing advance dated releases is inappropriate if the news conference, statement, or speech includes major revelations. Although the release instructions may be specific, its mailing might discourage reporters from covering the news conference or campaign event. On the other hand, if the candidate is generally newsworthy and the campaign is an intensive, well-covered one, the mailing can be a convenience for the news media, without compromising the event's publicity potential. Reporters know the candidate is always worth covering, and they will attend the news conference.

Exhibit 7-4
Guidelines for Audio Delivery Systems (Statewide Campaign)

Preparations (based on appropriate tape recorder/telephone system)

1. *Lists*. The campaign should compile a comprehensive list of all radio stations that have newscasts.
2. *Telephone systems*. The campaign should experiment with alternative systems and formats within its budget.
3. *Personnel*. The campaign will require at least one full-time staff member to oversee the audio delivery system; depending on the system and response, one or two additional staff members may be a wise investment and can be added as response is evaluated.

Alternative Systems (not necessarily mutually exclusive)

1. *Incoming telephones*. These are for receiving calls from radio stations and can be regular or WATs (800 toll free number); they are answered by a staff member or automatic machine that provides recording and disconnects automatically.
2. *Outgoing telephones*. These are for making calls to radio stations and can be regular or WATs (unlimited or a bulk-rate telephone line is more economical if the system to be used regularly); they are used by a staff member to initiate talks and offer recordings.

Types of Audio Feeds (actualities or reaction statements)[a]

1. *No choice*. The radio station is offered a single actuality, usually no more than 30 or 40 seconds.
2. *Choice*. The radio station is offered some choice, in terms of subject or time:
   (a) Subject—the campaign staff member offers two different actualities or reaction statements; the station can take one or both, air either or both, or take both but delay decision on which to air;
   (b) Time—the campaign staff member offers the same actuality or reaction statement in two different lengths, one 20-30 seconds, the other 30-50 seconds.
3. *Experimentation*. The campaign should survey and work with radio stations to determine types of subjects to be used for tapes, length of tapes, and so forth.

Audio/Video

Most television stations refuse film footage supplied by the campaign; if the policy of local stations is flexible, the campaign should consider supplying its own footage to generate television news. Radio stations, especially smaller and rural stations, are more flexible. Although the major radio stations in large metropolitan markets will probably turn down campaign tapes, many other stations, especially in the suburbs, will accept taped actualities. For example, if the candidate holds a Thursday news conference, the campaign can supply radio stations with a brief excerpt of the most newsworthy part of the opening statement—usually the lead. Actually, there are several alternative ways of supplying actualities to radio stations (Exhibit 7-4). The objective is to supply *audio* material, rather than, or in addition to, standard news releases. The audio delivery system is not an alternative to an active program of telephone interviews with radio stations, appearances on radio programs, or radio coverage of news con-

---

Procedure

The campaign staff member who initiates calls establishes rapport with radio station personnel, obtains direct telephone numbers, and deals will individuals by name. The staff member knows which stations are partisan or have less-demanding standards and which stations will use tapes less frequently. The candidate's voice is taped the night before, or early the morning of, the actuality. The staff member begins calling radio stations early each morning;[b] the sooner the actuality gets out, the more times it will be used throughout the day.[c] Weekend calls can be especially productive because radio station news operations may be understaffed, and they can use the tapes. If the campaign also uses an incoming telephone system, it can put an advisory out on the wire tickers that an actuality tape on a certain subject is available by calling the telephone number.

---

[a]The actuality is a taped excerpt of the candidate's voice from a speech, news conference, or other campaign event (with a time and place context). If a reaction statement, the tape of the candidate's voice may be accepted as an actuality even without a time/place context, if it concerns a major newsworthy story.

[b]The campaign staff member explains the time and place of the news conference; the radio station uses the candidate's voice as if its reporter actually taped the candidate that day; the announcer will probably refer to the place and the time ("earlier today," "this morning," and so forth).

[c]The candidate can record the actuality on the telephone from any location and at virtually any time. When the campaign staff member calls radio stations with the actuality, the release time is emphasized. For example, if the staff member calls a radio station at 8 a.m. with an actuality from a 10 a.m. news conference (i.e., what will be billed by the radio station as an excerpt from what the candidate said at 10 a.m.), the actuality has a release time of 10:15 a.m. The alternative is permitting the radio station to say, "We asked Mr. Smith what he intended to say later today, and he said . . . ."

ferences and other campaign events. Audio delivery is the most effective way of securing widespread radio coverage.

Hand Delivery

The campaign can use a professional messenger service, staff or volunteer messengers or it can also combine all three systems. The campaign should use the same individuals repeatedly, because they are most familiar with the route, traffic conditions, the building entrance, and possible parking problems, and they are known to the media outlet's security guards or receptionists. For the local campaign the volunteer who gives the release to the weekly newspaper editor can also promote it.

The fastest delivery method relies on messenger teams. One person stays with the automobile while the other drops the release. This avoids the parking problem. Many professional messenger services use motorcycle messengers. The campaign that hand delivers many releases in a large metropolitan media market may need several messengers or teams to insure that all of the releases are delivered quickly. The wire services and media outlets closest to their deadlines usually receive the releases first.

The release should be in an envelope that is addressed to an individual by name and title and includes the complete name and address of the media outlet. Alternatively, or in addition, another envelope may simply be addressed "newsroom" or "city desk," followed by the media outlet's name and address. The envelope should have the words BY HAND or BY MESSENGER printed or rubber-stamped on it.

The Level A or Level B campaign should strive for simultaneous hand delivery of releases in different media markets. For example, when a news release is completed at the main headquarters of a statewide candidate, it can be sent by telecopier to other campaign headquarters or volunteers' homes in major media markets. Each recipient campaign staff member or volunteer can then make several copies of the news release to deliver to major media outlets in that city. The objective is to deliver the release at about the same time in major media markets throughout the state.

Traveling Media

The level of campaign activity and the news director's ability to promote the campaign with the news media can spur networks, television stations, magazines, newspapers, news and wire services to send a reporter to travel with the candidate—for a day or two days or for a campaign swing. When the campaign is planning a major rally or other campaign event, or a campaign swing is expected to be intensive and successful and to generate large crowds, the news director should try to increase the number of traveling media. When the candidate is traveling through a state, or part of a state, the news director should invite local reporters to join the candidate's traveling entourage during that part of the trip.

When the candidate generates news while campaigning, the traveling media can telephone or wire their copy. The campaign is responsible for the logistics of the campaign tour; in any major campaign, the advance staff makes certain that media requirements are in order. Regarding travel, media outlets are responsible for the cost of reporters' travel and accommodations, although the campaign may make the reservations. If reporters travel on the campaign plane, their media outlet can be billed for an amount *at least* equal to first-class airfare.

To accommodate the traveling media as well as the media in each city or area visited, the candidate's aides travel with a supply of news releases that have been prepared in advance and datelined for each event. Aides also have a supply of speech texts and covering releases for any speaking commitments, news releases for news conferences or visuals, campaign schedules, and media information kits. In the precision campaign, the candidate who issues a reaction statement while campaigning can receive instant publicity throughout the state (see Exhibit 7-5).

Exhibit 7-5
Publicizing the Reaction Statement

1. When the wire service ticker installed at the campaign headquarters reports a major news development that provides an opportunity for the candidate's reaction, a short draft statement is immediately completed and telecopied to the candidate's traveling aide.
2. The candidate reviews the draft statement with his news director or aide, makes modifications, talks by telephone with the research division or other aides in the campaign headquarters, and authorizes a final version of the reaction statement.
3. If the statement is short, the candidate records the entire statement by telephone with the campaign headquarters; otherwise, he records the best excerpt.
4. The statement is duplicated by the candidate's aide and given to the traveling media; if possible, the candidate inserts the statement in his next public appearance, news conference, or speech, to provide a dateline (i.e., actuality) for the statement. The dateline is used in news releases.
5. The statement is duplicated at campaign headquarters and sent by telecopier to other headquarters or volunteers' homes strategically situated in important media markets throughout the state; the main headquarters has the release hand delivered to many media outlets in its city, and each recipient of the telecopier release makes additional copies for immediate hand delivery to several important media outlets in his city.
6. The audio operation makes a recording of the reaction statement available to radio stations throughout the state—either by calling stations or by putting an advisory on wire service tickers that a statement is available by calling a certain telephone number.
7. As releases are given to the traveling media and, at about the same time or shortly thereafter, hand delivered in major media markets throughout the state, radio stations obtain the audio feed. Meanwhile, the campaign mailing operation is integrating the news release into the day's mailings; the mailed news release may be used for print or broadcast news by some media, but it is used primarily for background and future reference. The mailed release also provides the formal record indicating that the candidate did issue a statement that day. Also, since the campaign's key volunteer leaders receive such mailings, they are kept informed.

8

Advertising and Direct Mail

The same theme and issues should be emphasized by the campaign in generating news or purchasing advertising. The exception is specially targeted advertising directed at specific constituencies interested in a single issue or several issues. This chapter supplements the earlier discussion of advertising and includes a brief review of direct mail, which, in the classic marketing sense, is a form of advertising.

Advertising Theory and Practice

Advertising is the paid, nonpersonal presentation and promotion of the candidate and campaign. Advertising is inferior to generating news because (a) it costs money and (b) its credibility is less than that of news. Although advertising messages are usually perceived by the electorate as paid propaganda and therefore tainted, advertising, unlike news, affords the campaign control over content. Advertising permits greater targeting of specific messages to an identifiable readership or broadcast audience. If the utilization of media through news and advertising has strategic unity, the campaign may achieve the ultimate media objective—that is, the electorate finds it difficult to separate campaign news from campaign advertising.

Advertising strategy is a function of the overall campaign strategy of reaching certain kinds of voters with a theme or issues relevant to them. Since the campaign does not have an infinite advertising budget, it cannot reach every eligible voter, nor can it reach everyone the same number of times. The advertising strategy and its budget is simply a delineation of priorities governing the use of two types of media. The first type of media—the print or broadcast media—can be used for either news or advertising, and strategy must relate the dual use of each medium to expose readers, listeners, or viewers to similar messages through news and advertising. The second type of media—outdoor and transportation advertising and the many kinds of advertising specialties—can be used only for advertising, and strategy is less demanding for these media (which are likely to reach fewer voters) and has a limited goal—perhaps name identification.

In the local campaign, advertising, rather than news, is more important to its marketing task. The modest campaign often cannot generate significant news for television, most radio stations, and even daily newspapers;

with limited news potential, it relies on selective advertising, including advertising specialties. In contrast, the Level A or Level B campaign cannot be effective unless it purchases advertising *and* makes news; its advertising program, although hopefully consistent with its news program, is the responsibility of an advertising agency.

Types of Advertising

The advertising agency has access to market research services, demographic data, circulation figures, Nielsen television ratings, and other valuable resource materials. The campaign can secure some of these materials if its staff is willing to incur a significant cost—the time needed to collect the information. However, some of the most important information, especially the Nielsen television reports, are available on a subscription only basis.

The local campaign that emphasizes personal campaigning by the candidate, precinct work, and direct mail may place little or no *media* advertising. Hence, one of the advertising agency's major functions, placing advertisements, is irrelevant. The modest campaign needs staff members who can handle marketing and communications within the framework of the campaign—that is, press relations, layout and graphics, copywriting, editing, and so forth. If the campaign strategy is correct, the manager is mainly interested in printed material that implements the strategy. Perhaps a local printer and artist can be recruited to help with problems of typography, layout, and design, and the campaign itself can supply the ideas for issues and the text.

The manager and senior staff of any political campaign must understand advertising fundamentals. If there is no advertising agency, the campaign must relate directly to advertising media. If there is an advertising agency, the campaign must relate to the agency. Some political campaigns advertise in newspapers or on radio without an advertising agency, because their advertising budget is not large enough to justify an agency (whose compensation is based on space and time purchased). Since an advertising agency is virtually indispensable for purchasing television spots, television advertising is discussed only briefly in this chapter.

Newspaper. Newspaper advertising can achieve name identification and issue orientation; it can also consolidate support, secure volunteers, raise funds, persuade the uncommitted, and turn out the vote. It can usually achieve issue orientation better than any other objective. Although its readership is limited, relative to television audiences, and it is easier for the reader to avoid reading the advertisement than for the viewer to avoid seeing it, the quality of readership is important. Newspaper advertising, like newspaper articles on the campaign, can reach those with a higher probability of voting, especially the community activist, joiner and member of fraternal, religious, community, and service organizations—in short, the person who actively interacts with others.

Newspaper advertising featuring a "campaign platform" usually alienates more voters than it persuades. There is always at least one issue among the many listed that turns off a possible supporter. The newspaper advertisement should concentrate on a single issue or two or three major issues deemed strategically important. Even the ideological diehards who urge lengthy dissertations on every conceivable issue will usually be upset by an issue, sentence, phrase, or word in the ad.

The cost of newspaper advertising is usually based on a line rate—that is, the number of lines per column inch multiplied by the number of column inches. Most newspapers have six or eight columns, and their advertising rates reflect the varied format. The advertising rates may assume camera-ready copy—that is, the campaign supplies a reproducible proof of the advertisement exactly as it is expected to appear. Even if the newspaper will absorb typesetting and layout costs, the campaign is wise to have the design, layout, and typography done by a professional artist and then prepare reproducible proofs (for photo offset newspapers) or suitable mats (for letterpress newspapers). This method insures consistency for all campaign advertising. The campaign also is confident that the advertisement will look professional and pleasing to the eye. If the campaign supplies the finished product, the deadline will be more advantageous, because the newspaper will not have to design the ad, fit the copy, or set the type. Whether the campaign uses an advertising agency or deals direct, it must make certain its material conforms to the newspaper's technical size specifications.

Advertising strategy calls for selecting the newspapers, and sections of each newspaper, best able to reach the priority voters and then varying the advertisements according to the newspaper or section of newspaper. Advertising strategy also considers the relative benefits of daily versus Sunday advertising. Although the Sunday edition may have more readers, the advertisement can be buried; yet, readers spend more time on the Sunday newspaper. The Monday newspaper is thinner and the advertisement may be more prominent, but will readers be too rushed to read it? Finally, the strategy must consider the impact of the ad if it is seen and not read. The headline or the candidate's name are, for many newspaper readers, the most important message, since it is the only message they receive.

Small advertisements placed throughout the newspaper can achieve name identification or help get out the vote. Testimonial ads, either in the form of short, signed messages or excerpts from an endorsement, can be effective; often copies of endorsement letters are used with a photograph of the prominent elected official or citizen who has made the endorsement. The overriding consideration for endorsement advertising is whether the endorsement will sway any voter. If so, which voters and how many will be persuaded to vote for the candidate? If a single endorsement is much more important than others, newspaper advertising may be more effective if it concentrates on the most important endorsement. Newspaper advertising can also include a coupon to enlist volunteers or secure contributions; sometimes these coupons are used as much for a humble, grassroots image as for their value in getting volunteers or money.

Radio. Small radio stations, like weekly newspapers, will bend their dead-lines to increase advertising revenue, especially as election day (and the end of campaign advertising) approaches. However, stations must program advertising spots and also log them for the Federal Communications Commission, so there is a limit to exploiting radio's immediacy. The best method is analogous to "riding" newspaper deadlines; in each case, buy space or time for specified days or times. This strategy reserves the preferred space or time before the opponent can purchase it, and allows the actual tape, proof, or mat to be produced at the last minute in time for the final airing or publication deadline.

Radio time is most effective if spots, 60 seconds or less, are purchased, although programs are cheaper on a cost per minute basis. The short radio spot, like the short television spot, penetrates the listener's (or viewer's) consciousness before he can switch stations or leave the room. Given a fixed budget, shorter spots mean a greater number of exposures, which is an important factor since broadcast spots require substantial repetition over time. The heavy purchase of broadcast spots during the final phase of the campaign, or in the last week or closing days, is desirable because it coincides with maximum voter interest. However, it cannot substitute for a phased advertising campaign that gradually shifts public opinion. In short, changes in voter perception are usually not sudden; they are a function of repeated exposures to broadcast spots.

Since the radio spot can use the candidate's voice, it is potentially a more personal message than the print media advertisement. The candidate's voice can be used alone, or preceded or followed by an announcer, or in a question and answer format. If the candidate's voice is not pleasing or audio identification is not a priority goal, a professional announcer, as well as special sound and musical effects, may be used. Even the local campaign should not depend on the station announcers to read from advertising copy; it is preferable to supply the tape of the advertisement to insure uniformity and professionalism. An exception is if the radio announcer or disc jockey has high credibility and a wide following.

The campaign should never buy a single spot or a few radio spots. It should always buy a package of purchases tailored to the campaign's needs. If the station does not have a suitable package, the campaign should seek to negotiate its own package. The campaign should not purchase advertising on low-priority programs or at disadvantageous times in order to secure its ideal "buys." Unless the radio budget is minimal, the campaign should use an advertising agency or professional time buyer.

Television. The cost of producing television spots is substantially higher than production costs for other advertising. This constraint discourages campaigns that can only afford to purchase a limited amount of time, since production costs are a disproportionate share of the overall advertising budget. Television is usually inefficient for any campaign in which it reaches significantly more voters than are eligible to vote for the candidate, since the advertising rates are based on the entire audience. Despite wastage, Level B campaigns must use television because of its reach—the sheer numbers of voters exposed to television. For example, a station within a state may also reach many voters outside the state, but the campaign has no alternative if it is to reach voters in its area. Similarly, suppose a statewide candidate in New Jersey wanted to reach voters; both New York City and Philadelphia television stations are critically important, despite their wastage (i.e., reaching so many non-New Jersey voters who cannot vote for the candidate) and high rates that are based on the total audience reached.

The most effective television spots are usually short and simple. Television programs are generally wasteful and inefficient, and even 60 second spots lose many viewers, although they may be appropriate during the campaign's identification or introductory phase. Unless the candidate is exceptionally well known, the spot should emphasize the candidate's appearance and voice. The candidate should be shown in people-oriented situations that are nonpolitical and noncontroversial. References to issues should be nonideological; survey research is important in pinpointing the precise issues to be utilized and important words and phrases to be used or avoided. Often, the most effective spots present the candidate interacting naturally with people of all kinds and ages; the voice over, either the candidate or an announcer, can supply the substance. The major mistake made in producing political campaign television spots is not using television's unique characteristics—sight, sound, and motion. Despite the importance of the *video* rather than the audio portion of television, too many spots do not use the opportunity to tell a story by picture.

A detailed discussion of types of television spots and production mechanics is far beyond the scope of this book. Campaigners who produce spots without professional assistance will not communicate well with the voters. Equally important, the purchase of television time is both a science

Exhibit 8-1
Advertising Budget Items

Purchase of Time and Space[a]

Newspapers (daily and/or weekly);

Magazines;

Radio Stations;

Television Stations;

Specialty Media (trade, professional, union, fraternal, and other newspapers and magazines);

Ethnic Media (if not included in other categories);

Outdoor (billboards);

Transportation (bus, trolley, subway, commuter train, taxi; bus, subway or train station).

Production Costs[b]

1. Newspapers and Magazines: Creative costs, writing, editing, layout, design, typesetting, composition, photography, reproduction proofs and mats, shipping, and postage.
2. Broadcast Media (itemize for radio and television): Creative costs, writing, scripting, editing, film and sound crews, equipment rental, purchase of raw tape or film, sound, recording, music, announcer, travel, studio rental, production of duplicate tapes or film spots, shipping, and postage.
3. Specialty and Ethnic Media: Includes above costs, plus adaptation costs; specific costs for any unique advertisements involving special copy or translations; production costs for reproduction proofs and mats, duplicate video tape or film spots.
4. Outdoor:
   (a) Billboards (24-sheet posters [104″ by 234″], 30-sheet [115″ by 259″], and other variations; also painted display, multi-vision or tri-vision animated signs): Creative costs, graphics, design, and related costs, printing of sheets and painting, electrical, or specialty costs for extraordinary billboards.
   (b) Cards, posters, sheets for store and home windows; snipe sheets for building sites; telephone pole posters; and lawn and yard signs: Creative and other production costs, including mass printing.
5. Transportation (cards, posters, or sheets for inside or outside of public transportation vehicles or inside public transportation facilities; bumperstrips; car toppers): Normal creative and production costs, plus mass printing.
6. Advertising specialties (calendars, matchbooks, pens, potholders, key chains, photograph records, sewing kits, balloons, buttons, and so forth): Extraordinary production costs.

Printed Matter and Direct Mail[c]

Candidate cards, basic campaign brochure, specialty and ethnic brochures, issues brochures, issues papers, fliers, tabloids, letters, questionnaires, postcards, simulated telegrams, and so forth: Creative costs, writing, editing, layout, design, typesetting, and so forth; actual printing costs (function of quantity); and postage costs, if direct mail used (itemized per mailing).

---

[a]If an advertising agency is used, the budget for purchasing time and space does not have to be increased to cover the agency compensation. Typically, the agency receives a 15 percent discount from the price the campaign would have paid for the time or space; thus it pays 85 percent of the rate billed to the campaign (i.e., the rate the campaign would have paid without the agency). The 15 percent commission, which costs the campaign nothing, is the advertising agency's compensation. An in-house advertising agency, formed as part of the campaign, can pay advertising agency rates.

---

[b]If an advertising agency is used, most or all of the creative costs are included with the agency commission. However, the agency will, unless provided otherwise, bill for all production costs and add a markup charge of about 17.6 percent. This is a form of additional compensation for the agency. Often, the campaign can save this commission by negotiating production costs with various vendors on the basis of bids; however, campaign personnel may have to take time to work with the vendors, rather than having advertising agency personnel do the work. Direct, reimbursable expenses, such as telephone, telegraph, travel, and entertainment are usually billed to the campaign without a markup charge.

[c]Although included in any advertising textbook, printed matter and direct mail are usually not considered part of an advertising budget for a political campaign, but are budgeted separately. They are included here for the same reason they are discussed in this book—that is, their theme or message must be consistent with the campaign's mass media advertising and its news.

and an art, and the margin of error is considerable. The importance of the television spot in reaching voters and the principles of buying strategy were summarized by New York advertising executive Daniel J. McGrath in a classic memorandum.[a]

Advertising Budget

Many political campaigns budget too little for mass media advertising and too much for other parts of the campaign, such as overhead, consultants, salaries, and traditional advertising (printed materials and advertising specialties). Another problem is the campaign that spends less than the budgeted amount, because other expenditures are permitted to take precedence over advertising; ideally, the campaign should set aside a kind of trust fund clearly earmarked for advertising. Many advertising budgets underestimate such production costs as design, layout, graphics, copywriting, typesetting, composition, paste-up, reproduction proofs, and mats or studio rental, scripting, music, sound, recording, filming, raw stock, editing, duplicate video tapes or film spots, and so forth.

The advertising budget should be classified in different ways. It should be divided into phases—months, periods of weeks, or by week—and the last week or two may include daily breakdowns. The budget should also be divided by type of media: print or broadcast, daily newspaper or weekly newspaper, radio, television, magazine, ethnic media, and so forth. The budget should distinguish clearly between production costs and the actual cost of purchasing space or time. Often, the former are relatively fixed— that is, they do not vary at all, or vary only a little, with the space and time budget. The advertising budget should be comprehensive (Exhibit 8-1); but its overall dollar amount, and the distribution of dollars within the budget,

[a]The McGrath memorandum and related principles of political television buying are summarized in the author's companion volume, *Political Campaign Management: A Systems Approach* (Lexington, Mass.: D.C. Heath, 1976).

should be based on explicit assumptions, such as alternative amounts of revenue. For example, a statewide campaign may budget $500,000 for advertising, including $450,000 for television time and $50,000 for other media; an alternative budget of $700,000 might allow $600,000 for television and $100,000 for other media.

Advertising Agency

The campaign can retain an advertising agency or form its own agency; the latter affords more control and can save part of the normal commission, but there are disadvantages.[b] Many advertising agencies are reluctant to accept campaign accounts, because if the campaign's revenue projections fall short, advertising billings are less than expected. Since the agency's primary income is from the commission generated by billings, it could risk investing substantial time and resources in planning and creating advertising that is not placed or partially placed. To avoid this problem, many agencies charge a monthly retainer that is charged against future commissions or they operate on a fixed fee, rather than commission, compensation.

Responsibilities. Whether an advertising agency is used or not, the candidate and campaign are responsible for advertising content. The campaign counsel should review all advertising to insure conformity with applicable laws. Most advertising must include a disclaimer—the line of type in a print media advertisement or the announcer's voice in a broadcast spot that indicates the name of the political committee (and its chairman) that paid for the advertising. Many states or local jurisdictions have laws governing wording, placement, and type size of the disclaimer.

The responsibilities of the advertising agency are detailed in the contract between the campaign and the agency (Exhibit 8-2). The campaign's legal counsel should review the contract carefully to insure that the campaign retains decision-making power, is not forced into a difficult cash flow situation, and negotiates some compromise between the agency's normal commission and markup charges and the compensation proposed by the campaign.

The political campaign's time span is so brief that the campaign's monitoring of advertising can be careless. It is the agency's responsibility to insure that every advertisement purchased appears as specified; if not,

---

[b] The managerial implications of the advertising agency structure, budgeting strategy, and related topics are discussed by the author in *Political Campaign Management: A Systems Approach* (Lexington, Mass.: D.C. Heath, 1976).

Exhibit 8-2
Excerpts from a Typical Advertising Agency Contract

Agency Responsibilities

1. Prepare preliminary plans to make best possible use of the appropriation deemed necessary or appropriation made available by the campaign or committee.

2. Prepare cost schedules for advertising expenditures and other related costs.

3. Prepare layouts and, when requested, finished comprehensive layouts; prepare all actual copy for use in advertisements of all types.

4. Exercise its best efforts to purchase at the most favorable rates quality art work, engravings, printed matter, and other collateral materials, from artists, designers, photographers, engravers, printers, and others.

5. Contract in behalf of the campaign for advertising media and exercise its best efforts to obtain the most advantageous rates.

6. Check insertion of advertisements in publications for appearance, date, position, size, and mechanical reproduction.

7. Prepare radio and television commercials and programs and provide the necessary supervisory services in connection with such broadcast production.

8. Check by examination of affidavits furnished by stations the broadcast of radio and television advertising for time, accuracy, extent, and related factors.[a]

9. Check the display of outdoor advertising for the date of appearance, position, site, workmanship, and mechanical reproduction.

Control

"Before incurring liability to third parties for the purchase of advertising time or space, or for talent or services within the scope of this agreement, the Agency shall first secure written authorization from the campaign, specifically, from the following: . . . The Agency shall not place any advertising without first submitting the text and design to the campaign for written approval, to be granted only by the following . . . ."

Compensation[b]

1. Where an agency commission of 15 percent is allowed by the medium, the campaign agrees to pay the agency at that rate; where less than 15 percent is allowed by the medium, the campaign agrees to pay the medium rate plus an additional amount to yield the agency 15 percent.

2. For all services and materials (artwork, comprehensive layouts, mechanicals, engravings, typography, musical arrangements, and so forth), the campaign shall pay the agency the charge to the agency plus 17.6 percent of such charge, unless agreed to otherwise in writing.

3. The campaign shall reimburse the agency for cash disbursements related to telephone, telegraph, travel, postage, and shipping.

---

[a] Checking by affidavits is insufficient; the agency or campaign must use professional or volunteer monitoring (perhaps the same volunteers who monitor news broadcasts) to verify broadcast spots, since refunds or compensatory time is permitted for spots aired incorrectly or cut short.

[b] Most campaigns should negotiate these provisions to secure a more favorable arrangement.

the campaign can secure compensatory space or time. The campaign should also survey volunteer leaders to gauge reactions to the advertising. Questions can also be inserted in telephone or in-person public opinion polls to determine how many voters have been exposed to the candidate's advertisements, and how effective they are. If print or broadcast advertising solicits volunteers or funds, there are more refined methods to measure effectiveness.[c]

Schedules and Traffic. One of the advertising agency's most important functions is to prepare the detailed advertising schedules, showing precisely when and in which media specific advertisements will be placed or aired, and to route the correct advertisement to each media outlet before the deadline. Even the modest campaign that cannot afford an advertising agency *must* prepare an advertising schedule to plan and execute its advertising program. For example, a campaign for state senate in a rural area might advertise in the campaign's final week in weekly newspapers (Exhibit 8-3) and on local radio stations (Exhibit 8-4).

The advertising agency's functions, while they include market research and the "creative" tasks, include the precise and detailed work required to allocate the advertising budget most productively—that is, formulating the best schedule to buy time and space at the most advantageous rates, in the most effective media, with the best placement. In short, each advertisement should have an appropriate message and should appear at a propitious time in relation to the campaign's overall strategy. The local campaign may be able to develop its own ideas, create its own advertising themes, and work directly with artists, printers, announcers, and so forth, but it also must formulate schedules and oversee the traffic function; for example, delivering the appropriate reproduction proof, mat, tape, film, and so forth, with payment, to each media outlet. (See Figure 8-1 for a sample instruction form.) Messengers are more reliable and faster than mail service, but regardless of the delivery method, advertising material should be routed to specific individuals. In almost all cases, advance payment is required, either because the media outlet's policy requires advance payment for any political advertising, or because federal, state, or local law (whichever applies to the particular race) requires campaigns to pay in advance for all advertising.

---

[c] For example, assume that television spots and newspaper advertisements solicit campaign contributions. By using a method developed by campaign consultant and survey researcher Arthur J. Finkelstein of DirAction Services, Inc., the campaign can monitor daily responses; newspaper advertisements can include coded coupons, and 3- and 6-day projections can be made; response can be measured in terms of response per thousand circulation, dollar response as a percentage of the advertisement cost, and so forth for each newspaper. Contributions in response to television spots can be coded by county with the number of responses and dollar amounts compared to county population, or the expected strength of the candidate. In short, response to print or broadcast media solicitation may provide valuable insights about the progress the campaign is making in different areas.

Exhibit 8-3
Advertising Schedule for Weekly Newspapers

Name of Newspaper; Town	Circulation	Cost of Half Page	Mechanical Method	Size of Entire Printed Half Page (height; width)	Date of Publication	Due Date
Jefferson Banner (Jefferson)	2,300	$55.00	Letterpress Mat	H: 10 3/4" W: 16 5/8"	Thursday, Oct. 30	Tuesday, Oct. 28, Noon
Lake Mills Leader (Lake Mills)	2,500	$55.00	Offset Repro Proof	H: 10 1/2" W: 16"	Thursday, Oct. 30	Tuesday, Oct. 28, Noon
Watertown Daily Times[a] (Watertown)	8,500	$132.30	Letterpress Mat	H: 10 1/4" W: 16"	Saturday, Nov. 1	Wednesday, Oct. 29, anytime
Mayville Independent (Mayville)	4,000	$82.32	Offset Repro Proof	H: 9 1/2" W: 15 1/4"	Thursday, Oct. 30	Tuesday, Oct. 28, 9 a.m.
Daily Jefferson County Union (Ft. Atkinson)	5,700	$83.60	Letterpress Mat	H: 11" W: 15 1/2"	Friday, Oct. 31	Wednesday, Oct. 29, anytime

Note: Excerpted from an actual advertising schedule for a state senate campaign in a rural district, this compilation was prepared by the campaign without using an advertising agency. The actual total schedule included nine weeklies, one biweekly, and two daily newspapers. The quoted rates are no longer applicable. In addition, the actual schedule included a Contact Column that provided such information as the names of the newspapers' advertising managers or editor-publishers and relevant telephone numbers.

[a]The *Watertown Daily Times* and *Daily Jefferson County Union* were the only two daily newspapers in the state senate district.

DATE: _____

NOTE: Photocopy of contract or correspondence attached for reference.

TO: _____

ADDRESS: _____

_____

ATTENTION: _____

You are hereby accepting delivery of:

_____ mat for letterpress

_____ reproduction proof for photo offset

SUBJECT OF AD: _____ SIZE: _____

FOR YOUR ISSUE PUBLISHED: _____

SPECIAL PLACEMENT INSTRUCTIONS _____

_____

CHECK ENCLOSED FOR FULL PAYMENT AMOUNTING TO: $ _____

(GROSS AMOUNT OF $ _____ LESS AGREED UPON DISCOUNT OF $ _____.)

- -

_____ radio tapes, as indicated below, which include the following spot commercials.

CHECK ENCLOSED FOR FULL PAYMENT: $ _____

Tape Number	Commercial Number	Time (Seconds)	Subject	Begin Airing	End Airing	Frequency During Day	Time of Day or Program

SPECIAL AIRING INSTRUCTIONS REGARDING ROTATION OF SPOTS:

SPECIAL AIRING INSTRUCTIONS REGARDING NUMBER OF SPOTS AIRED PER DAY, IF NOT SPECIFIED ABOVE: _____

Note: This is the substance of the advertising instructions form that should be duplicated on official campaign stationery. If an advertising agency is used, it will have its own advertising instructions correspondence and memoranda.

Figure 8-1. Sample Advertising Instructions Form.

Exhibit 8-4
Advertising Schedule for Radio Stations

Station and Town	Total Budget	Number of Spots	Length of Spot	Beginning and Ending Days	Distribution of Spots[a]
WTTN-AM (Watertown)	$175.00	50	30 seconds	Wednesday, Oct. 29, thru Monday, Nov. 3	Taxes: W-5; Th-5; F-10; Sat-10; Get out the vote: Sun-10; M-10
WTKM-AM (Hartford)	$105.00	60	30 seconds	Wednesday, Oct. 29, thru Monday, Nov. 3	Taxes: W-10; Th-10; F-10; Get out the vote: Sat-10; Sun-10; M-10
WYLO-AM (Jackson)	$86.80	28	30 seconds	Thursday, Oct. 30, thru Sunday, Nov. 2	Taxes: Th-7; F-7 Get out the vote: Sat-7; Sun-7

Note: Excerpted from an actual advertising schedule for a state senate campaign in a rural district, this compilation was prepared by the campaign without using an advertising agency. Like the prior table, this schedule is for the campaign's final phase—the week before election. The quoted rates are no longer applicable. The actual schedule also included a Remarks Column for comments on tape specifications, deadline time for payment and for delivery of tapes (if different), and the name and telephone number of the contact.

[a]This column indicates the number of spots per day. Note that this phase of the campaign has two spots, one stressing the tax issue, the other a get-out-the-vote theme. For this advertising schedule, different spots are not used in the same day.

Advertising Errors. The advertising agency can provide an independent, dispassionate analysis of the campaign's marketing problem. Is the candidate really as well known as the campaign believes or claims? What will be the actual effect on identification of the campaign's planned advertising? What issues should be used in advertising? How can they be communicated in simple terms so the average voter remembers the message? Is the candidate's political party an asset or liability and how, if at all, should it be used? The advertising agency selected should have experience in solving varied commercial marketing and communications problems; however, the agency personnel assigned to the account should also have political advertising experience.

If the political campaign does not use an advertising agency, it is more likely to make some of the mistakes common to novice political advertising (Exhibit 8-5).

Direct Mail

This discussion, a brief elaboration of the summary of direct mail in Chapter 3, should not be confused with direct mail fund raising.[d] Although the mailings discussed here can also solicit volunteers or money, their primary purpose is persuasion. Major direct mail efforts should not be undertaken without professional counsel, unless the campaign staff is experienced in graphics, copywriting, editing, and the logistics of putting together and mailing a direct mail package—that is, the envelope and its enclosures.

Direct mail precedes or begins with the formal announcement of candidacy. The basic list is the candidate's most likely supporters; for example, friends, relatives, neighbors, business associates, and peers (those who attend the same church or are members of the same fraternal lodge, service group, professional association, and so forth). For Level A and Level B campaigns, this list is expanded eventually to include anyone who has something in common with the candidate. The direct mail strategy must resolve whether recipients should receive letters over the signature of the candidate or someone else (the chairman, campaign manager, or a prominent supporter). The most effective letters are signed by someone known to recipients and perceived favorably by them. The opening letter, or any future letters, should be modified, in terms of content, style, and the signatory, for mailing to each specific list. Letters are only one method of direct mail, but the technology for mailing letters, or the many types of brochures, requires the strategist to make many decisions (Exhibit 8-6).

---

[d] The importance of forecasting in direct mail fund raising is illustrated by an example cited in a discussion of campaign finance in the author's related book, *Political Campaign Management: A Systems Approach* (Lexington, Mass.: D.C. Heath, 1976).

Exhibit 8-5
Advertising Errors in Novice Political Campaigns

1. The candidate insists on overseeing advertising, creating ideas, or even writing copy.
2. The candidate is given veto power over style, technique, or mechanical questions related to the creative function (as opposed to substantive content, which he should be able to veto).
3. The advertising theme and issues selected are irrelevant to the voters who must be reached.
4. The advertising theme, issues, media, or specific media outlets chosen for advertising reflect too much concern for diehard supporters and too little concern for reaching uncommitted, independent, or switchable voters.
5. The list of media outlets in the advertising schedule is incomplete; it omits many outlets that can reach relevant voter groups.
6. The data about media outlets is incomplete, inaccurate, outdated, or nonexistent, because the campaign cannot secure, does not try to secure, or does not understand market research (especially in terms of readership, listenership, viewing habits).
7. The campaign overcommits itself to advertising and is unable to purchase all the space and time reserved; hence, because it reneged on early commitments, it receives poor service and placement during the campaign's crucial, final phase.
8. Negotiations for space and time rates are inept because the campaign accepts the media outlet's first offer, often for space or time no one else will buy, or because the campaign does not negotiate package rates.
9. Production costs are curtailed to the extent that advertising is cheap, shoddy, and unprofessional and severely compromises the candidate's image.
10. Advertising is inconsistent in terms of theme, slogan, color, logos, typography, and so forth.
11. Advertising strategy does not empathize with the apathetic voter but assumes he is highly conscious of the campaign; hence it assumes the need for too many different ads. The campaign needlessly fears the voter will read, hear, or see the same ad several times; in advertising, especially broadcasting, repetition is important. One or two effective ads are preferable to six less effective, even if repeated many times.
12. Advertising is unclear. Typography is too complex, of varied size and type, aesthetically displeasing; there is too little white space. In radio spots, there are too many words for the time, or the announcer or candidate talks too fast. In television, too much is happening for the viewer to absorb, or the video message is compromised by too many spoken words.
13. Advertising is general—treating too many issues; its message is amorphous—the reader, listener, or viewer is confused over what is important, remembering little or nothing about the ad.
14. Photographs, sound, or films are unoriginal and unimaginative; they involve little or no action on the candidate's part; lighting, contrast, or reproductive quality is amateurish.
15. Too much advertising per exposure is purchased. The 60-second spot is bought when the 30-second spot will be adequate; the entire newspaper page is bought when half a page, 3/4 of a page, or 7/8th of a page will be relatively effective.
16. The broadcast spot is rhetorical, polemic, pedantic, dull; little or no use is made of animation or music.
17. The judgment as to which theme, issues, or approach should be used is left to the candidate, campaign manager, or their close allies; instead, these factors, as well as the specific approach in the ad, must be tested among less partisan, committed, or opinionated observers.
18. In an effort to save a few dollars, major advertising chores are delegated to volunteers; a good advertising message is compromised; (e.g., the newspaper ad is not read because layout is poor, or the broadcast spot does not get across its point because the announcer is incompetent).

19. Photographs, sound, films, video tapes of the candidate are unnatural and seem contrived.
20. The advertising schedule has no relationship to the campaign's phased development; the schedule is not graduated in expenditure to help the campaign's momentum, or it fails to consider the need for an identification phase.
21. Scripts for broadcast spots are written as if they are for the print media; full sentences are used, when phrases are more effective; the words are written to be read by the voter when they will be heard by him.
22. The advertising lacks a strong opening; the newspaper ad does not have an eyecatching headline, the broadcast ad has a weak beginning.
23. The advertising does not end affirmatively; the newspaper or broadcast ad goes nowhere; it does not develop to a conclusion to stimulate and excite the reader, listener, or viewer to act or vote for the candidate.
24. The advertising omits important information, such as the date of election, number of the district, the candidate's political party, and so forth, if such information is important. Alternatively, the advertising includes such information when it is not important or, in the case of party identification, could be negative in a general election if the party is a minority party.
25. The advertising campaign's approach is nebulous, mixed, or cannot be defined. It seems too hard hitting and aggressive by boldly projecting simple themes; other times, the approach is too subtle, low key, or symbolic.

Local campaigns are likely to spend much of their total budget on direct mail, because it can more effectively reach a limited constituency than television, radio, and many newspapers. Although well-financed local campaigns have sponsored several mailings to every registered voter, the increasing costs of design, paper, printing, and postage often make it impossible for a candidate to afford more than a single districtwide mailing—usually scheduled for the campaign's final week. As an alternative or a supplement to the single districtwide mailing, the resourceful strategist considers many different mailings, each tailored to a limited constituency within the electorate. The campaign may have four or five mailings or even dozens of mailings that vary in emphasizing either the issues or the signatories, depending on the characteristics of voters on the specific list.

Direct mail is compromised if low-priority lists are selected or if the list is technically deficient (many names are of persons deceased, unregistered to vote, not living in the district or eligible voting area, or who have moved since the last election). The most effective package is also compromised by insufficient attention to post office regulations, laws governing disclaimers, or the strict adherence to a series of deadlines prescribed by the ultimate deadline—the "drop date" or date scheduled for delivering the mail to the post office.

Since many voters toss away mail that is impersonal or has bulk-rate

Exhibit 8-6
Methodology and Technology of Direct Mail Voter Contact

Purpose of Mailings

1. Candidacy announcement;
2. Fund-raising solicitation (dinner or reception invitation, finance committee solicitation, or mass solicitation);
3. Volunteer solicitation;
4. Endorsement solicitation;
5. Precinct (e.g., seeking unregistered voters);
6. Persuasion (directed mainly at uncommitted, independent, or switchable voters);
7. Reinforcement (e.g., campaign newsletter to reinforce supporters);
8. Multi-purpose.

Characteristics of Letter Mailings

Size and Color:

1. Monarch stationery and envelope (7¼" by 10½" letter folded in thirds to fit in 7½" by 3 7/8" envelope) creates a personal effect.
2. Business-size stationery and envelope (standard 8½" by 11" letter folded in thirds to fit in #10 size envelope, 4 1/8" by 9½"), with the option of window envelope for recipient's name and address to show through window, is more impersonal.
3. Use of color can vary for paper and ink.

Personal versus Impersonal Effect:

1. Postage can be treated by using (a) commemorative postage stamps especially chosen for effect; (b) regular postage stamps; (c) a postage meter; (d) a postage meter with a message imprint; or (e) bulk-rate postage printed in a box in place of the stamp (but note regulations governing bulk-rate mailings, especially restrictions governing enclosures).
2. Dates can be (a) individually typed, just as the letter is individually typed; (b) individually typed to blend with the body of the letter (i.e., letter text is duplicated or printed to look as if individually typed); (c) simply printed as is the rest of the letter; (d) printed with only the month and year (precise date avoided); or (e) not used (i.e., letter is undated).
3. Addressee sections of letter mailings can be (a) individually typed, as is the entire letter; (b) individually typed to blend with the letter text that is duplicated or printed; or (c) omitted (i.e., letter is not addressed to a specific person or audience).
4. Salutations may be (a) personal (first- or last-name basis) or impersonal (i.e., "Dear Fellow Rotarian" or "Dear Friend") and part of an individually typed letter; (b) part of an automatically typed letter (made to look personal); or (c) typed in to blend with duplicated or printed text.
5. Signatures can be (a) individually penned in by the signatory on an individually typed letter; (b) individually penned in by someone else on an individually typed letter; (c) signed by signature machine on a mass letter; (d) included as part of the duplicating or printed process; or (e) omitted altogether.
6. Method of duplication (printing) can be treated in any of the following ways. (a) Each letter is individually typed (no duplication or printing). (b) The letters are typed on an automatic typewriter or by computer. (Note: In methods (a) and (b), addressee portions and salutations may be personalized, with additional personalization created by insertion of recipient's name and possibly other personalized data within text; only the addressee portions and salutations are personalized; or if there is no addressee portion, only the salutation is personalized.) (c) Camera-ready text to be used for all letters is *typewritten*, then photographed, and printed. (d) Copy (camera-ready text) is *typeset* for duplication/printing.

7. Quality of paper for stationery and envelopes may be (a) expensive stock; (b) quality bond; (c) medium bond; (d) inexpensive bond; or (e) cheap offset paper.

8. Envelope addresses can be (a) individually typed on each envelope; (b) typed on labels that are placed on the envelopes; (c) shown through window envelopes (d) printed on envelopes by addressograph or similar plates; or either (e) data processing labels or (f) non-name labels ("occupant" mailing) can be used.

Enclosures:

1. Brochures require attention to variables that include size, type, subject, cost, color, layout, photographs, paper, folding, and so forth. As an enclosure, the size and folding of the brochure may affect the mailing envelope size—that is, 8½" by 11" brochure, folded once, fits in 6" by 9" envelope; 8½" by 11" brochure, folded twice, fits in #10 size envelope; same brochure, unfolded or mailed flats, fits in 9" by 12" envelope.

2. Reply envelopes or reply postcards present choices for (a) Postage—envelopes with postage stamps; envelopes that require postage be placed on a printed box; or standard business reply envelopes (pre-stamped); (b) Type of envelope—large sealing flap printed with questions for recipient to provide information; or simple return envelope to contain recipient's completed information card; and (c) type of information desired on envelope flap or card—volunteer or contribution solicitation, or both; precise questions asked or boxes to be checked off by respondent.

Characteristics of Printed Brochures

1. Enclosure brochures may be with or without letter or additional enclosures. Other variables include type and size of envelope, labels, mailing method, and so forth.

2. Self-mailer brochures are usually folded and usually include space for addressing by label, typewriter or handwriting; postage method is usually bulk postage—that is, permit obtained, fee paid, printed box on mailer.

Characteristics of Postcard Mailings

1. Endorsement cards are printed postcards addressed by local supporters and mailed to their neighbors, relatives, and friends. They are signed by the supporter, possibly with a handwritten message added.

2. Polling place cards are guides that can be taken by the voter to polling places. The cards can be designed to (a) promote one candidate (possibly with a photograph) or (b) promote a slate of candidates or the candidates of the same political party and can be (c) computer-produced to provide personalized salutation and show precise address of each voter's polling place (even without computer salutation, cards can vary to show different polling place for voters in different precinct).

Characteristics of Simulated Telegrams

1. Simulated telegram mailings are usually mass printed on yellow paper and inserted in yellow envelopes; all capital letters are used in the text.

2. They can be computer produced to personalize recipient's name and address and to allow for insertion of a polling place that is appropriate to the recipient.

Characteristics of Ballot Mailings

Ballot mailings resemble a ballot with emphasis on a single candidate's name or on his party's slate, (other candidate's names may be printed in a way as to be unclear or covered, or the preferred candidate's name can be in a different color, larger type, and so forth).

Characteristics of Simulated Newspapers

Simulated newspapers (usually tabloid, printed on newsprint paper) resemble actual newspa-

158

Exhibit 8-6 (cont.)

pers; the mailing is merely a campaign publication designed to promote a single candidate or slate of candidates and is usually in form of a self-mailer.

Sources of Mailing Lists

1. Candidate's personal list;
2. Affiliate chapter membership lists of organizations in which candidate is active;
3. Political party membership lists (national, state, local chairmen of party central committees, volunteer clubs; for example, Young Republican, Young Democrat, Women's Republican Federation, and so forth);
4. Lists purchased or rented from direct mail firms (can include lists of almost every conceivable type of voter);
5. Voter registration rolls (available from registrar of voters, often on a one-time-only basis, free to each candidate, or at a nominal cost; or on computer lists rented by commercial firms; or from political parties);
6. Publicly available lists (telephone books, property tax rolls, automobile registration, civic and business directories);
7. Lists from supporters active in various organizations (corporate employee lists, union membership, church membership, service and community group membership lists);
8. Campaign house list (financial contributors, volunteers).

Methods of Addressing Mailings

1. Addresses (placed directly on mailing material or on a separate label) can be (a) hand addressed; (b) individually typed; (c) computer typed (based on tape of automatic typewriter); or (d) shown through window envelopes.
2. Addressograph plates can be used to put addresses on labels or directly onto mailings; or printing can be computer produced, usually on cheshire or heat transfer labels suitable for mass mailings (pressure sensitive labels are usually impractical).
3. All addresses must be complete with zip code.

Types of Postage

Postage can be (a) first-class postage—expensive, but most reliable—or (b) bulk-rate postage—inexpensive, but requires carefully planned, coordinated mailing and close rapport with post office to avoid delay.

Note: This compilation, although abbreviated, illustrates the diversity of direct mail advertising; the discussion of the letter mailing is more complete than other options to illustrate the number of decisions required for any direct mail package.

postage, a political return address, or a political appearance when opened, direct mail has its obvious limitations. Many voters only read the headlines, scan the photographs, or skim the text. Any mailing should be designed to arouse attention by skillful use of color or copy on the envelope or front of the self-mailer, especially the use of a teaser line—that is, an interesting statement or question. As an added inducement for recipients to read the mailing, or at least skim it for a longer time before tossing it, the mailing should use all space efficiently by emphasizing, for example, a few important issues or points with large type, plenty of white space, and several, or even many, clear, action photographs. The most eloquent copy is irrelevant if it is not read, and much of political direct mail is either not read or is only read by already committed supporters or by opponents of the candidate. Contrary to the mythology of political novices, the most aesthetically pleasing direct mail package, complete with effective copy on the most important issues and quality, attention-getting photographs, will not convert *masses* of voters from one candidate to another.

In sum, direct mail is an insurance policy to guarantee *exposing* the candidate and his message to a known list of voters. It is helpful for identification, especially of the party label, and it can achieve some issue identification for more thoughtful, serious voters who are, however, only a small minority within the total electorate. Direct mail is most useful in local races that lack fierce, competetive political activity and will be won by the candidate whose name is most prominent or who is a member of the dominant party.

For most campaigns, direct mail should be primarily used for carefully planned mailings to priority lists and rarely used for general mailings to registered voters who cannot be defined or categorized by additional characteristics. In the latter case, direct mail might be considered for the candidate who does not project well in personal appearances or through other media, and in either case, adjunct committees could provide valuable letterheads for mailings on related issues of parochial concern.

**Part III
Scheduling and Advance**

Introduction to Part III

Scheduling, like media, is a marketing tool for the campaign. As will be seen in the chapters in this section, the difference between scheduling and advance is often a matter of degree. Scheduling the candidate, even in the modest campaign, must include a minimum amount of verification and detailed checking of the proposed and finalized schedules. Thus, the scheduling secretary in the local campaign should know the fundamentals of advance. However, although correspondence, telephone calls, and personal meetings are important in arranging the candidate's schedule, they are an imperfect substitute for the advance man who visits the proposed or agreed upon site of the candidate's appearance. In many ways, the chapters on advance are simply more detailed applications of scheduling methodology, except for the assumption of at least one visit to the site before the candidate's appearance.

9

Scheduling as a Marketing Tool

Every political campaign, regardless of level, has a finite resource that must be allocated to its most highly valued uses. That precious resource is the candidate's time. Although scheduling is imperfect, if only because the decision maker lacks perfect information, the goal of scheduling should be perfection—that is, allocating the candidate's time in such a way as to produce the most votes on election day. This suggests an overall strategy or plan, within which scheduling, like other campaign divisions, has a precise role. The nature of this role creates a difference between scheduling and other components of the modern political campaign: since campaigns vary in size, complexity, and use of technology (i.e., precinct workers, direct mail, or other advertising) and since some campaigns can win without advertising or without direct mail, the success matrix for each campaign is a particular blend of all components except scheduling, which is fundamental and constant. The campaign is nothing without a candidate, and the candidate cannot relate his goals and plans to campaigning without a personal schedule.

Scheduling is a marketing tool for the campaign, but unlike other marketing tools—news, printed brochures, communications through local and adjunct committees, and other means of informing the electorate—scheduling is the basic marketing tool. There is a philosophy or theory of scheduling that presupposes the need to relate scheduling strategy to overall strategy. Scheduling decisions cannot be made without reference to criteria. Each campaign must define and judge the relative importance of the relevant, and often competing, criteria. These standards are applied in evaluating alternative uses of the candidate's time in an effort to optimize the composition of the schedule.

Thus, scheduling is two sides of the same coin. One side concerns its philosophy, theory, strategy, criteria, and the judgments and discretion used to select time options for the candidate. The other side concerns mechanics, methodology, techniques, details, and follow-up. Although the size, structure, and demands of the scheduling operation vary considerably from the Level C campaign to the Level A campaign, all campaigns must first formulate a scheduling strategy and then implement it.[a]

---

[a] Exhibits 1-3 and 2-2 summarize the scheduling and advance functions at different levels of campaigning.

Philosophy of Scheduling

Which voters should be reached? Obviously, the national campaign must reach tens of millions of voters; the local campaign may have a constituency of tens of thousands. This is the quantitative consideration; but scheduling must also confront the qualitative consideration of which kinds of voters are more important to reach than others? The qualitative consideration is a strategic plan evolved by campaign management; if it is poorly conceived, irrelevant, or nonexistent, methodical scheduling and the most conscientious scheduling staff are of limited use. Conversely, the most brilliant marketing plan that precisely describes the characteristics of voters who need to be reached with a certain perception of the candidate, or with the candidate's position on certain paramount issues, cannot be implemented without a properly functioning scheduling operation.

As a marketing tool, scheduling relies on the campaign strategy's delineation of the priority consumers—that is, the voters who are most important to reach. If the campaign cannot define who it must reach, how can it schedule the candidate? Why accept one kind of invitation and reject another? Why visit one area and decline to visit another? As a marketing tool, scheduling relies on the campaign strategy's assumption that the product can be defined on a constant, not erratic, basis. If the candidate's image and positions are not authentic and stable, then how can the campaign, or scheduling, effectively market an undefinable product?

There are two sides to the scheduling equation: demand for and supply of the candidate's time. The supply has a finite limit, although it may not seem so if skillful schedulers make better use of the time. The demand varies with the momentum of the campaign; the campaign going nowhere will generate a disappointing number of invitations. However, invitations comprise only a part of the schedule; the rest includes negotiating invitations to events and initiating dates, times, and conditions that *create* events. However, before the tour or scheduling director can try to solve the scheduling equation, he must understand the candidate.[b]

Relationship to Candidate

Many campaigns try to schedule the candidate without considering his unique personality, temperament, and needs and without explaining the scheduling process to the candidate. Intensive scheduling requires a serious, committed candidate. The reluctant candidate who may be unin-

---

[b] Larger campaigns have a tour or scheduling director; the senior scheduling decision maker may also be termed the scheduler. Local campaigns may have only one person in charge, the scheduling secretary.

terested in the election outcome, or the candidate beset by personal problems, will be less inclined to accept a demanding schedule. The half-hearted or preoccupied candidate is psychologically unprepared for rigorous scheduling and specific, difficult commitments. When he does travel or appear or speak at campaign events, his attitude will affect his performance. The candidate is likely to project poorly both to the audience as a whole and in conversation with individuals. He may seem disinterested, apathetic, lethargic, even hostile or rude. If he works hard to hide his discomfort, the mental strain will put added pressure on him.

Inept scheduling can demoralize even the most enthusiastic candidate. The symptoms just cited can occur if the candidate is tired and exhausted because of overscheduling, or disgusted because of a poor crowd turnout, inadequate briefing, or sloppy advance work that caused him to be late. It is premature to discuss dividing the schedule between the apparent and public needs of the campaign and the candidate's personal needs, unless the candidate and his tour director understand each other (see Exhibit 9-1).

Targeting and Media Orientation

Targeting means that scheduling places priority on reaching certain groups rather than others. These groups of voters may be defined by where they live (geography), how they are registered to vote (party), their past voting behavior (voting history), or any of the standard demographic variables of income, education, religion, race, and so forth. Most target groups probably represent two or more variables, but a single variable may be a reasonable approximation. Targeting is theoretically more precise for campaigns that rely on survey research; but smaller campaigns that rely more on voting history, judgment, and intuition can canvass local neighborhoods and identify target voters by name, as opposed to the statistics used by major campaigns to describe important groups of voters.

Media orientation is the degree to which the schedule is oriented to produce news coverage. The local campaign that generates little news coverage is primarily or solely person oriented; the major campaign that makes news and has traveling media reaches its much larger constituency through the media *via* scheduling. The number of persons reached *directly* by scheduling is statistically insignificant; the number of persons reached *indirectly* by the news generated by scheduling is statistically significant. The schedule is media oriented in two ways. First, it includes items that are newsworthy and emphasizes locations and times of day most conducive to news coverage. Second, it includes such items that are directly media oriented as interviews, editorial and other meetings with journalists, news conferences, tapings, and so forth.

Exhibit 9-1
Relating Scheduling to the Candidate

---

1. The candidate should be committed, serious, and willing to devote full time to the campaign; he should be in good physical condition and able to devote long hours to campaigning that includes a rigorous travel schedule.

2. Before declaring his candidacy, the candidate should understand how much time is required as well as the intensity of commitment; at an early stage, the campaign manager and scheduler should discuss the time commitment in terms of its effect on the candidate's spouse, family, business commitments, weekends, and other factors; the candidate should not subsequently disrupt the scheduling operation by pleading ignorance or surprise at the demands of the schedule.

3. The level of the campaign and the strategy determine the schedule's media orientation, the weight assigned to different criteria, and the types of events that will dominate the schedule; the candidate should understand the rationale of the composition of the schedule. The candidate must understand the importance of scheduling to overall strategy.

4. Once the candidate understands the philosophy of scheduling and its application to his campaign, he should agree never to accept or reject invitations but always refer inquiries to the scheduler. The candidate should understand the decision-making process, and he should help formulate and understand guidelines governing the scheduler's discretionary authority to commit the candidate—for example, how many hours daily, for which kinds of events, at what times of day, on what days of the week. Certain exceptions that require the candidate's personal authorization should be outlined.

5. Each candidate has a unique personality, temperament, and physical constitution; for example, the candidate may be an early or late riser and may prefer early morning flights to late evening flights. The schedule should reflect the candidate as much as possible.

6. The most overbearing schedule is tolerable if the candidate's personal comfort is considered; the minimal schedule can be unbearable if the candidate's personal needs are ignored. The candidate should never drive, even in a local race; a traveling aide should be responsible for the schedule, speech text, news releases, telephone calls, and so forth; larger campaigns divide functions among the traveling staff.

7. The candidate is more confident and relaxed if he knows what will happen and what to expect next (i.e., if his briefings are complete, timely, and accurate). The candidate should expect to be scheduled for activities that emphasize his strengths and obscure his weaknesses; in part, the schedule reflects how well the candidate can relate to nonsupporters, independents, and ticket splitters, and how well he relates to party supporters, stalwarts, and diehards.

8. The level of exposure should be graduated, not just in terms of the campaign's momentum, but so the candidate does not become tired, ill, or hot tempered. The campaign should have programmed rest periods, not just a day set aside, but planned hour or two-hour breaks at propitious times for relaxation and privacy. Besides adequate sleep and rest, the candidate's attitude can be bolstered if a trusted friend or confidante joins the traveling campaign entourage.

9. The overall campaign schedule must reflect the commitment, if any, made by the candidate's spouse and family to campaign, separately, or in joint appearances with the candidate.

10. If the candidate is an incumbent, the scheduler must consider the responsibilities of the office, especially attendance required in any legislative body.

Strategy

The candidate's daily activity is not unplanned and spontaneous; it should reflect a plan to use the candidate's time to get votes. Each day's activities should be part of a weekly, monthly, or phased pattern with proportions of the candidate's time allocated to different types of events and different areas, and to satisfying well-defined goals of raising money, motivating volunteers, inspiring supporters to turn out to vote, and reaching the uncommitted. Scheduling strategy operates under the campaign's universal constraint—that is, its limited time span. If the candidate's time is poorly allocated, there is no second chance after election day; therefore, each week, day, and hour must count, and every activity and item on the schedule should be there for a reason. There are only so many days in a week, and so many hours in a day; travel time can be minimized, but not eliminated; the candidate requires a minimum amount of sleep and rest. In sum, scheduling is like generating news: there are severe limitations on compensating for lost opportunities. If the candidate should have visited a city four times during the campaign and instead was there only once, he cannot fly there three times during the last week; conversely, if the city was worth only a single visit and the candidate accepted invitations for four visits, the time expended cannot be retrieved—it has already been lost.

Any campaign has two opposite strategies vying for attention. The *consolidation* strategy emphasizes the need to keep the candidate's present supporters happy and motivated; the *persuasion* strategy emphasizes the need to recruit new supporters. Consolidation strategy is based on present or actual strength; persuasion strategy is based on future or potential strength.

Consolidation. This strategy is most appropriate for the leading candidate or the candidate whose political party has a registration edge, especially in a local race. The campaign not only gives scheduling priority to areas of strength and groups of known supporters, but its media orientation is designed for news coverage that will reach the candidate's supporters. The candidate who campaigns in a given area will receive the most media coverage in that area; the candidate who campaigns before a particular group will receive media coverage that notes the type of audience. People in the area will know the candidate was there; people sympathetic with the group will know the candidate addressed it.

Advocates of scheduling to consolidate support argue that the candidate should spend his time where the votes are, not where they might be. This strategy suggests that certain kinds of voters are virtually certain to vote for the candidate, if they are properly cultivated and motivated—that is, if the candidate personally seeks, or is reported to be seeking, their support. The same amount of the candidate's time invested in supportive areas or before supportive audiences will produce more votes on election day than a corresponding increment of time in a heterogeneous area or before a mixed audience. Consolidation scheduling also rewards past support, volunteer effort, and financial contributors; indeed, such scheduling may do more than reinforce support, it may be essential to maintain the current flow of contributions and level of volunteer activity.

Persuasion. This strategy assumes the need to reach voters who are classified as uncommitted, independent, ticket splitters, or even committed to the opposition, but vulnerable ("soft support"). Persuasion strategy may be designed for a more modest goal than moving someone from the opposition column to the candidate's side. It may move certain voters from the opposition candidate to the undecided and ultimately fail in changing their preference, but in the meanwhile, it *lowers their probability of voter turnout* for the opposition. One goal of this strategy is to shake the voter's commitment to the opposition candidate—that is, diminish the intensity of support. Scheduling the candidate before mixed audiences can show them that he is not as undesirable as perceived or depicted. Persuasion may not mean intellectual conversion; often, the voter need only see or hear the candidate or know he exists (i.e., the candidate achieves some minimum level of identification) to opt for him.

Perhaps the strongest argument for persuasion strategy is the increasing volatility of the electorate, which reflects the decline in party loyalty. As the number of independent voters rise, the "swing" element becomes more important—and can be crucially important—even for the party with the most registered voters. The ideal is to identify and reach those voters who can make the difference in electoral results—that is, those who can tip the balance of the election. Certain types of voters require considerable effort; others require limited attention. The campaign should schedule the candidate to reach the swing voters easiest to reach rather than emphasize the impossible task of reaching the voter irrevocably committed to the opposition.

Contingency. Partisans tend to be myopic in two ways. First, they are preoccupied with satisfying the candidate's supporters, whom they feel should be rewarded for their early wisdom, volunteer work, and financial contributions. Often, they do not realize that most candidates cannot win without reaching significantly beyond their base of support; the more narrow the base, the greater the need to find new support. Second, partisans write off or dismiss too many possible areas or types of voter support, partly because they resent the candidate importuning seemingly hostile voters. They exaggerate the resistance or hostility of certain voters, and they resent any strategy that seems to take them for granted.

The paradox is that extreme partisans can simultaneously maintain that (a) the candidate's base of support is sufficient for victory, if only he would dutifully spend his time in "important areas" or with the "right people," and (b) any voter personally exposed to the candidate will vote for him. This is the *myth of conversion*, an evangelical belief among diehard supporters that the more the candidate gets around before new audiences, the greater the support—seemingly without limit. Public apathy, party loyalty, commitment to the opposition candidate, preconceptions and biases are all conveniently overlooked in this messianic strategy.

It should be apparent by now that, as noted earlier, scheduling strategy is dependent on campaign strategy. Since no single campaign strategy is universally applicable, no scheduling strategy applies across the board. Campaigns are different, and a *contingency* strategy must fully consider the unique character of each campaign. Such a strategy embodies both consolidation and persuasion, as elements dictate. The strategy is almost always internal and confidential, because no voter wants to read either that he is taken for granted or is written off. Even committed supporters will become contentious if they are privy to the campaign strategy, parts of which will offend everyone.

What is the mix between keeping present support and motivating these supporters to go the polls, and cultivating new support? Each campaign has a different optimum, but the theoretical optimum is easy to find. The candidate should be scheduled for *just enough* appearances so that his supporters continue contributing time and money and that a satisfactory voter turnout is assured. Allocating additional time beyond this point, which is subjectively determined, is wasteful; volunteer effort, money, voter turnout will be increased only marginally by progressive increments of the candidate's time. Allocating significantly less time is also a misallocation of the candidate's time; partisans resent the time and attention given to broadening the support base, and the candidate, in his zeal for new support, loses more votes than he gains or simply does not get the support he took for granted.[c]

Consolidation scheduling often reflects the scheduler's laziness or his

---

[c] The question is, what is the ratio of votes received on election day to time spent? The balance, or trade-off, between consolidation and persuasion strategy can be represented by the equation,

$$\frac{T_c}{V_c} = \frac{T_p}{V_p},$$

where the ratio of the time spent for a consolidation event or activity to the votes received on election day is equal to the corresponding ratio for persuasion strategy, at the margin or tradeoff point. T_c is the time spent for the consolidation activity; V_c is the votes received for lack of courage or imagination. It is *easier* to schedule the candidate before friendly, committed audiences; these groups extend the most invitations, and they are the most persistent. It requires courage to say no to supporters and patience to explain why the candidate cannot appear or speak at their function. It requires effort and imagination to seek out invitations—that is, to *create* events—and it is especially difficult to identify that segment of the electorate that can swing the election. Even if survey research identifies these voters by demographic characteristics, it is especially challenging to correlate the candidate's schedule with reaching those voters. The corollary tool is, of course, media; the scheduler is concerned not only with the schedule's direct reach, but also, based on the counsel of the news director, with its indirect reach through news reporting of what the candidate does.

The nature of news coverage can alter the scheduler's perspective. For example, it may make no sense for the candidate to speak to a certain group; its membership is irrevocably committed to the opposition. Nevertheless, the invitation is accepted, not because the candidate wants to reach the group, but because he wants news coverage of the appearance to project a certain perception to the electorate or a part of it or because he wants to use the occasion to emphasize certain issues likely to be reported in the media. In the Level A or Level B campaign, the candidate is concerned with overall news coverage. Thus, scheduling must consider the traveling media: news coverage of an appearance in one area or before one group will be pervasive. Turning down or snubbing an invitation can result in negative publicity; voters do not like either the candidate who writes off support and seems to give up, or the campaign that is perceived as unresponsive, snobbish, or discourteous.

The scheduler's task is a balancing act between satisfying present supporters and cultivating potential supporters. The basic political fact of life is that the candidate cannot spend all of his time with diehard supporters, but he cannot ignore them with impunity to seek expanded support. The distinction between the consolidation and persuasion scheduling strategies is not discrete; the campaign not only combines the two strategies, but it usually does so on a daily basis. For example, although the campaign may allocate its initial period to securing its base of support, it still spends some time trying to broaden it; in later phases, when it primarily emphasizes broadening the support base, it still spends some time with the original supporters.

---

the consolidation activity; T_p and V_p are analogous for persuasion strategy. The equation is only valid if the time spent is correlated with votes based on the time spent; hence, the more appropriate equation uses Δ to allow for the change in the amount of time spent and the corresponding change in votes, if the time had not been spent:

$$\frac{\Delta T_c}{\Delta V_c} = \frac{\Delta T_p}{\Delta V_p}.$$

Exhibit 9-2
Scheduling Criteria

---

1. *Geographical balance*. Level C campaigns are concerned with sections of a district, residential and commercial areas, or even neighborhoods; Level A and Level B campaigns are concerned not just with geographical boundaries, but with media market boundaries.
2. *Constituency balance*. Examples are (a) labor versus business—that is, blue collar versus white collar; major corporate versus small business; and varying business, trade, manufacturing associations versus professional and occupational groups, different unions—and (b) ethnic groups or organizations that are based on religious, racial, or nationality orientations. Standard demographic variables help define different constituencies (e.g., age, sex, income level, education).
3. *Political balance*. This criterion is defined in terms of party registration.
4. *Audience*. This criterion includes not only the number of people expected to attend an event, but also the quality—that is, the percentage eligible to vote for the candidate; the committed versus uncommitted; the propensity to donate time or money, and so forth.
5. *Event Balance*. Examples are (a) mass attendance event versus private event attended by few; (b) event requiring speech versus nonspeaking event; and (c) rigorous versus more relaxed event (e.g., walking tour versus sitting at head table at dinner).
6. *Media Orientation*. Factors to be considered are (a) media perception and depiction of event; (b) probability of coverage (location, time of day, crowd turnout, and so forth); and (c) pacing (Is event too close to competing candidate activity, just before, or just after, proposed event, hence compromising potential media coverage?).
7. *Contribution to Victory Margin*. How many votes will the appearance get?
8. *Other Benefits* (direct or indirect). Examples are endorsements, volunteers, and contributions.

Note: It is impossible to achieve total balance simultaneously, (i.e., criteria are competitive or are even mutually exclusive). Therefore, the campaign seeks balance over the course of the campaign; no single event can satisfy perfectly every criterion.

Scheduling Criteria

Perhaps the best way to distinguish between the scheduling operations for different levels of campaigns is to compare criteria with standards. Most campaigns have identical or similar criteria—for example, crowd size, publicity potential, and so forth. But the Level A and Level C campaigns have different standards; the former may seek a minimum audience of 5,000 and network television coverage; the latter may want at least 50 present and would be delighted with an article in the local weekly newspaper. All campaigns require scheduling criteria (Exhibit 9-2), but the criteria must be defined in terms relevant to the specific campaign by establishing quantitative standards. Even if a proposed schedule item satisfies the criteria established by the campaign (which also must weight each criterion for relative importance) and meets the campaign's standards, the item may not be placed on the candidate's schedule because the answers to other questions (Exhibit 9-3) are unacceptable.

The overriding debate often concerns an issue that the scheduler or

Exhibit 9-3
Questions Relating to Scheduling Criteria

1. What are the candidate's personal and confidential wishes? How does he feel about the type of activity, area to be visited, specific event, host?

2. Will the event require a new speech by the candidate or significant revision of an existing speech; is the customary speech acceptable as is or with minor revision? How long a speech is required?

3. How much effort is required by the campaign to make the event a success? Will it require considerable advance work to put together loose ends, advertising to stir attendance, research and the news operations to devote more time than usual? Will local campaign staff and volunteers have to devote extraordinary time, and could their time be more profitably used in other pursuits?

4. What is the event or invitation's prior history? Has the campaign previously rejected similar invitations from the area or group, reneged on a prior commitment to appear, or does the campaign in some other way feel obligated to accept?

5. How was the invitation extended, in writing or by telephone? Promptly and courteously? Was the person extending the invitation persistent? Does the person extending the invitation have the authority to extend the invitation?

6. Is the host or group reliable?

7. What are the objectives of the event, according to those extending the invitation? Will the objectives be attained? What would be the candidate's purpose for going? What is the likelihood the purpose will be served?

8. Does the local volunteer chairman recommend or approve the invitation? Is there any opposition among volunteer leaders or workers? Do they feel strongly either way? Has the scheduler queried everyone whose views, recommendation, or opposition should be known?

9. Do the local fund raisers or major contributors recommend or approve the invitation? Do they oppose it? Do they feel strongly either way? Has the scheduler been in touch with any key money contacts regarding the invitation?

10. Is the invitation important to any important segment of the campaign—for example, volunteer leaders, financial contributors, elected officials, and others who have endorsed the candidate, party leaders, candidates on the same slate? How important would they rank this invitation over another favor they might ask?

11. How is the candidate presently doing in the area or among the constituency represented by the invitation? What effect will the appearance have?

12. When was the last time the candidate was in the area or spoke before the group? When is the next scheduled visit? Is this visit really necessary?

13. Is the invitation an annual or one of a kind event? Or is it repetitious—for example, a weekly Rotary Club luncheon? Is the date specific and fixed, or is it negotiable, subject to change by the campaign? Is the date totally open, subject to the candidate picking the ideal date and time?

14. Regarding the specific invitation, is the candidate already scheduled to be in the area? If so, what effect will the event have on the schedule, especially the events preceding and following it? If not, does the event justify a trip into the area; also, could a constructive schedule of other events be built around this event?

15. Do the day, date, and time of the event adversely affect the candidate's overall schedule? Does it interfere with the candidate's private time needed for rest, relaxation, research, or staff meetings? Will the event make the candidate tired so that he does poorly at a more important event?

16. What are the event or activity's travel implications? How much travel is required? Can the event fit in with a larger travel itinerary? Will the travel be inconvenient, possibly subject to bad weather, road construction, or other problems? How much will the travel cost?

17. Could someone other than the candidate attend in his place—for example, a surrogate, prominent supporter, spouse, family member?
18. What would happen if the candidate did not attend? Could a telegram or message be sent? If the candidate or a surrogate is not present, what will be the real, rather than claimed, political repercussions?

local chairman does not want to confront: should present support or potential support tip the scheduling decision? Present and potential support advocates both use voting statistics, current registration figures, and prior electoral history as evidence, and the former use survey research to measure current support, while the latter use it to discern how to reach potential support. The implication for scheduling is the *self-fulfilling prophecy* approach—that is, schedule the candidate with the theory that certain assumptions about support will prove valid, and they will be proven on election day. If the strategy posits a certain numerical or percentage showing by the candidate in a given county or area, scheduling the candidate consistent with the hypothesis will validate it on election day.

The preeminent question is not the absolute value of an activity or event, but the relative value: What is the alternative use of the candidate's time? A rally with 10,000 people is an invitation that should not be passed up, unless the alternative is a rally somewhere else with 20,000 people. The subtle consideration is the need for the candidate to have some time for rest, relaxation, research, and other *private* time. There are times when it is preferable for the candidate to have private time—in effect, to be doing nothing (public)—than to accept an invitation. This subtlety must be grasped by anyone aspiring to the fine art of scheduling.

Time Budgeting

The campaign formulates its budget in dollars; the scheduler formulates a budget in time. Any campaign tour, activity, or event consumes part of the budget; is it worth the expenditure in time? The time budget is formulated by calculating the number of weeks, days, and possibly the number of hours available for campaigning between the beginning of the campaign and election day. Major rest periods or days off must be factored out of the budget to present a net figure of available time.

For example, consider a candidate for statewide office whose campaign will last approximately two months (Labor Day through election day) and comprise six days each week for a total budget of about 48 days. Assume that a county chairman, either of the candidate's political party or of a local campaign committee, requests three visits by the candidate. The scheduler determines that *any* visit to the county even for just one event, will consume a half day (based on the round-trip air and auto transportation). To satisfy the chairman's wishes (for several events per trip), the candidate's three visits would consume two to three days.

Does the county justify about 5 percent of the time budget? The scheduler checks with the political staff and finds the county will contribute about 1 percent of the candidate's expected (i.e., hoped for) statewide vote total. This criterion suggests that about half a day would be a fair allocation of time. Assume, however, that other criteria lead the scheduler to recommend allocating an entire day, or about 2 percent of the budget, for visits to the area. The consequent decision is, then, how should the candidate spend this entire day in the county—that is, should he make a single visit or spend a half day on two separate occasions. The latter obviously involves greater travel time, and probably one event on each trip, rather than the three or four events during the one-day swing. However, two visits provide the visibility afforded by *frequency*, and greater news coverage will result from two distinct trips to the area. The one-day trip may be more intensive than two limited trips, but the candidate's workers will probably remember the two trips, especially if they are scheduled at intervals—one near the beginning, one near the end—of the campaign.

Unit Budgeting. Generally, the candidate should be profitably occupied during the times of day normally used for meals. This goal leads to unit budgeting, or dividing the day into three parts: breakfast and the morning, lunch and the afternoon, and dinner and the evening. Each part or unit of the day is built around a meal function, although the function might not be a banquet; it could be a private meeting, or even a strategy or staff session. The point is that the candidate rarely eats alone, unless the meal is during a programmed private interval for rest or research.

Often a candidate visits an area to appear at a single event, and the scheduler must work with the local chairman to "flesh in" the schedule. For example, suppose the candidate accepted an invitation to appear at or address a major fund-raising dinner. The dinner reception, meal, and program will consume most of the evening unit. Given the candidate's investment in travel time, how can the campaign exploit the trip? Assume the news director recommended an afternoon luncheon meeting with the editorial board of the city's major newspaper. This luncheon could occur the day of the evening banquet or the next day (if both are open on the campaign schedule). If the luncheon occurs the same day, the campaign can decide whether to schedule additional activities that morning or to schedule travel time from somewhere else prior to the luncheon; it must also decide whether to schedule a breakfast activity for the next day as well as when to fly out. If the luncheon occurs the next day, this leaves the morning after the dinner open; there is an *automatic* incentive to create a breakfast function. For example, the scheduler might apprise the campaign manager and other ranking staff members of the open time, either formally in a scheduling meeting or informally if the schedule must be formulated quickly; perhaps someone will suggest and arrange a breakfast meeting with major labor leaders that can be hosted by the candidate in his hotel suite.

In the example just given, the candidate started with an expenditure of approximately one unit, then graduated to two, then three, units. Once the meal functions are set, other activities and events can be scheduled to fill in the schedule. However, and this is an important principle of scheduling, events scheduled first usually deserve priority; if the candidate must change the agreed upon or confirmed arrival or departure time to arrive late or leave early, the scheduler must negotiate with the first function, before disrupting it by a second function.

Reviewing the example, the scheduler must work with the news director to consider the publicity potential of expending three units by arriving early and leaving late the same day, or arriving in late afternoon just before the dinner and leaving in mid-afternoon the next day, which is also about three units. The latter may mean two days' publicity, rather than one day's publicity. Another consideration, similar to whether different times of day are more or less conducive to certain kinds of news coverage, is whether desired events can be scheduled on a particular day or at a particular time. When the scheduler consults the inventory file of general ideas, or specific invitations from the area, he finds opportunities with various constraints (e.g., morning events or late afternoon events). Perhaps someone has offered to host a late afternoon cocktail party to raise funds; the scheduler must determine if this event can be held successfully only at that time and place, or whether the host could sponsor a similar reception at a location near the newspaper, just before the scheduled editorial board meeting.

Media Budgeting. Geographical budgeting concerns political subdivisions that guide the expenditure of time. However, since the media-oriented schedule relies on news coverage to reach many more voters than are present at any activity on the schedule, time budgeting must consider the event in terms of how many people in which areas will be reached by the publicity.

The most sophisticated media budgeting is *media market budgeting*— the ultimate recognition that media market boundaries, rather than political boundaries, should govern scheduling for a statewide candidate. Media market budgeting allocates the candidate's time in the same way that the advertising budget is allocated; a percentage of the candidate's time, like a percentage of the advertising budget, is allocated to each media market. The percentage reflects the contribution in votes that the media market will make to the state's overall total. The media market is much larger than the city or county in which the activity or event occurs; for example, the New York City media market includes the Long Island counties of Nassau and Suffolk and the area north of New York City, notably Westchester; similarly, the the Los Angeles media market extends far beyond the city or even county boundaries. Media market budgeting often recognizes that the best way to get television coverage is to engage in a visual in the center of the media market—that is, the candidate attending an event far out in the suburbs of New York or Los Angeles is less likely to get television coverage, or will not get any television coverage, than if the activity is in Manhattan or metropolitan Los Angeles. This recognition implies a schedule bias in favor of urban activity.[d]

Travel Time

Minimizing travel time, whether for the airplane-oriented Level A or Level B campaigns or for the Level C campaign that relies primarily on the automobile, is a fundamental schedule constraint. Time spent in traveling is time that cannot be spent in meeting voters. Hence, the adept scheduler tries to construct an itinerary that flows from one nearby location to the next. For example, the local candidate may begin at one end of the district and drive across the district, attending one event after another, until he finds himself at the end of the district; the longest leg of the journey will be the return drive at the end of the day. Even more preferable is the circular-type route that begins and ends at the candidate's home base, but follows a continuous, almost circular course.

The alternative is the candidate beginning at one end of the district and rushing across the district to a commitment, then rushing back to the first location for another commitment, with similar excursions throughout the day. The Level A or Level B candidate has the same problem; only the geography is different. The travel constraint accounts for the candidate's scheduled swings through parts of a state or several states; each leg of the trip involves minimal travel. Whatever travel time is required can be used by the candidate for debriefing from the prior stop and briefing for the next campaign stop. Perhaps the candidate is scheduled for an interview during the auto or plane ride. The alert scheduler suggests to the candidate, on his private, internal schedule, how the candidate might wish to utilize the time. This involves working with the candidate's aide to determine what research

---

[d] For a discussion of extrapolating political and advertising data to formulate an advertising budget and the candidate's schedule, based on media markets, see Arnold Steinberg, *Political Campaign Management: A Systems Approach* (Lexington, Mass.: D.C. Heath, 1976).

material, possible speech text, future statements, briefing papers, newsclip files, staff memoranda, and other reading matter require the candidate's attention.

Fixed versus Flexible. Once the campaign accepts an invitation and issues an official confirmation, this event "freezes" a portion of the schedule. The location, date, and time of day inevitably circumscribe the options available before and after the event. When the campaign accepts an event, it not only is betting that a superior alternative for the same date or time is unlikely to be available, but that the event will probably not interfere with accepting a superior alternative scheduled before or following the original event. The missing variable is, of course, travel time; acceptance of an event necessitates travel time to go from the prior destination to the event, and from the event to the next destination. This seems obvious; yet, if prior and subsequent schedule entries are speculative, they will depend on the first decision.

This extended discussion points up the problem of early commitments. Sometimes they are necessary, but they may conflict with the principle of minimizing travel. The statewide candidate in California accepts a luncheon in San Francisco; then, the finance chairman arranges an important breakfast meeting that must be held the same day in Los Angeles, or not at all. Finally, the candidate has a chance to speak at the keynote session of a major statewide convention the same evening in Los Angeles. After all of these events have been confirmed, the scheduler learns that the opposition candidate will finally agree to a television debate, but it must be taped late that afternoon at a San Diego station. Thus, the candidate begins in Los Angeles, flies to San Francisco, then to San Diego, then back to Los Angeles. This is hardly an extreme case; fortunately, for the candidate, each location is easily accessible by rapid commercial aircraft.

Difficult itineraries cannot be avoided altogether, but they are less likely to occur if scheduling is cautious and does not *freeze* days or parts of days by committing the candidate too far in advance. Once a date is confirmed, it is difficult, but not impossible, to modify the date or time. The preferable technique is to create or build events around scheduled commitments, especially news conferences, visuals, media meetings, receptions, private meetings with potential endorsers or contributors, and other activities that the campaign can initiate. When the scheduler uses his inventory of open invitations, proposals by local campaign committees, or priority news conferences, visuals, or other media activities suggested by the news director, he can creatively fill in the gaps in a schedule.

Travel and Publicity. Minimizing travel time can conflict with maximizing publicity. Suppose a statewide candidate plans to devote two days to each of two cities. He can allocate the four days by visiting each city once for a two-day period, or each city twice for two one-day visits, or each city four times for four half-day visits. If the aforementioned times do not include an allowance for travel time, then the more times the candidate visits each city, the more time must be allowed for travel. Although multiple visits seem wasteful, the scheduler must work with the news director to estimate the ratio of the candidate's time spent in the city to the publicity generated. The half-day visit may generate almost or approximately as much publicity as the full-day visit. In addition, multiple visits relate to the *frequency* of publicity; the repetition factor is important; especially if multiple visits are scheduled at reasonable intervals.

A practical application of the stress on frequency of visits is when the candidate visits each of these two cities the same day. For example, suppose he holds a visual in one city in the morning, then immediately flies to the second city for another visual, perhaps by one o'clock. The travel time seems oppressive, yet the candidate succeeds in penetrating two television markets the same day. Although his schedule is hurried and his *personal* exposure is limited in each of the two cities, the average person in each city, as distinct from the typical person who attended the candidate's event, is conscious of the candidate's trip. The news media publicized the candidate's presence in each city; thus, more voters were reached.

If the candidate had stayed in the first city all day, he would have received a similar article in the next morning's newspaper, similar radio coverage, and virtually identical coverage on the evening news. By traveling to the second city, the candidate received nearly twice the publicity, since the media in the second city also covered the candidate.

10 Composition of the Schedule

The schedule offers a variety of activities, both because different types of activities are better suited for varying objectives and because some activities are more appropriate for different times of day. The varied schedule is also more tolerable for the candidate. From one vantage point, the schedule can be divided into public and private portions; the first concerns visible activities and events involving people, the second concerns the candidate working alone, resting, participating in staff meetings, or meeting privately with present or potential contributors, endorsers, or volunteer leaders. The public schedule is media oriented both because it includes many direct media entries (e.g., news conferences, visuals, interviews) and because its schedule is constructed to generate news.

The common denominator of any schedule entry is that it revolves around the candidate. The schedule reflects his strengths and accentuates his positive qualities. The schedule deemphasizes events in which he does poorly, even if that means deemphasizing news conferences or visuals, although the campaign's media orientation will be severely compromised. The scheduler assumes that if the candidate does well or poorly in a particular type or style of campaigning, such as walking tours or rallies, that he will perform appreciably better if the media is present. In other words, the news director works harder for a media turnout at events in which the candidate is expected to do well or the campaign has confidence—that is, it expects a heavy crowd turnout. The news director does not push for coverage of activites or events of questionable merit, and gracefully and nonchalantly discourages reporters from covering such items on the schedule.

Types of Activity

Most campaign activity falls into the general classifications outlined in the following pages. Each activity has intrinsic worth as an end in itself and may also be a means to an end—publicity. The campaign should seek invitations and events in which the candidate is the central figure. It may accept or even solicit events in which the candidate plays a subsidiary role, if the events are important and the candidate can do no better or if media considerations are involved. The scheduler soon discovers that unless the campaign committee, its local counterpart, or an adjunct committee organizes the event or activity, the campaign cannot control the situation totally; this is especially the case if an important outside group invites the candidate. As a supplicant, the candidate wants the exposure; the scheduler can only negotiate so far, and then must accept the host group's terms or decline the invitation.

The passive scheduler is concerned only with the invitations extended to the candidate; the active scheduler negotiates the conditions of those invitations, tries to change dates and times, stimulates additional invitations, and creates campaign activities to achieve defined objectives. These objectives reflect overall strategy, especially whether the campaign is a primary or general election race. For example, the Republican candidate's scheduler solicits invitations from Republican groups or nonpolitical groups with a high percentage of Republicans, during the primary campaign; however, he seeks more diverse audiences during the general election. The active scheduler researches all possible events by communicating with the Chamber of Commerce, tourist bureaus, cultural organizations, and any other groups that maintain calendars of events, dinners, fairs, or other public gatherings. Each local area has its own distinctive events that are potential candidate appearances.

The campaign can only exert full control if it creates and is the sole sponsor of an event. If the campaign cosponsors an event, it should be prepared to negotiate with the other sponsors who have their own objectives. This is especially true with political parties, and other political organizations, particularly cause- or issue-oriented groups that are more interested in their project than the candidate. If the host or sponsoring group is nonpolitical or nonpartisan, the scheduler must assure the hosts or sponsors that the campaign will not overly politicize the event.

The most important element inherent in all campaign activity is the candidate; the schedule must revolve around him. The scheduler and candidate should know when an event begins and ends, but far more important is when the candidate arrives and departs. The competent scheduler plans carefully so that the candidate arrives at the most propitious time; never so early that his time is wasted, never so late that the crowd has become disappointed or has thinned out. The candidate never stays longer than required to make the desired impression, shake the proper number of hands, speak the required length of time, and fulfill the requirements of protocol and courtesy. The scheduler's objective is for the candidate to arrive at any event at the peak of activity and crowd attendance. The candidate is rarely the first to arrive, or the last to leave.

Fund Raising

The campaign manager and finance committee must decide how much money must be raised and how; these decisions affect how much of the candidate's schedule must be allocated to fund raising. The scheduler usually relies on the campaign manager or finance chairman for guidance on scheduling fund-raising activities involving the candidate; in effect, much of the scheduler's discretionary authority is removed. Even so, the scheduler is responsible for formulating the candidate's detailed schedule, including such fund-raising entries as small meetings, receptions, banquets, and other activities.

Small Meetings. The small meeting is a private appointment with the candidate and a present or potential contributor or fund raiser, or several such persons. The meeting can involve breakfast, lunch, dinner, or cocktails. The candidate is usually accompanied by the finance chairman or a senior staff person, possibly both. Although the scheduler is usually *told* to schedule such a meeting by the manager, who determines the necessity for it, the scheduler must answer basic questions (Exhibit 10-1) required to prepare the candidate's internal schedule and briefing.

Receptions. The fund-raising reception either precedes a luncheon or dinner banquet or is an independent event. Unlike the small meeting, with an attendance limited to perhaps a dozen, the fund-raising reception has 25, 50, or even 100 people; in the extreme case, several hundred or thousand may attend. The larger the reception, the less intimate and personal the affair; larger receptions are usually for smaller givers. Sometimes the fund-raising dinner is preceded by two or three receptions, each segregated according to the contributor's past contributions, present contributions, or the kind or amount of dinner tickets purchased.

Any fund-raising reception is either free or has a price of admission; the reception may be open to anyone who is attending the dinner or who has purchased an entire table of tickets. The free reception may be a reward for past contributions. If the free reception is a gathering of potential contributors, there must be a planned program of follow-up solicitation, or the reception will be a failure. It is also advisable to convince a contributor to underwrite the cost of such a reception.

Finance chairmen and committee members interact socially with potential givers; many aspiring fund-raisers exaggerate the importance of a possible reception, but their friend in the campaign (i.e., the finance chairman) finds it difficult to question their judgment or say no. The campaign manager and scheduler must ask the hard questions that determine whether the reception is a social or fund-raising event; the reception can be both, but it should not be social *instead* of fund raising. The scheduler implicitly or even explicitly attaches a monetary value to the candidate's time—that is, how much of a dollar guarantee is required for the candidate to attend a fund raising reception?

The scheduler should be skeptical of hastily scheduled receptions that

Exhibit 10-1
Questions for Small Fund-Raising Meetings (or Receptions)

1. Is the meeting breakfast, luncheon, dinner, cocktails, or just an appointment? Why the time and setting, and is an alternative format or setting more desirable? Where would be the ideal location? Is there sufficient privacy?

2. How many people were invited, how were they invited and when? Who is following up the invitations? If a written invitation has been extended, has the candidate seen a copy?

3. Who will actually attend? Does the candidate's briefing include a guest list annotated for corporate or other descriptive affiliation? Does the briefing include other pertinent information (e.g., issues likely to be raised or the attitudes, preferences, and biases of those attending)?

4. What is the purpose of the meeting? Does everyone invited understand the purpose? Do they know the time, location, and expected length of the meeting?

5. Who is officially calling or hosting the meeting? Is the host only lending his name or home, or is he picking up the tab also?

6. Who is responsible for the meeting—that is, even in the small meeting, who will open it, lead the conversation, and close it? Who will introduce the candidate? Is there at least one person in the meeting who will act as a kind of cheerleader? Does everyone with a role know what they are supposed to do?

7. Is the plan to discuss finances directly, or other matters? If finances will be discussed at the meeting, by whom? If not, who will follow up the meeting and when?

8. If someone other than the candidate will raise the money issue, will it be done while the candidate is present, or has it been decided (this is usually advisable) to continue the meeting after the candidate departs and *then* discuss money?

9. What is the minimum amount of time the candidate can devote to the meeting or reception? Can someone move the meeting along before and after the candidate's presence?

10. Is this meeting absolutely necessary? Is the candidate's presence critical, or can someone else—spouse, family member, elected official, prominent citizen, campaign manager, finance chairman—represent him?

Note: Many of these questions should be applied by the scheduler to *any* small meeting.

allow insufficient time for designing, printing, mailing invitations, and making follow-up telephone calls. The more affluent the guest list, the more advance notice required. The reception that is poorly conceived and compromises quantity and quality of guests can be a waste of the candidate's time, although it is a status or social event for the host. Moreover, even if the finance committee is holding the reception, or it will be in a private home, the scheduler must review the details.[a]

Banquets. The legendary $100-a-plate dinner is the most common banquet fund-raising event, but the price should be varied according to the affluence of the candidate's constituency. The dinner price reflects a calculated

[a]Many sections of this chapter overlap; for example, a reception can be part of a banquet event or separate; a fund-raising function or related to an ethnic event or forum-type group; a speech-making event or simply a "handshaker"; an extended visit or a "quick drop by" as part of personal campaigning. Details for many events mentioned in this chapter are noted in later discussion of scheduling or treated as part of advance work.

decison by the dinner or finance committee: What price will produce the greatest net (after cost) revenue? The banquet, sponsored by the campaign, its finance committee, or a local counterpart, is usually for the sole financial benefit of the campaign. Another possible sponsor is an adjunct committee that solicits ticket sales among the committee's constituency. If a political party sponsors the dinner, the proceeds may be split between the candidate and the party or a group of candidates.

The candidate usually is the main speaker or makes remarks, at his own fund-raising dinner; generally, the main speaker is someone from outside the area who can generate attendance. The guest speaker delivers the principal address, which includes a tribute to the candidate who is the guest of honor. If the dinner has several beneficiaries, protocol may require the candidate's presence at the head table, but he may speak only briefly or is just recognized or introduced. The scheduler must verify all details, even if the campaign does not have full control over the banquet. If a speaker is addressing a dinner in honor of the candidate, the scheduler should insure that someone in the campaign is acting as liaison to brief the speaker.

The fund-raising banquet is scheduled two months in advance, sometimes longer. The date and facilities are reserved far in advance, although the selection of a guest speaker may be delayed. It is possible, but difficult, to have a major fund-raising banquet on less than 30 days' notice. However, such events should usually be among the first confirmed schedule entries, and they should be determined in the campaign's earliest stages or before the public campaigning begins; for example, the date for a fall dinner should be selected in the spring or summer, before the Labor Day campaign period actually begins. These decisions are usually outside the scheduler's responsibility; however, the campaign manager, finance chairman, and others must determine whether the dinner can be a success, which is the best location and date, and whether the expected proceeds justify the staff and volunteer labor required for banquet arrangements and ticket sales.

Other Fund Raisers. Many campaigns, especially at the local level, sponsor a variety of fund-raising activities such as bazaars, auctions, fashion shows, rummage sales, car washes, book sales, cookie sales, and so forth. Local components of Level A and Level B campaigns also sponsor such activities. These fund-raising events are only relevant to the scheduler if they require the candidate's presence or if the candidate can gain something by appearing or speaking at such an activity. The candidate's appearance may boost the morale of volunteers; it can be symbolically important to volunteers engaged in similar and other types of activity. Even the candidate for major office may be scheduled to participate in such an activity if the candidate's appearance will generate favorable publicity, especially television coverage.

Exhibit 10-2
Types of Direct Media Contact

1. Interviews with media personnel that are conducted by telephone or in person (at a hotel suite, an event, the campaign office, the candidate's home, or on the campaign plane);
2. News conferences that are sponsored by the campaign or by other groups (alone or joint);
3. Visuals;
4. Tapings and live broadcast interviews (television and radio):
5. Editorial board and other media meetings;
6. Availabilities.

Media

From one perspective, any schedule entry with publicity potential is a media event; for the Level A or Level B campaign, most schedule entries are usually media oriented. Activity is scheduled or rescheduled at locations and times of day to increase the chance of media coverage. The lower level campaign is more concerned with an event's intrinsic worth; the higher level campaign may accept an event with limited intrinsic worth, but high media potential. For example, the major candidate may engage in a half hour or hour walking tour of a busy shopping area. Given past newspaper and television coverage of his campaign along with his television spot advertising, the candidate is a celebrity. The advance staff produces a band, balloons, and pretty girls in campaign outfits. The event has questionable intrinsic worth, in that the candidate does not meet a statistically significant number of voters relative to his statewide or national candidacy. However, the event is worthwhile primarily because of its media orientation: the candidate reaches a statistically significant number of voters through newspaper and (especially) television coverage.

Each campaign schedule must allocate time not only to activities that may be covered by the media (i.e., indirect media activities), but also to direct interaction with the media. The two tests of a media-oriented schedule are whether its activities are newsworthy and the media is made aware of them *and* whether the schedule emphasizes direct media contact (Exhibit 10-2).

Forums

A forum event gives the candidate an opportunity to speak—whether a prepared or formal speech or merely brief remarks. If the candidate wants exposure before a group but cannot get a speaking invitation (e.g., the group is nonpolitical), the scheduler may compromise by negotiating an appearance by the candidate, with a public introduction so everyone knows he is there. The forum event that involves questions and answers is more rigorous; this format can be natural for the fluent performer. The local candidate who is a poor public speaker, who does not wish to state his views, or who does poorly in question periods may find excuses to refuse forum events. This is often the case with a local candidate who is favored because of his party's registration edge; the scheduler decides he has more to lose, than to gain, by such exposure.[b]

Any speaking commitment is a forum event. The types of speaking invitations accepted or solicited reflect the campaign's strategy choice of persuasion, consolidation, or contingency. The candidate in a primary election is scheduled for forum audiences relevant to the primary; the scheduling priorities for the general election are quite different. Many speaking commitments are scheduled to reward volunteers and financial contributors for past effort or to stimulate high voter turnout in certain areas or among constituencies of strength.

Nonpolitical Groups. The list includes Lions, Kiwanis, Rotary, Chamber of Commerce, local manufacturers, industrial, business, and professional associations and groups, as well as unions, service groups, fraternal and social organizations, churches and religious groups, and so forth. These audiences can provide an important way for the local candidate to broaden his base. They include community leaders, opinion molders, and activists—that is, the kinds of citizens who communicate frequently with others and who have a higher than average probability of voter turnout. The national or statewide candidate may speak to national, regional, or state conventions or conferences, or even to a joint meeting of two or more organizations, or several chapters of the same organization.

The best way to speak to such groups is *before* the campaign begins. The unannounced candidate should find a supporter who can secure an invitation for the candidate to speak on a "nonpolitical" topic. This avoids politicizing the group and permits the organization to state that it sponsored the candidate before he became an announced candidate. Occasionally, such groups permit both candidates to speak, on separate occasions, or in a discussion or debate before election day.

Ethnic Groups. Just as the persistent scheduler discovers an array of occupational and professional organizations representing the diversity of work in America, he can also find a seemingly endless variety of ethnic,

---

[b] Each candidate has his own style for holding forums. Sen. Jesse Helms (R.-N.C.) was elected in 1972 in a campaign that featured numerous, well-attended breakfast functions, following which the candidate spoke and sometimes took questions. Former Governor Ronald Reagan's 1976 campaign for president included many public question-and-answer sessions, because Reagan did well in such a setting.

nationality, racial, and religious groups. The same guidelines apply here as for other nonpolitical groups; the candidate should speak at such gatherings before he is an official candidate. Regardless of when he speaks, he should use an adjunct committee leader or other campaign supporter to secure an official invitation. This person, someone who is known, respected, and admired by the group, can escort the candidate; however, if this person is not an active member of the group, another person who is intimately involved should be recruited. This person shares the common ethnic, racial, religious, or national heritage of the group's members and can brief the candidate on the organization's history, purposes, membership, and leadership, with particular emphasis on traditions, customs, and pronouncing difficult names.

Schools and Campuses. The local candidate can build quite a following by speaking in public schools in his district before he is perceived as a candidate. Although the students cannot vote, they can influence their parents; also, if the candidate speaks over a period of years before becoming a candidate, the junior and senior high school students may be of registration age. Appearances during campaigns are usually not high-priority events, unless the students are older, especially high school, and the audience is quite large.

The Level A or Level B candidate, unlike the local candidate, will find little intrinsic worth in high school speaking commitments; however, the publicity potential can be vast. Since virtually all candidate appearances in a school involve question periods, this type of interaction with students, as well as the socializing before and after the talk, can provide good visuals. However, the scheduler should avoid such commitments if the candidate is impatient, cannot relate to youth, or cannot handle questions.

Whether the candidate speaks at a public or private high school, or at a university campus, he should not only try to boost the morale of his youthful supporters, but he should be seen with students who are respected and admired by their peers. Students are especially socially conscious, and the scheduler should ask hard questions of the candidate's youth group to find out what the candidate should say and do to make supporting him the fashionable thing to do. Although particular attention should be paid to political science, civics, government, and debate classes or clubs, the candidate should meet as many individual students as possible, providing the campaign's youth affiliate has done its job. It is usually inadvisable for a candidate to speak at a school or campus if the campaign has no students who can advance the trip, unless the campaign is in its formative stages and the local candidate hopes his appearance will net some campaign workers.

The scheduler must always ask: What is the objective of the school or campus visit? How many registered voters are at the university? Are they eligible to vote in the election? What are the followup plans after the candidate's appearance? For the Level A or Level B campaign, perhaps the most crucial consideration is media coverage—is it likely to be positive or negative? How will the campaign's target groups react to the candidate's campus appearance? What is the risk, if any, that the candidate will be treated discourteously, disrespectfully, or in a way that makes the candidate look like too much of a supplicant? If the campaign decides to go forward with the campus visit, the news director should notify the campus newspaper, arrange for coverage of the candidate's activities, and possibly an interview.

Joint Appearances. The leading candidate avoids joint appearances with the opponent; even if promoted as a discussion, they are likely to become a debate. Sponsoring such appearances is the goal of many groups; but the leading candidate should try to avoid appearing on the same platform as the opponent, unless stalling tactics or refusals result in significant negative publicity. The campaign policy toward joint appearances or debates should be consistent; it should not be the scheduler's problem. Once such an event is accepted, the campaign manager decides who will brief the candidate, and who will be in charge of advancing the event, especially encouraging the candidate's supporters to attend the event. It is the scheduler's problem to allow adequate candidate time for preparation and rest.

Issue Groups. These organizations are permanent and on-going, or they can be ad hoc groups created in response to a particular controversy. As has been repeatedly emphasized, it is important for the candidate to have a key supporter inside the host group; if not, everything possible should be done to have an invitation extended on the campaign's terms. If the candidate has precisely the opposite position than that advocated by the group, an appearance is usually a waste of time, unless the news director sees the potential for favorable publicity in that the appearance will not result in a confrontation that might have negative media impact. Creative campaigns may encourage the formation of noncampaign, ad hoc groups concerned with issues emphasized by the candidate. However, in all cases, the candidate and scheduler must remember that the issue group is usually more interested in the issue than the candidate. In many cases, the candidate can never satisfy the extreme elements of the group; for example, the candidate opposed to abortion may not be opposed vociferously enough to satisfy the local "Right to Life" group.

It seems heretical to many of the candidate's most ardent and faithful supporters who either want to reassure the committed or convert all of the opponent's supporters, but the scheduler must always ask the hard questions. Why should the candidate go? How many votes will the appearance get? What are the consequences or costs of not going?

Varied Formats. If an organization or group is important, the aggressive scheduler does not wait for an invitation; he works with the campaign manager, volunteer leaders, and important contacts to make the invitation occur. If the campaign cannot secure an invitation for a major speech, it tries for remarks; if not remarks, then for a place on the head table and an introduction; otherwise, an introduction from a seat off the head table. The scheduler's persistence is entirely a function of the group or constituency's importance to the campaign. The scheduler always asks: Is the organization doing the candidate a favor by inviting him, or by the type of invitation extended, or is the candidate doing the group a favor by accepting?

The scheduler should not rule out the candidate's visiting a banquet reception, as long as the candidate is invited or his visit is not considered an impropriety. Whether the candidate is publicly introduced at the banquet, or escorted through the reception, the person or persons making the introduction or escorting the candidate should be prominent and liked. Whether the candidate formally addresses the group or speaks informally to its leaders and members as he "works" the reception, he should be briefed to say the right thing. The candidate should be briefed to make shorter and less political (or nonpolitical) presentations before nonpolitical groups, especially if the invitation or candidate's presence is controversial. Remarks should be low key, affirmative, and on issues of concern to the audience; ideally, the remarks should be perceived as on a higher level than campaign polemics or political rhetoric.

Rallies and Mini Rallies

It is almost impossible for a campaign to sponsor a major rally, either in an indoor or outdoor context, unless the candidate has achieved substantial recognition through television news and spot advertising. Even major campaigns with skilled advance staffs are reluctant to schedule the traditional giant rally, because too much staff and volunteer time is required to turn out a respectable crowd. The experienced scheduler fears unfavorable media coverage generated by a poorly attended rally. Indoor locations are preferred because they are usually easier to fill, and there are no weather problems, and fewer sound problems. The outdoor location is speculative, can pose security problems, and risks bad weather. The scheduler usually provides for a contingency plan if bad weather threatens any outdoor rally. Also, the crowd is usually densely packed in a small area.

The scheduler often considers other activities in the context of mini rallies. These are related to the candidate's appearance, but there is less pressure for the massive attendance required to fill a certain number of seats or outdoor area. These mini rallies can be in the form of visiting shopping centers, walking tours, headquarters openings, or some of the tours discussed later in the chapter.

Shopping Centers. The mini rally can be held at a shopping center, either in an indoor mall or on the parking lot. The campaign must select the best day and time; in urban areas, the noon hour is often best to take advantage of the lunchtime crowds; in suburbs, Saturday mornings may be best. The scheduler selects the time of the candidate's appearance, especially any remarks, to coincide with the height of shopping and pedestrian activity to exaggerate overall attendance. The mini rally, which may precede or follow personal campaigning, requires vast technical support, including volunteers to distribute handbills, brochures, balloons; careful negotiations with shopping center or store managers; provision for sound; and any other problems associated with the candidate's appearance. The campaign always distinguishes between public and private property; the latter requires permission, and it is helpful to have such permission in writing.

Walking Tours. Without a mini rally, a walking tour is simply personal campaigning. However, if there are any provisions for the candidate to speak to a group, the walking tour becomes a kind of mini rally. This can be the case if the candidate's schedule includes a series of campaign stops at shopping centers, bus terminals, or other congested areas, and there is some provision (perhaps even a platform or microphone) for the candidate to speak to a group of voters, either before or after the walking tour.

The walking tour is often depicted as a mini rally when the candidate is virtually surrounded by well wishers and accompanied by supporters carrying banners or placards, a band, pretty girls in costume, children with balloons, and so forth. This is really a mini rally without the customary speech or remarks, speaking platform, sound equipment, or other formal preparations. However, there must be considerable preparations and advance work to turn out the crowd; otherwise, the walking tour and mini rally are not a good visual. Finally, it is essential to emphasize that advance work is based upon a *walking formation*, which is planned in advance so that staff members do not surround the candidate and prevent him from meeting people. Staff members should never walk directly in front of the candidate; they should be either at the side or rear, or perhaps 50 feet ahead. It is highly questionable whether any staff member other than a single aide or security personnel should be directly adjacent to the candidate. Needless to say, this same standard applies to overzealous volunteers who stay too close to the candidate.

Headquarters Openings. The opening of any campaign headquarters presents an opportunity for a mini rally to stir interest in the headquarters, encourage volunteers to work, and secure local media attention. If a headquarters is already open, the candidate may "officially" open it with a celebration and remarks inside the headquarters or on the sidewalk or in an adjacent parking lot. Alternatively, the candidate may simply plan a visit to the local headquarters to thank volunteers. In either case, advance work is required to assure a crowd turnout, invite as many local people as possible, and handle sound and other logistical problems. Whenever the news media is expected to be present, advance work is even more important.

Personal Campaigning

Personal campaigning is not only desirable for the local candidate, it is essential. Unfortunately, most local candidates are too preoccupied with useless strategy sessions or addressing groups of diehard supporters to engage in valuable personal campaigning. For the Level A or Level B candidate, such campaigning is a farce, because the number of voters reached directly is statistically insignificant. However, as a visual, personal campaigning for the major candidate can be extremely useful, if advance work assures good pictures and filming of the candidate interacting with a continuous number of pedestrians.

Street and Merchant. The candidate can introduce himself to pedestrians and consumers in a high-density shopping area. He can go door to door among storeowners and shopkeepers and shake hands and distribute campaign brochures. However, if the candidate is accompanied by a large entourage of staff, volunteers, and reporters, advance work is required to secure permission for the candidate to use private property. Many commercial operations do not want candidates walking through their stores, either because they feel business activity is disrupted, or they don't want to be accused of favoritism or feel obligated to invite the opposition candidate. The local candidate politely asks storeowners or managers to display his window sign and keep a supply of campaign brochures on the counter. The major candidate may also make such requests, but his visit should have been preceded by advance work to get posters and signs in windows and brochures distributed, since his street or merchant campaigning is mainly for media attention. In either case, the candidate or advance men are never unduly persistent, since owners are apathetic, interested only in business, or afraid to offend the opposition candidate; the manager is often afraid to do anything without the owner's permission. The candidate will campaign more effectively if he is confident and is accompanied by others, who help distribute literature and entice voters into meeting the candidate. It is also helpful to distribute advertising specialties or premium gifts to voters—for example, shopping bags are especially effective for consumers.

Door to Door. Like street and merchant campaigning, this can be crucial for the local candidate if the residential area is well chosen. The candidate should make certain to avoid meal times. He should carry campaign materials and be prepared to enlist volunteer support. Ideally, the candidate should be accompanied by volunteer workers who are also going door to door. If the candidate has a limited time, he can select strategic neighborhoods and visit several households per block or neighborhood to create the impression of pervasiveness. The effective campaigner knows that he cannot spend more than a couple of minutes per household, just as he cannot spend too much time with any one individual in street campaigning. The organized campaign follows up door-to-door visits with targeted mailings, especially letters produced by automatic typewriters.

The Level A or Level B candidate who walks door to door in a residential area can provide a powerful boost to statewide and even national volunteer efforts. The candidate is scheduled for an hour or even two hours of precinct work, and different reporters and camera crews accompany the candidate during different times. Of course, the advance staff carefully selects the area for any personal campaigning, if the local and traveling media will be present; part of the visual should be the favorable response the candidate receives.

Coffees. The aggressive scheduler works closely with volunteer leaders to organize and schedule several coffee sessions each week, even several per day or morning. These events are usually hosted by a housewife in her home; they are practically useless unless they involve potential, rather than just present supporters. The candidate should probably spend at least 15 minutes at each coffee, rarely more than 30; he should meet each person, speak to the group for a few minutes, and possibly take several questions. The greater the attendance, the more time the candidate should invest; the scheduler must determine the probable attendance. The effective hostess, using written invitations and a telephone committee of neighbors to follow up the invitations, can organize a successful event; if the home is large, the coffee could have as many as 50 or 100 guests. There is no reason to discourage men from attending.

Receptions. The assumption here is that the reception is not part of a dinner or banquet function. Like any other *scheduled* personal campaigning, the candidate should arrive at the peak attendance point. He should be escorted by two individuals; one should probably be the host. They should know the people present and should introduce the candidate to as many as possible. It is often difficult to set up a receiving line; in either case, it is essential that those who have the responsibility of moving the candidate around the room know their task and take is it seriously.

Tours

Although an incumbent is in a superior position to be invited, or to invite himself, for tours, especially of government and military facilities, the creative scheduler can arrange tours for the challenger. Although some tours are depicted as fact finding missions, the candidate is usually involved in personal campaigning; the facilities should be selected in terms of the number and type of people the candidate will meet. For the major campaign such tours may have substantial publicity value, or are pursued principally as a visual.

Factory, Industrial Plant, Farm. Such invitations usually must be solicited by the candidate and require the cooperation of management. Management is often reluctant to disrupt production; also, employees who work piecemeal, rather than on an hourly or salaried basis, will probably react negatively to the candidate's disrupting their work. The scheduler should decide whether touring the operation, even with management's permission, will gain or lose votes. The candidate should not be accompanied by management, but should be accompanied by both management and workers.

Some factories may permit the candidate to address a group of employees and may even provide sound equipment. Some corporations sponsor an employees forum, where the candidates appear separately or jointly. In terms of publicity, especially for visuals, the interaction between candidate and workers on the assembly line is preferable to the forum. This is especially true if the tour is related to an issue; for example, the candidate supporting a particular defense program visits a plant that would get the contract or subcontract.

The farm is the rural counterpart of the factory; in other areas, the cannery may provide an appropriate tour context. The standards are identical. How many people will the candidate see? Will the tour gain or lose votes? Can it be related to an issue? Does the candidate at least enjoy a base of support within the worker ranks, so that sympathetic workers will help advance the tour? What is the media, especially television, value?

The scheduler should consider, in addition to, or instead of, the tours, visiting the plant entrance during a change in work shifts, which usually occur very early in the morning, often at six or seven o'clock, or in mid-afternoon, or occasionally, very late at night, if the plant is on three shifts. It is essential that the candidate be accompanied by volunteers who help distribute literature. If the candidate is in a Level A or Level B campaign, the image of the candidate greeting early morning workers can be an appealing visual; it is also a dramatic boost for volunteer workers who need to know their candidate is working as hard as they are. Early morning campaigning, if reported in the print media and seen on television, symbolizes a serious campaign to the public. Also, depending on the media market, it can be a good story for the television station that has at least one early morning crew on duty.

Health, Welfare, and Other Facilities. Examples include drug rehabilitation centers, hospitals, mental hospitals, welfare centers, unemployment offices, nursing and senior citizen homes, and prisons. It is misleading to consider so many diverse types of facilities together; their only common denominator is possible inclusion on a candidate's schedule. Clearly, the mental hospital or prison is not toured to gain votes within the facility, but to generate favorable publicity. Like the factory tour, the tour of a health center, methadone clinic, or facility for the handicapped should be related to a campaign issue; for example, the candidate could be proposing a new government program or opposing an existing one. Obviously, the candidate's scheduler must be quite skillful to arrange a tour of a facility that can be criticized or condemned by the candidate without a resulting negative impact. However, the hosts may cooperate; for example, the physicians in a veterans hospital who believe its budget cuts should be restored might welcome the publicity resulting from the candidate's tour.

The focus on publicity and visuals should not obscure the fact that some public or private facilities can present opportunities for personal campaigning, especially for the local candidate. The senior citizen home may include many residents who are registered to vote and who, if they are registered, can be persuaded to vote for the candidate. In this example, the candidate's visit can be followed up by a special operation to insure that anyone who cannot travel to the polls can vote by absentee ballot.

One final point: the candidate must be briefed on whether the facilities are governmental, private, or mixed (partially government funded); he must know what levels of government are involved. The facts are especially important if the tour is tied to a visual. The same point could be made about tours of universities or schools. Private and public institutions have different problems, and the candidate should know what kind of facility he is touring, and how its peculiar problems relate to campaign issues.

Other Appearances

Each state, county, or area has its own distinctive events, such as annual fairs, barbecues, fish frys, civic celebrations, and parades. Many of these activites are related to nationality and ethnic holidays and commemorations. The scheduler must assign staff and volunteers to researching all possible events in all relevant areas and to making sure the candidate gets invited, usually through the intervention of a supporter who is a member of the group or the fair or parade committee. The scheduler must determine what mode of appearance—walking tour, booth, reviewing stand (for a parade), speech before a luncheon, and so forth—will produce optimum results. In certain parts of the country, the state or county fair is an unparalleled opportunity for personal campaigning (and for a good visual); in other areas, parades are more likely to draw the crowds.

Sports and Exhibitions. One way to "humanize" the candidate is for him to be seen at major sporting events and exhibitions. It makes little sense for the candidate to attend such an event for exposure unless he can at least get introduced. This is especially important if the introduction is broadcast on television or radio or if good advance work insures that the camera zooms in on the candidate. Such visits are most effective if the scheduler works with the volunteers leaders to find supporters among the owners, sponsors, or participants of the sports event or exhibit. The myth among some campaign publicists is that the candidate must be on the political news page (wherever that is). However, a photograph of the candidate in the players locker room will reach many voters, even if it is on the sports page; it could also be a good visual.

These events can also provide an opportunity for handshakes and "working the crowd" as it is entering or leaving the game or exhibition. However, such campaigning requires volunteer support and literature distribution as well as the considerable amount of advance work mentioned earlier. Unless the candidate is well known (principally through television), this approach can be disheartening and unproductive. Also, if it is too far from election day, the candidate's visit may be forgotten.

Commuter Stops. Apart from train and bus stations, many communities do not have commuter stops; these typify the East coast. Like any other massive confrontation with groups of apathetic voters, the candidate who campaigns at train, bus, and subway terminals needs plenty of volunteers, especially in distinctive outfits. Music or free premiums are helpful. It is essential that the advance staff survey the optimum (most crowded) commuter stops and determine the train schedules. If the candidate actually rides the train, this can be a good visual.

Caravans. The car caravan can be an effective method of reaching voters in a district. A motorcade of neatly decorated cars can convey momentum and enthusiasm. If the route is well chosen, many voters will remember the candidate's name and this demonstration of support. If the schedule is formulated carefully, the car caravan can feature a series of short stops at campaign headquarters, shopping centers, or public gathering places. The car caravan can be related to a series of mini rallies, but only if advance work is done to assure precise scheduling—especially by making a dry run of the route—and an acceptable crowd turnout. The advance man measures exactly how much time is needed at each stop for getting in and out of the car, shaking hands, walking a prescribed route, and possibly addressing the crowd.

The caravan can include other types of vehicles. One major candidate once sponsored a caravan of campers to drive through an important area of his state. The use of campers also symbolized his support among the large number of voters who owned campers or recreational vehicles. In this case, or for the caravan traveling short distances on a Saturday morning or afternoon, the campaign should determine that the idea is a net plus—that is, for example, it does not unduly disrupt traffic and thereby antagonize voters.

Private Time. This chapter concludes by treating the candidate's private schedule apart from other types of activity. Because of the misconception that unless the candidate is visibly campaigning, he is not productive, it should be emphasized that the best interests of the candidate require that time be set aside for important private meetings as well as for rest. Some candidates spend too much time in strategy sessions or sleeping; but it is possible to overschedule the candidate's public time. The best way to allow for sufficient private time (see Exhibit 10-3) is for the scheduler to monitor and review the schedule continuously to insure that it is built around the candidate. The scheduler is concerned with when events start and end only insofar as they affect the candidate's arrival and departure time; he always spends the least possible time at an event, an amount that is consistent with achieving the campaign's desired objectives in scheduling the event.

Exhibit 10-3
Planning Private Time

The schedule must allow time for both regular and special private meetings; it must also allow for planned breaks during which the candidate can initiate and return telephone calls. The candidate must interact, in person and by telephone, with a variety of individuals, including some of the following on a daily basis:

1. Volunteer campaign chairman, possibly cochairman;
2. Major volunteer leaders, including adjunct committee chairmen;
3. Campaign manager or campaign director;
4. News director or press secretary;
5. Tour director or scheduling secretary;
6. Finance chairman (volunteer) or finance director (staff);
7. Research director and research source people;
8. Past, present, and potential major contributors;
9. Past, present, and potential major endorsers, especially prominent citizens and elected officials;
10. Leaders of major corporations, unions, and a variety of membership organizations.

Private time also includes the following nonvisible media efforts that can help generate news and advertising:

11. Private interviews with reporters in hotel suite, aboard campaign plane, or at home;
12. Editorial and other media meetings;
13. Telephone interviews, especially audio releases;
14. Reviewing advertising plans, primarily for strategy, policy, and major substantive content (candidate must know what advertising will say);
15. Filming or taping broadcast media spots or programs (always preceded by adequate rest period).

The scheduler must plan time for such candidate briefings as the following:

16. Review of news clippings file and broadcast media coverage;
17. Review of news releases (including occasional writing and editing);
18. Reading of research briefings and some original source material (including issue analyses);
19. Reading of briefing materials for visits to various areas and locations;
20. Review of upcoming weekly schedule and of daily schedule.

Finally, the candidate can only be at his best if he is properly rested. The activity is graduated, rather than too harsh at the outset; the scheduler knows that the candidate's illness could jeopardize the entire schedule. Accordingly, formulating the schedule entails:

21. Programming for no more than six days of campaigning per week;
22. Programming for an appropriate amount of sleep;
23. Scheduling breaks during the day—at least one, probably two, possibly three—with adequate time for personal needs plus contingency time for possible telephone calls, reaction statements, and other decisions;
24. Building in a special cushion of time for rest before major debates, intense trips, filming of television commercials, and so forth;
25. Planning so candidate can spend some time with spouse and family.

11 Administering Scheduling

Political scheduling markets the candidate to voter subgroups by strategic targeting. This approach requires the delineation of criteria and standards in order to budget the candidate's time in the most advantageous way. Implementing the schedule involves detail work, but administering scheduling is more much than correspondence, files, telephoning, and logistics. The orchestration of scheduling is a creative process that depends on excellent communications between the scheduling division and contacts outside the campaign. This interaction reflects the scheduler's emphasis on details, correspondence, and files, not to enhance the status of bureaucracy, but to support the creative function. The basis of the scheduler's actions must be his authority.

Scheduling is a science and an art. It is a science because its theory, methodolgy, and techniques are known and subject to constant testing. It is an art because, although a dedicated clerk can master the *routine* of scheduling, each day is unique and constructing the schedule requires innovative, adaptive processes. The creative scheduler is imaginative and never satisifed with the schedule. The complacent, bureaucratic scheduler is like the news director who does nothing more than mail news releases.

The concepts relevant to overall campaign and media strategy also apply to scheduling. The schedule should be graduated or paced to reflect an escalating scale of activity, in terms of both the number and intensity of events. Although the opening week may be more active than the second week, or one campaign tour may be more intense than a subsequent tour, the overall direction is upward. Like generating news or purchasing advertising, the scheduler wants to cause momentum; the schedule is planned to include more frequent appearances and larger crowd turnouts as voter consciousness rises toward the end of the campaign. The master scheduler knows that productive scheduling must be both a cause and an effect of momentum.

Just as advertising space and time are reserved and purchased far in advance of the campaign's final phase or week, the scheduler carefully blocks out time for the candidate's final push. When the scheduler delays accepting an invitation or proposal, because he hopes for a superior invitation or alternative proposal, he risks losing lead time to plan for whatever is ultimately accepted. In addition, procrastination may mean that the number of options decreases over time. Hence, scheduling for the last part of the campaign requires keen intuition and judgment; playing this game of holding open days for better scheduling opportunities is like Russian roulette, in that the days can only be held open so long before local chairmen or prospective hosts become disenchanted, or the campaign ends up with lower-priority activities than the original proposals or with empty days or parts of days that must be filled.

Communications

The scheduler must concentrate both on the strategic and relatively long-term schedule—that is, he must be planning for several weeks ahead while handling the immediate needs of the current week's schedule or even monitoring *that day's* schedule, which includes many last minute revisions, changes in travel or hotel reservations, and implementation of contingency plans. The experienced scheduler knows that frenetic activity, crises, and emergencies are normal and to be expected in the campaign. Only the static campaign that does not try to adapt to changing circumstances will have a quiet scheduling office. The scheduler must have contingency plans for every phase of the schedule, so that necessary changes can be made quickly, and staff members do not have to waste time discovering what the alternatives are; the options are already known.

Like the news operation, the scheduling office requires at least two staff members—one to deal with the immediate crisis, the other to continue working on scheduling for the coming weeks. Even in a small campaign with a single scheduling secretary, there must be at least one other person qualified in scheduling. The goal is for the operation to process correspondence and telephone inquiries efficiently, yet oversee the candidate's activities while he is campaigning—that is, for example, by tracking his travel, compensating for lateness, and reconfirming that everything is in readiness at the next campaign stop. Even if the campaign has an advance staff, the scheduling office is still the nerve center that charts the candidate's daily course.

As a practical matter, the telephone system for scheduling should include a rotary direct line; alternatively, or in addition, the candidate should have one "hot line" telephone number for his personal use or for his traveling aide's use. There should never be a problem for the candidate or an aide who must communicate by telephone with the scheduling office. In larger campaigns, the office is staffed whenever the candidate is campaigning; the scheduling office starts and ends the day with the candidate. If the candidate is campaigning a half day or not at all, scheduling may still be operating. If the tour director or scheduler is away from the office, he is always available by telephone. The absence of any person on the scheduling staff should not confuse or disrupt the operation; notes and files should be accessible and understandable to anyone on the scheduling staff.

Policy

The scheduling staff is friendly, courteous, and cooperative. Its staff is especially recruited not only for superior work habits, dedication, and conscientiousness, but for ability to work under stress. Regardless of inevitable daily scheduling crises, the scheduler and staff must be able to remain calm and make decisions dispassionately and quickly. An attitude of confidence and self-assurance is important, both in dealing with the candidate and others—within or outside the campaign. The competent scheduler is not always liked by others, but he is always respected. Regardless of his decisions, he seeks to convince any offended individual that the decisions are made solely in the best interest of the candidate and campaign. The scheduling staff has its own distinctive style of turning people down as gently and graciously as possible; the daily immediacies of scheduling usually require such conversations to be as brief as possible, but the skilled staff is succinct and to the point without being abrupt.

The attitude is characterized by a polite, but definite, skepticism. Simply put, the scheduler trusts no one. He knows that those inviting the candidate or proposing an activity, including some of the candidate's best supporters, will lie or mislead the scheduler to get a favorable decision. They are prone to exaggerate the importance of their event; often they deceive themselves. If pressured by their own colleagues or local supporters, local campaign chairmen will say almost anything in order to be able to deliver the candidate. The persistent scheduler always verifies information and is especially suspicious of crowd turnout figures, the number of people invited, tickets sold, expected media coverage, presence of elected officials and other notables, and the amount of time requested of the candidate.

"We guarantee that the candidate will be out by ten o'clock," are famous last words given to entice the candidate into attending a banquet whose program actually ends at midnight. The experienced scheduler asks tough, hard questions to determine the real starting and ending times; then, once he has the facts, he begins negotiating the schedule to compress the event or activity to its essentials, so that the candidate can arrive later or leave earlier than proposed, or both.

Generally, it is important to give the local chairman or supporter advance notice of the campaign's decision on an invitation or proposal, especially if that person brought the matter to the campaign's attention. The local chairman should not learn from someone else or from the newspaper that the candidate will visit his area or has accepted a particular speaking invitation; otherwise, this valued supporter feels slighted. Whenever possible, the campaign should build the image and enhance the status of its local chairmen by giving them the credit for an invitation's acceptance or by enlisting their help in turning down the invitation.

Consecutive/Concurrent Scheduling. The local campaign chairman or prospective host is inclined to schedule activities too loosely. The candidate is forced into an unrealistic schedule, in which he spends too much time at each activity. Therefore, any major activities that require printed invitations or otherwise "lock in" the candidate's time must be reviewed at an early stage—for example, before the invitations are mailed—to avoid the misallocation of the candidate's time caused by consecutive scheduling. Consecutive scheduling occurs, for instance, when the local chairman proposes a 5 p.m. news conference; a 5:30 meeting (for about 15 minutes) in the candidate's suite with local elected officials; a 6 p.m. reception; then dinner at 7 p.m. The schedule is consecutive because no activity begins until after the prior activity has ended. The candidate must spend more time than necessary at each activity, because another activity has not yet started. Also, the schedule includes "dead time"—that is, the time between each activity is unproductive because it is insufficient for research or rest. In the above example, the candidate's 5:30 meeting with local elected officials will necessarily be followed by 15 minutes of dead time, or the meeting could be extended to a full half hour, which is longer than necessary.

Concurrent scheduling examines the goal of each activity and redefines it by correlating the time the candidate spends to the objective sought. In the consecutive scheduling example, additional dead time or wasteful "over time" occurs because there is no reason for the candidate to spend more than thirty minutes at the 6 o'clock reception (in fact, the height of the crowd will be during the latter half of the time period). If the candidate remains at the reception until 7 p.m. and thus avoids dead time, then the dinner cannot start promptly because political scheduling assumes that *the candidate cannot be in two places simultaneously*. What is more, if the candidate is among the last to leave the reception, the crowd will be slow going into the dinner, which now may not begin until 7:15 or 7:20.

In concurrent scheduling, activities and events overlap so that the schedule can be built around the candidate who, accordingly, invests only the appropriate amount of time in any activity and has limited or no dead time (see Exhibit 11-1). In consecutive scheduling, the candidate appears to be doing things logically, but in fact, he is compromising the optimum by adapting to a poor schedule. In concurrent scheduling, the schedule is constructed to make the best use of the candidate's time.

Exhibit 11-1
Concurrent Scheduling

Proposed Consecutive Schedule	Revised Concurrent Schedule
5:00—News Conference.	6:00-6:15—Candidate meets with local leaders in suite; press aide is downstairs in room set aside for news availability.
5:30-5:45—Candidate meets with local leaders in suite.	
6:00—Candidate attends reception.	6:17—Candidate departs suite for room (adjacent to reception room) set aside for news availability.
7:00—Dinner begins.	
	6:20-6:30—News availability.
	6:32-6:52—Candidate circulates throughout reception (reception had started at 6:00).[a]
	6:55—Head table forms for entrance into dinner.[b]

Note: Concurrent scheduling revisions to the consecutive schedule proposed in the text increase the candidate's private time by about one hour.

[a]At 6:45 the bar closes; shortly afterwards, at two minute intervals, the lights flash intermittently to move people from the reception to the dinner; after the candidate leaves, the lights are flashed more often, then dimmed.

[b]Assumes head table will enter in a procession.

Details. Each campaign sets its own standards for the amount and type of information required—that is, criteria are established to determine whether an invitation or proposal can be accepted and then, if the event is scheduled, what type of information is needed to facilitate the candidate's appearance. These standards partly reflect the number of scheduling staff; the more limited staff has less time to devote to each schedule entry. Also, the campaign with an advance operation takes some of the burden for detail work from the scheduling secretaries. Regardless of the level of campaign, size of the scheduling staff, or presence of an advance operation, the scheduler's files must include basic information for each event.

It will often save time if the prospective host provides the required information by completing a form or questionnaire and returning it to the scheduling office. Another possibility is for the campaign to prepare a checklist of questions for any prospective hosts and to mail the checklist with the acceptance letter. The scheduling office may prepare several different checklists, each suited to specific types of events. Thus, no host is given a more extensive checklist than is required and recieves a checklist or questionnaire covering only the most pertinent items. Use of either forms or checklists indicates to people that the campaign takes scheduling seriously; prospective hosts know what is expected of them. However, the scheduler should realize that many people are busy, lazy, apathetic, uncommitted to the candidate, or just undependable. These people may require a shorter form, or most of the information may have to be obtained by telephone; of course, the campaign with an advance staff has a major advantage in verifying details.[a]

Whether the campaign mails out questionnaires or checklists, or whether it gets much of its information over the telephone, it should prepare its own standard forms to record basic information. These forms (see Figures 11-1 and 11-2) can summarize the file for each event.

Responses

Any invitation should be acknowledged the day it is received. Even if the reply is not definitive (i.e., yes or no), it should acknowledge the invitation and indicate when a decision will be reached. In addition to this *interim* reply, the scheduler may wish to acknowledge the invitation by telephone to indicate the campaign's interest. If the invitation was written at the suggestion of someone, the scheduler may send that person a copy of the reply. If the invitation is by telephone, the scheduler will, if time permits, request an invitation in writing. Generally, any correspondence should not be signed by the candidate, but by the scheduler.[b]

Correspondence should be individually typed or on an automatic typewriter. In either case, the letter should be sufficiently personalized and should not appear to be a form (although it probably is an adaptation of one of several alternative forms used by the scheduling office.). The letter should refer to any prior correspondence or telephone calls, and it should always mention the invitation, especially the place, date, and time. The latter information avoids future confusion and could provide a useful index for filing purposes. If possible, the campaign should send a letter that confirms a telephone call in which an invitation was extended but, based on the information received, turned down in the same conversation.

Although the secretarial staff may prepare all response letters, the scheduler or a senior aide should review each letter before it is mailed. In addition, the office should prepare a daily or weekly summary of invitations

[a] Individuals who most resent the scheduler's requests for details are usually most likely to host a poorly conceived and executed event. Nevertheless, the scheduler must be persistent. The scheduler should not lower the campaign's standards to placate the local chairman who says "everything will work out."

[b] The local candidate may sign all scheduling correspondence prepared by the scheduling secretary. Although it is best to keep the candidate outside the scheduling process, some campaigns sign the candidate's name to acceptance letters, and the scheduler's to regrets. The safest policy is that all scheduling correspondence is signed by the scheduler.

or at least the important invitations. This summary can indicate whether the invitation was accepted, turned down, or is in the pending file. Larger campaigns sometimes maintain a card file to keep abreast of invitations, especially if copies of the invitation are being distributed to various campaign officials for comment. The card file is probably unnecessary if the scheduling filing system is efficient and includes appropriate forms in each event's file to summarize information. Regardless of the filing system, the summary keeps key campaign leaders and staff informed, so they are never embarrassed because they did not know about an invitation or the campaign's response.

Regrets. If the campaign is run properly, it stimulates far more invitations than the candidate can accept or many that do not meet the campaign's high standards. If an invitation will not be accepted, a letter of "regrets" should be mailed as soon as possible; this policy is simple courtesy. Delaying the news that the candidate will not attend a function does not make it more palatable and may be a hardship for the group that could spend the time looking for another speaker. Some delay is excusable if the campaign is truly uncertain or is making an effort to find a substitute speaker; however, it is best to keep the group informed not only of the reason for the delay but when the final reply can be expected.

The turndown letter, or letter of regrets, should be written carefully and skillfully. The scheduler should assume that any such letter can be part of the public record. Hence, its wording should be cordial and its response factual; vagueness is usually preferable to a misstatement of fact. The tone of the letter should make the recipient feel that the candidate and campaign were genuinely pleased and honored to receive the invitation and gave it most serious consideration. The regrets letter, if prompt, responsive, and graciously worded, can keep the campaign's supporters happy and make new friends.

Reasons. If an invitation does not meet the campaign's criteria or standards, this reason should probably not be stated directly in the letter. The safest language is that the invitation or proposal conflicts with "prior commitments"; note that the vague "prior commitments" is preferable to the specific "a prior commitment." An exception is when the criterion or standard can be stated succinctly and in an unoffensive manner or when the candidate will clearly be at another end of the country, state, county, or district, as appropriate. The specific conflicting engagement should probably not be mentioned, because the recipient of the letter may be jealous or question the campaign's judgment in allocating the candidate's time. This can even be true if the candidate is in another area; the person cannot understand why the candidate is scheduled in that city rather than his city.

Summary of Invitation or Event

Print information
in pencil if
subject to change.

File #: _____

Date form completed _____

By: _____

Updated (when/by whom)

1. ____ / ____
2. ____ / ____
3. ____ / ____
4. ____ / ____
5. ____ / ____

Date/Location of Event: _____

_____ _____ _____
Date   State   County   City/town/neighborhood

Time of event: _____
Title of Event: _____

Sponsor: _____

DATE INVITATION EXTENDED: _____

Type of event: Meal/banquet: Breakfast   Lunch   Dinner

Circle as appropriate

Fund Raising: Small Meeting   Reception   Banquet   Other: _____

Personal Campaigning: Coffee   Street and Merchant   Door to Door

Other: _____

Forum: Type of group: _____

Rally: Indoor   Outdoor   Capacity: _____

Tours: Type of facility: _____

OTHER OR ADDITIONAL INFORMATION: _____

Exact name of location or facility —————————————————

Precise address —————————————————

————————————————— City   State   Zip

ATTENDANCE: ———— PRICE PER TICKET: $ ——— CAPACITY: ———

Name of main contact ——————————— Telephones (o) ——— (h) ———

Title ——————— Mailing Address ———————

Name of alternate contact ——————— Telephones (o) ——— (h) ———

Title ——————— Mailing Address ———————

Person who extended invitation (if different than above)

Name ——————— Title ——————— Tel: (o) ——— (h) ———

Mailing Address ———————

List name of head of organization (if different than above)

Name ——————— Title ——————— Tel: (o) ——— (h) ———

Mailing Address ———————

Figure 11-1. Sample Internal Scheduling Form: Summary of Event.

Supporting Information for Scheduled Event

Event begins_____ ends_____ Candidate should arrive_____ depart_____

Purpose of event _____

Candidate's spouse invited _____ Family _____

Candidate's attire: White Tie   Black Tie   Business Suit   Casual   Other:_____

VIP's present: 1._____ 2._____ 3._____

4._____ 5._____ 6._____ 7._____

8._____ 9._____ 10._____

Head table comments (if different than above) _____

_____

Transportation—Method _____ Cost _____

Possible problems _____

Contingency reservations made as indicated below: _____

_____

_____

Lodging required for overnight visit: YES   NO

If yes, expected location _____ Tel.: _____

Address _____

Reservations made as indicated below: _____

Media coverage expected: _____

Staff contingent—candidate plus _____ staff, to include _____

Possible problems: POLICE _____ PERMITS _____ PERMISSIONS _____ OTHER: _____

Speech required: YES _____ NO _____ LENGTH: _____ Min: _____ Max: _____ Suggested: _____

Topic: _____ Include _____ Avoid: _____

RATING—YES, NO, NO OPINION

Local Chairman _____ Local Finance Chairman _____ Campaign Manager _____

RECOMMENDATION—Scheduling _____ Advance _____

Liaison required: YOUTH _____ FINANCE _____ NEWS _____ SUPPLIES _____ ADVERTISING _____

VOLUNTEER _____ RESEARCH _____ ADJUNCT COMMITTEE _____

Numbers and types of campaign materials needed _____

Figure 11-2. Sample Internal Scheduling Form: Supporting Information for Scheduled Event.

Once the turndown letter is mailed, the campaign is committed against the event. It is difficult, although sometimes possible, to resurrect the event, if the campaign's schedule changes or if new information suggests that the invitation should have been accepted. Schedule changes are unavoidable, but when new information casts doubt on the scheduler's original decision to reject the invitation, it suggests that perhaps the decision was rash. Hence, an invitation should not be turned down unless the scheduler is certain of the decision and reason. For example, do the date and time definitely conflict with another commitment—that is, is the information concerning the first event correct? Can the date or time of the first commitment be modified? If travel or lodging plans are changed, can the second invitation be accepted? Finally, if the second invitation is worthwhile, should it be turned down altogether because of conflict, or is there a possibility for negotiating a different date or time for it?

Whenever criteria or standards are involved, the scheduler should be certain he has all the necessary information. If the letter or telephone call inviting the candidate provides insufficient information, the scheduler should assign someone to get more information or to verify the points affecting the decision. If a single standard is involved (e.g., crowd size), the scheduler may wish to explain the problem to the person extending the invitation. Perhaps the event can be modified or enlarged, the location changed, or the date, time, ticket price, or some other variable affected. Here is where the scheduler's creativity can rescue a poorly conceived event destined for the regrets file and turn it into a success.[c]

The scheduler must also check with anyone else in the campaign who may have a special interest in the invitation. Perhaps it should be accepted for fund-raising purposes, or because the person extending it is an important political supporter. Obviously, standards cannot be waived indiscriminately, but sometimes other staff members can give the scheduler new input; for example, the youth division can comment on a college invitation. At the least, certain campaign leaders or staff should know about invitations that concern their area of responsibility and have a chance to comment on the merits of the invitation before it is turned down.

The scheduler always weighs the security of a vague regrets letter versus the greater credibility of a specific regrets letter. The specific reason, if stated inoffensively, tells the person that the invitation received serious consideration and that there was a reason for turning down the invitation. Each campaign must develop several form letters for turning down invitations; these forms reflect the scheduling policy of the campaign, but they also allow for adapting or personalizing the form, or for

[c] An activity that seems unlikely may have redeeming news value; yet, the news director will never know the option exists unless the discerning scheduler takes the initiative in seeking the counsel of the news director.

Exhibit 11-2
Text Suggestions for Regrets Letters

1. Thank you very much for your letter of _____ inviting me [Mr. Smith] to attend . . . .
2. Many thanks for your thoughtful invitation to Mr. Smith to . . . .
3. John Smith has given me your kind letter of _____ and asked me to thank you for your gracious invitation to . . . .
4. Your invitation was deeply appreciated . . . .
5. Mr. Smith greatly appreciated your kindness in inviting him . . . .
6. Your thoughtful invitation was most appreciated . . . .
7. Your kind invitation was most appreciated . . . .
8. We are grateful for your interest in the campaign . . . .

9. Unfortunately, Mr. Smith will be unable to accept your [kind, gracious] thoughtful invitation because . . . .
10. Unfortunately, Mr. Smith will be unable to attend the _____ because of prior commitments.
11. Mr. and Mrs. Smith deeply regret that prior commitments will prevent them from accepting your thoughtful invitation.
12. Your kind invitation would certainly have tempted Mr. Smith, but . . . .
13. Mr. Smith has asked me to convey to you his regrets at being unable to attend . . . .
14. Mr. Smith wishes he could join you and your colleagues at _____, but . . . .

15. Mr. Smith had asked me to give your invitation priority consideration.
16. Mr. Smith has asked our scheduling staff to give your proposal the most serious consideration.
17. I know how disappointed Mr. Smith is that prior commitments preclude his joining you in _____ on _____. Mr. Smith is keenly interested in _____ and would have been delighted to join you.
18. Mr. Smith would have liked to accept your fine invitation, but he is already committed for . . . .

19. Although prior commitments make it impossible for Mr. Smith to accept your invitation [attend your event/be with you and your colleagues/join you on . . . .], he hopes that he can send a personal representative in his place.
20. Mr. Smith is so disappointed that he is unable to be on hand at your annual _____, and he has asked me to assure you that the campaign will be sending a representative. If you believe it would be appropriate for this person to address the gathering . . . .

---

stating a specific, understandable reason ("Unfortunately, the commercial airplane schedule would require Mr. Smith to arrive in the morning for your evening commitment, and . . ."). In sum, the language of regrets letters is very important. (See Exhibit 11-2 for sample wordings.)

Follow-up. Many regrets letters will require some kind of follow-up activity. Although the letter should be so gracious and warm that it can be shown by the recipient to his colleagues or others on the program committee, the campaign may also wish to send a telegram to be read at the occasion. If so, a staff member must maintain a *futures* file for telegrams, so that the appropriate telegram is sent on time; it is important that the address be correct, especially if the telegram is to be delivered to someone the day of the event, perhaps while the person is at the event.

Another possibility is that the candidate will send someone in his behalf to deliver a message or short remarks. This may be a local person or someone sent from headquarters especially for the purpose. If the event is important, the campaign may try to convince the group to have a surrogate speaker—the candidate's spouse, a family member, someone who has endorsed the candidate, or someone from the campaign speakers bureau (if one exists).

Pending. Unless an invitation or proposal is accepted or rejected immediately, it receives an interim reply and is placed in the pending file. No letter should be put in the pending file before an acknowledgment or interim letter is mailed, a copy of which is included in the file. No correspondence should remain in this file indefinitely; each matter must have a deadline for reply and resolution. If this deadline cannot be met, it may have to be changed, and the group should be notified. Whatever the reason, an invitation should never be allowed to just stay in the file without receiving proper attention. The scheduler should also determine whether the delay caused by placing the matter in the pending file poses a hardship for the group; for example, a group may need an early reply because facilities have to be reserved, a speaker chosen, a date selected, and so forth. Ideally, the group and scheduler should agree on a deadline for the decision; the scheduler should never delay the decision until the last moment, but should try to reply as early as possible.

The pending file must be reviewed informally each day, and it should be reviewed weekly on a formal basis. Whenever the scheduling staff meets, or the senior campaign decision makers convene to review the progress of recent campaign events and decide on future events, each participant in the meeting should be given a summary of priority pending events. If the list is of all pending decisions, those that require decision at that meeting or are recommended strongly by the scheduler should be marked appropriately. The summary should include the salient facts about each invitation or proposal; if necessary, copies of the internal information summaries or the actual invitations may be distributed.

Invitations in the pending file either have clear merit or cannot be rejected without additional information. In many campaigns, almost every invitation is in the pending file because invitations are not decided individually, but considered together in a meeting held once or twice a week, or as the need arises. One reason for placing an invitation in the pending file is that the campaign is reluctant to become committed to a date or time too far in advance, especially if it involves the final phase or week of the campaign. Often, the campaign simply wants to check with its local leaders, or the scheduler wants to survey ranking staff members in the campaign head-quarters.

The pending file must distinguish between invitations for particular dates or times and open invitations ("Whenever you come to Buffalo, we would like you to consider speaking to our employees' luncheon forum"). Open invitations may be totally flexible or conditional ("Our luncheon forum is held every Thursday, and we only need one week's notice"). The *priority* pending file may indicate those invitations that require a quick decision, because the prospective host so requests, the scheduler must decide because other decisions are in the balance, or the scheduler is afraid of losing the option altogether.

Acceptances. Once an invitation is accepted, the event's file is reviewed immediately for thoroughness and accuracy. The scheduler notes what information is missing and anticipates possible problems. The scheduler knows what deadlines are imposed by the event, and he makes certain anyone affected by the deadlines is informed of the acceptance, if necessary, in advance of a formal campaign staff meeting. As the date of the event approaches, it receives progressively more attention; however, as soon as the event is accepted, hotel, airplane, and other reservations are made, and contingency plans are developed.

The scheduler confirms that the host group understands the conditions of acceptance, so there can be no misunderstanding later, when it is too late to alter the event or for the candidate to renege. Other individuals involved in the event may receive copies of the acceptance letter; however, the scheduler determines early the single individual who can represent and negotiate for the group. The group and this individual must understand at the outset the parameters of the commitment. These conditions should be detailed in the initial acceptance, an accompanying memorandum, or other written communications sent shortly after the acceptance. The group must understand when the candidate will arrive and leave; whether the candidate will speak, how long, and on what topic; and any other substantive matters. Both the group and the campaign must have the *same* interpretation of the conditions of acceptance. Also, if an advance man will be assigned to the event, the acceptance letter should so indicate; this letter or a subsequent one should state the name of the advance man and indicate clearly his responsibilities and authority, and the reason why the campaign is using an advance staff.

Files. The importance of files cannot be overemphasized. The campaign is fast moving, and decisions must be made quickly; the filing system should be accessible and understandable to anyone involved in scheduling. The scheduling operation should have such a well-organized filing system that if the scheduler or another member of the scheduling staff is absent, a substitute can find and use the information. The file for each event should include all relevant correspondence; copies of any printed invitation, advertising, or publicity for the event; and memoranda concerning relevant telephone conversations (see Figure 11-3). The telephone memoranda are important, since the fast moving campaign must use the telephone for seeking information, negotiations, and give and take.

Ideally, a copy is made of a letter as soon as it arrives to be used in the event the original is misplaced. (The well-staffed scheduling operation keeps a log book to "register" every letter and note its ultimate disposition—regrets, pending, acceptance). As the campaign moves to within about a week of an event, its file is probably moved from the acceptance to the *current* file. Since the current file is often an open filing system on top of a desk to permit accessibility, the scheduling office must be neat and orderly; otherwise the most urgent files are misplaced.

Except for the acceptance file, which is usually filed by date, both the regrets and pending files usually embody duplicate filing systems involving photocopying and possibly color coded carbons. The date filing system or subdivision includes specific dates or the open category. The other two subdivisions are alphabetical (by name of person or organization, or cross referenced) and geographical (the appropriate level for the campaign—state, county, city). These subdivisions are important, because they enable the scheduler to retrieve a file quickly even if only part of the information is known. Even regrets files are often valuable—either for follow-up or surrogate activity—because the turndown was controversial or is being reconsidered or simply because the campaign schedule or circumstances have changed and the scheduler may want to change a regret into an acceptance, if possible.

Authority

The scheduling operation must have a single person in charge; this individual's discretionary authority is defined by the campaign manager. The tour director makes most decisions, except in certain preestablished areas. At the other extreme, the scheduling secretary in the local campaign may be little more than a glorified clerk. However, the efficient campaign manager always finds a competent scheduler, even for the local campaign, and entrusts that person with maximum responsibility and commensurate authority. The scheduler's effectiveness is based on his authority; no one—the campaign manager, finance chairman, even the candidate—should schedule commitments without checking with the scheduler.

The scheduler operates the central clearing house of schedule informa-

Memorandum of Telephone Conversation

FOR FILE _____

Day _____ Date _____ Time _____ AM/PM _____ Length of call _____ (min)

Conversation with _____ Telephone (o) _____

Representing _____ Telephone (h) _____

Title _____

Representing campaign _____

Who initiated call? _____

_____

If no file exists on event, use *Summary of Invitation or Event* and attach; otherwise, summarize points raised and commitments made below.

Figure 11-3. Sample Telephone Memorandum Form.

tion; any proposals, invitations, schedule changes must be cleared through this individual, or someone with the responsibility and authority to act in his absence. Unlike the news operation, the scheduler and his staff often deal directly with individuals and groups outside the campaign. Although many campaign division chiefs—the finance chairman, youth chairman—or adjunct committee or local committee chairmen may refer inquiries or proposals to scheduling, individuals and groups who telephone the campaign headquarters can be routed immediately to scheduling. This is acceptable, since the scheduling staff is instructed not to give out confidential information, nor can it make commitments over the telephone. In the larger scheduling operations, one receptionist or secretary may specialize in routing or handling such telephone calls, just as another person may specialize in transportation and hotel arrangements; the Level A campaign may have a traffic manager who oversees the campaign plane and all other travel logistics.

The authority of the scheduler can be summarized as follows: only one person, the scheduler, has the authority to commit the candidate. Anyone else who promises to deliver the candidate is undermining the authority and *effectiveness* of the scheduler, just as anyone who speaks for the candidate undermines the authority of the news director and compromises the news operation.

Liaison

Scheduling, like the news media operation, is effective only if it is coordinated with the rest of the campaign. This means that scheduling must establish a system so that key staff members receive copies of the candidate's long-term schedule. Each time a copy is distributed, the staff member exchanges or destroys the outdated copy. Each new, updated schedule summary should be issued at least once every two weeks. The campaign manager personally approves any person on the distribution list for both this summary (or its weekly counterpart) and the candidate's daily internal schedule. The distribution is always by hand delivery; copies are never left on the recipient's desk. By distributing these materials, as well as personal memoranda to division heads regarding specific events, the scheduler encourages input. Unless the staff knows the schedule and its changes, it cannot make suggestions. Formal and informal liaison must be thorough (see Exhibit 11-3).

Preparing the Schedule

The schedule distributed to the media is the official campaign schedule; it emphasizes public events, avoids confidential information of concern to the candidate or staff, and includes special instructions to the media regarding transportation, lodging, or communications. In contrast, the schedule prepared by the tour or scheduling office is considered the *internal* schedule; it is longer than the public schedule because it has so much more information, such as names of car drivers or passenger rosters for each car. If the schedule becomes too cumbersome, the reader is referred to additional briefing materials, sometimes in an attached addendum. Detailed issue briefings are usually separate; very personal or sensitive information may also be apart from the schedule, perhaps in the candidate's daily briefing summary, where the topics can be itemized by event. In Level A campaigns, a single individual oversees the briefing. In addition, every candidate should receive a set of index cards (3″ by 5″ or 4″ by 6″) that list the schedule, by event, and what is expected of the candidate, especially length and type of speech or remarks.[d]

Calendar and Notebook

The scheduler and staff use a large, wall-mounted calendar to view an entire month at a glance. The calendar is covered with acetate, so that staff members can use grease pencils to write and cloth to erase. Also mounted on the wall are large maps of geographical and political (district) boundaries, highways, and airline routes. Since this room is the scheduling nerve center, it is accessible only to scheduling staff and others with a need to know. If guests are expected, the calendars are covered. These calendars should be removable from their frame so they can be taken to strategy or scheduling meetings.

The importance of the filing system is underscored by the scheduler's personal notebook (or, if necessary, two notebooks). This notebook, usually in a large loose leaf binder, is always at the scheduler's side or locked in a cabinet or safe. It contains the summary of the candidate's schedule, on a daily basis, as well as excerpts principally from the acceptances file. If more than one sheet is required for a day, each sheet has a page number and total number of pages ("page 2 of 4"). The worksheets should provide plenty of room between entries; often, ink is used for definite commitments and pencil for speculative entries. The scheduler may also use another color ink or code to indicate events that have been definitely confirmed (i.e., an acceptance letter has been sent), although pen/pencil is probably the superior system. Although the scheduler tries to keep this notebook updated, the detailed files for each event may provide even more elaborate and itemized schedules.

The scheduler knows that in addition to his notebook and the wall

---

[d] The candidate on an extended tour may have the cards prepared by the traveling entourage; the cards are based on the complete schedule communicated by telecopier.

Exhibit 11-3
Scheduling Liaison

1. *Candidate*. The candidate must know the aggregate amount of time committed in his behalf, the composition of the schedule, the additional briefing, research, and speechwriting requirements generated, and any possible problems.

2. *Campaign Manager*. The person on top of the campaign must know future commitments and where the candidate is. The campaign manager or someone he delegates is responsible for insuring that many of the individuals listed below are given definite, specific assignments arising out of the schedule, and they perform their assignments. He must know the schedule and changes as early as possible to decide which campaign staff members must be assigned to travel with the candidate, perform research, writing speeches, and so forth.

3. *News Director*. The news operation must gauge the media value of all events, know what time is available for media events, and prepare its own schedule and deadlines for various types of news releases. The news operation must also produce the campaign's official schedule for the media.

4. *Traveling Entourage*. Any staff member on the permanent traveling entourage or any staff member who may be needed for a specific tour or event must be aware of the schedule. This includes a single aide for the small campaign who does everything; for larger campaigns, there may be a personal aide, driver, news director or other press aide, researcher, writer, political aide, secretary, political or media consultant, photographer, security aide, one or two advance staff. For most statewide campaigns, the traveling entourage should be 2 to 5 persons, based on the size of the state and intensity of the particular tour.

5. *Candidate's Family*. The spouse and family members need to know the schedule, especially if they will be surrogates. The campaign must establish a policy early regarding joint and separate appearances; the latter are preferable because they allow for more extensive use of family members.

6. *Advance*. If advance is distinct from scheduling, the director of advance or chief advance man must be apprised of each new commitment so he can assign someone to it or to implement changes.

7. *Research*. The research director may need to provide material on areas to be visited, or data and analyses on subjects or issues likely to be raised in particular areas or at certain forums.

8. *Speechwriting*. The speechwriter needs access to the scheduling files not only to know what events require speeches and their length, but to have as much background as possible to prepare appropriate remarks; he also interacts with research and news.

9. *Materials and Supplies*. This section must know how much and what kinds of materials must be delivered or shipped for particular events, the deadline for delivery and the name and address of the recipient; sometimes, new materials may have to be printed or ordered.

10. *Divisions*. Each division of the campaign must be apprised not only of that part of the schedule most relevant to it, but of the entire schedule, since its staff may have ideas or see opportunities unapparent to others. These divisions include finance, youth, and any other parts of the central campaign headquarters.

11. *Adjunct Committees*. These specialized committees should be given an opportunity to comment on proposals, invitations, or parts of the schedule pertaining to their constituency or subject area (veterans, lawyers, doctors, senior citizens, and so forth); they may also initiate meritorious schedule proposals.

12. *Local Committees*. Schedulinq must interact with local chairmen to get information and ideas, especially when going into their areas.

13. *Political/Organization*. The political staff assists the campaign manager in evaluating the political implications of the schedule, negotiating endorsements, forming local and adjunct committees, and handling other commitments possibly requiring the candidate's time.

14. *Surrogates*. The scheduling staff must screen invitations for surrogate opportunities; an active surrogate or speakers bureau program requires at least one additional clerical staff member to book speakers. Also, the program requires liaison with research in order to be responsible for producing a briefing book on the candidate and on issues; this resource book is a must even for bright, informed speakers.

15. *Advertising Agency*. For the major campaign, certain activities may present excellent opportunities for still photographs, audio recording, or filming, for possible commercials. Also, advertising may be used to generate attendance.

16. *Political Party/Other Candidates*. The candidate's party leaders and other candidates running on the same ticket may be given the schedule as a courtesy, or to help coordinate common appearances; however, caution is exercised in distributing the entire schedule; a summary is preferred.

Note: Some of the campaign division heads may participate in formal meetings that review the schedule; others may simply receive memoranda or summaries. Particular divisions may receive information on a need-to-know basis (e.g., a deputy campaign manager may meet with the materials and supplies coordinator to decide on campaign materials shipments for events). Finally, liaison with the political party or other candidates may be cautious, since the candidate does not want his complete long-term schedule known to those outside the official campaign organization.

calendar, all of the detailed files for a given day must be reviewed and integrated for the preparation of a master schedule for that day. The master schedules for several days must then be combined and summarized so that the news division can issue a schedule news release as promptly and as far in advance of the included days as possible. The efficient news director is always pressing the scheduler for enough information to issue a new campaign schedule.

Another important section of the notebook is the scheduler's summary of the campaign's remaining days. While this summary is much more detailed than the wall calendar that is concerned with the "big picture," it is perhaps not as detailed as the worksheets. Once a week or every two weeks (and sometimes more often if this summary becomes too messy from corrections or just becomes too outdated), a new summary is prepared. The format is the same: more than one day per page, but with plenty of white space between typewritten entries and with special emphasis on major events, airplane and other travel plans, and overnight stops. Whenever a new typewritten summary is prepared, it is distributed to staff members who have been approved by the campaign manager; they can also use the white space between entries to pen in additions. When they receive a new summary, the old one is discarded. Since the summary covers the period from the day after issuance through the end of the campaign, the scheduler or anyone else using it for reference tears off sheets as the days pass.

The calendar, scheduling worksheets (usually on lined paper), and typewritten summary always indicate clearly those days that are reserved for the candidate's rest, family time, debate preparation, or any other "untouchables." None of these materials has as much information (for example, names of contacts, telephone numbers, history of information) as the file for each individual event. When the final daily schedule is typewritten, the information is integrated, checked, and rechecked.

Final Schedule

The final schedule reflects the shrewdness and experience of the scheduler, and it can only be as accurate and thorough as he is realistic. The schedule's validity is tested every time the candidate campaigns. Is he punctual or habitually late? Although it is fashionable to blame the advance staff, the candidate, local supporters, or unanticipated events, the scheduler is ultimately responsible. Of course, the absurd way for the schedule to be on time is for it to be so loosely constructed that too much time is allowed for each activity. But this results in a major misallocation of the candidate's time.

Whether the schedule is advanced in person or by telephone, the scheduler must determine absolutely exact times for every component of the schedule, no matter how minor the component. The scheduler trusts no one and always verifies information given; if the host says it is a ten minute ride from the airport to the hotel, the advance man times the ride at the same time of day; if there is no advance man, the scheduler asks another person who knows the area, route, and traffic conditions. If there is the slightest conflict, the scheduler pursues the matter. The scheduler knows that if several small items or components of the schedule are each a few minutes late, the schedule is soon thirty minutes late for that period; if each subsequent period is thirty minutes late, the end of the day is a disaster.

The scheduler builds the schedule around the candidate; hence, everything must be in readiness when he arrives at an event; if the candidate is delayed, the schedule is delayed. When the candidate is ready to leave, the car and driver must be ready. In order to be ready, preparations must begin five, ten, or fifteen minutes before departure time. The schedule also considers every possible cause for delay, such as extra applause, photographs, autographs, or a quick conversation with the host before leaving. Because the candidate's advance and traveling staff know the schedule, the candidate is unconcerned; even if he is accompanied by only one aide, it is that person's responsibility to move the candidate in and out of events. This person or the advance man knows the following two principles:

1. *The candidate cannot be two places simultaneously.* If departure from the hotel is scheduled for 10 p.m., then departure from the banquet

hall must be at 9:55, and since this may mean allowing another five minutes for small talk, autographs, or other delays, the program must end at 9:50. The amateur scheduler equates the 10 p.m. departure time with concluding the program; the experienced scheduler knows that 10 p.m. departure means the car departs at that time. Hence, at 10 p.m., the car must be parked in an unblocked position with the driver ready, and the candidate must step from the hotel exit directly into the adjacent, waiting car; thus, the driver must be ready before 10 p.m.

2. *The schedule must have built in cushions.* If an airplane is scheduled to arrive at 10 a.m. and driving time from the airport is one half hour, when can the candidate meet someone in the hotel suite? The novice says 10:30. The experienced scheduler checks the airline's punctuality record for that route; calculates the time required to walk from the gate to the car (and arranges to have one waiting to avoid delay); *then*, after verifying that the thirty-minute driving time is correct, he adds this to the equation; finally the scheduler computes the time for the candidate to go from the car to the hotel suite (assuming preregistration prevents any delay and that the car driver has the key to the suite).[e]

It is impossible for the schedule to be too detailed, or to be checked too frequently. Staff resources permitting, the schedule should be typed and retyped, until it is absolutely accurate and neat. Neatness is a discipline that makes the schedule easier to understand and follow and makes errors easier to spot. Inept schedulers fear the neat, typewritten schedule, because it is easy to spot their failures. Indeed, part of the debriefing for any trip is to review the schedule for any tardiness. The candidate's aide always puts a check mark next to each time on the schedule if it proves correct; he crosses out the time and substitutes the actual time if it is proven wrong. In a good campaign, the scheduler should be on time or occasionally up to ten or fifteen minutes late; time cushions inserted into the schedule should permit the campaign to catch up to its original schedule very quickly.

There is only one excuse for the schedule being substantially late: extremely bad weather. Even here, the campaign should have contingency plans to minimize delay.

Although most of the other scheduling tips are included within the following chapters on advance work, the preparation of the scheduling must reflect certain basic guidelines (Exhibit 11-4). Additional requirements are listed under appropriate subject headings in the final chapters. The internal (detail) schedule (Figure 11-4) incorporates the basic guidelines and requirements.

The novice scheduler is never on time; the experienced scheduler is rarely, if ever, late. When the schedule is formulated, it emphasizes realism

---

[e] Often, it is prudent to round off each time increment to the nearest five minutes. For example, if it takes three minutes to walk from the banquet hall to the waiting car, allow five minutes for a full time cushion.

Exhibit 11-4
Guidelines for the Final Schedule

1. Each entry has been reviewed by appropriate campaign staff; controversial items have been reviewed by both campaign manager and candidate.

2. The schedule is complete, specific, detailed, and accurate; it includes each item in the exact sequence (e.g., Invocation, Pledge of Allegiance, National Anthem) and indicates the person responsible (individual giving Invocation, leading Pledge of Allegiance, and so forth).

3. Each entry shows the complete location and telephone number; after the first full entry, subsequent entries show the precise location, floor of building, name of room, and so on; telephone numbers always permit instant communication with candidate or traveling entourage at any time, and the numbers are verified to be operational during the time of the event. The schedule is proofread carefully after typing.

4. The schedule notes the person responsible for keeping the schedule moving, (e.g., Master of Ceremonies) or for event preparations (e.g., host or hostess); this person and any others who can affect the time element must be briefed—that is, any person on the program knows how much time is allotted for his segment.

5. The candidate's arrival and departure time for each segment is clearly shown, with destination listed after each departure; the schedule includes cushions to allow for movement in and out of events. The schedule always shows who meets the candidate at each arrival point or stop.

6. The schedule indicates by their initials the staff members who will accompany the candidate, especially if the composition changes during the day; it also indicates any volunteer chairman, supporter, host, and so forth who will accompany the candidate. The candidate is always escorted by an appropriate person or persons who can introduce him and who are fully briefed on the schedule.

7. The time factor is rechecked so that the amount of time listed for each phase of the schedule is realistic, and the schedule has built-in flexibility to allow for inevitable delays; if these delays are anticipated, they do not compromise the schedule.

8. Each part of the schedule is again verified, after typing, to make sure the name and purpose of event are correct; the day, date, time, location, and telephone number are accurate; and any new location involving other than a room change shows a new address and telephone number. Each event must show a person in charge or the name of the contact, together with relevant telephone numbers.

9. After retyping, the travel components—airplane, car, and so on,—are reviewed again to verify that all information is listed, and every segment of the schedule, including brief car trips, is covered by an assigned driver and car.

10. The test of the final schedule is whether it is final; it has been explained to everyone involved in it (i.e., any person mentioned understands his role, responsibility, and time limitations); the candidate understands each item, and no major commitments were made without his approval; and each participant in the schedule has a copy of it or the portion applicable to him, including the latest changes.

Note: Also see Guidelines for Schedule News Releases (Exhibit 5-2); for elaboration on specific points discussed here, see the following chapters, especially the discussion of *travel* and *lodging*.

and punctuality; it is not *destined* to be late. The obvious sign of inept scheduling is a schedule clearly constructed in a dream world; each time segment typifies the scheduler's wishful thinking.

Tuesday, Oct. 19 (continued)
David Kreps, Advance

5:35 P.M.	Arrive KNXT-TV (CBS) NOTE: Arrive at SE Gate; 5800 Sunset Boulevard guard already alerted. Los Angeles CONTACT: Ray Chandler, producer (213-462-8000; 462-8021, 24) NOTE: HJ stays with candidate or near candidate.
5:40-5:45	Make up (adjacent to Studio C)
5:50-5:55	Pre interview discussion with George Marker (who will conduct live interview
5:56-6:05	Candidate reviews notes
6:06	In position for live interview
6:08-6:14	Scheduled live interview on "Six O'Clock News"
6:15-6:25	Take off make up, miscellaneous goodbyes.
6:30	Depart KNXT for Harold Grosline residence (3 cars, same passenger roster)
7:00	Arrive Harold Grosline residence 8301 Charlton Way Beverly Hills 213-652-0238 (NOTE: Reception open to media, but campaign not pushing it; probably only 2-3 major reporters attending.)

7:05	Join $50 a person reception (in progress from 6:30)
	   SEE ATTACHED BRIEFING for HTS. HANDSHAKER, escorted by Groslines.
	   (Expected turnout: 60) No remarks.

7:30	Depart reception for Majestic Hotel Auto A: Rex Peters, driver (213-348-7354-o; 873-0113-h) Passengers: HTS, Harold Grosline, Sally Grosline Auto B: George Brocker, driver (213-334-8000-o; 934-4990-h) Passengers: Staff--HJ, GR, SQ + Kreps Auto C: Peter Brocker, driver (son of George) Passengers: back up car in case needed for reporters; if so, this will become second car, and HJ will ride with reporters

8:15
Dick Dunnell
   and Dave Kreps,
   Advance
	Arrive Majestic Hotel for South Bay Republican Dinner
	8454 Via Tejon
	Palos Verdes (Mrs. Ralph Jackson, Chairperson:
	213-347-8567 o-347-3022; h-347-9887, 8344)
	
	Met by: Dunnell (at Towers Entrance)
	               --more--

Note: This illustration shows part of the third page of an internal (detail) schedule for the period of October 18-22 (five days). This schedule is distributed only to a limited number of campaign staff members.

Figure 11-4. Internal (Detail) Schedule.

12 Fundamentals of Advance

Advance work is the detailed planning, study, and verification of the candidate's travels and movements. The advance man or advance person confers personally with everyone involved in the schedule to insure that all arrangements are in order and the event occurs exactly as planned. Advancing, in its classic definition, is at least one trip to the location or site of the activity or event before the day of the "drill." The advance man literally walks the exact steps the candidate is expected to take; whenever driving is involved, the advancing is done at the same time of day the candidate will travel. During the drill itself, the advance man precedes the candidate by a few steps, as he confidently leads the way along the course he has charted.

If a campaign cannot afford an advance staff or cannot find volunteers to advance the candidate, the schedule is advanced by mail and telephone. *Mail* advance uses letters, memoranda, questionnaires, and checklists to explain the campaign's needs and verify details. *Telephone* advance requires the scheduler to ask probing questions over the telephone to evaluate the schedule for accuracy and thoroughness. Although mail and telephone advance are not real advance work, because they do not involve at least one preliminary visit to the site in advance of the drill, they can be useful, if the scheduler can easily discern possible problems and knows exactly what questions to ask.

Theory of Advance

The theory of advance is that there is only one reliable way to verify every entry and movement on the candidate's schedule—that is, by visiting the site of activity, inspecting the facilities, and tracing the candidate's anticipated itinerary by walking and driving the route personally. The advance man compares the planned or draft schedule with the reality he encounters; if the schedule includes blocks of time to fill, or time "opens up," he uses his experience, imagination, and skills to work with local supporters to construct the optimum schedule. Unlike the scheduler, who often relies on a third party (e.g., the dinner chairman insists the hotel can serve the banquet meal in sixty minutes), the advance man can confer with the banquet manager and maitre'd. When the advance man personally meets each individual who has a role in the candidate's schedule, he can judge his or her stability, dependability, and dedication. Based on the conversation, the advance man decides whether the individual has the competence to get the task done and then outlines the standards, goals, and guidelines to help do the job.

The job of advance is, by definition, never done; there is no limit to thoroughness. The schedule can always be improved; details can always be checked again. If the advance man truly felt the drill was flawless—that is, the schedule maximized the candidate's time and every detail was in place—then he could spend more time with local leaders to gather information that might be incorporated in the candidate's briefing. If he still had time, and everything was in order, he could join the volunteers in preparing for the candidate's arrival or in making telephone calls, selling tickets, blowing up balloons, putting up decorations, or anything else to help boost attendance or make the drill a success.

Advance work has several limitations. If the campaign is managed poorly, the news operation is ineptly run, or the candidate turns people off, the advance man cannot compensate for such deficiencies. Like the news director or tour director, the advance man is circumscribed by overall campaign strategy. If a poorly conceived strategy puts the candidate in an area or before a group that represents a low-priority use of his time, the advance man can only make the best of a bad situation. Thus, the advance man can suggest changes or modifications of the schedule within the limits of the commitment already made; the campaign is rarely in a position to renege. Generally, the advance man suggests reasonable changes instead of "scrubbing" (cancelling) the drill, and the tour director or campaign manager accept the recommendations.

Policy

The advance man is the official campaign representative and the personal representative of the candidate. Every campaign division—finance, youth, research, supplies and materials—must channel communications relevant to the drill through the assigned advance man; either they inform him or he takes the initiative to learn their relationship to the drill and then monitor their activities. Once the advance man is assigned to the drill, the scheduler or campaign manager makes no changes without working through, or informing, the advance man. No one in the campaign headquarters contradicts the advance man, nor does he ever contradict or criticize a campaign staff member. Differences are settled privately; the campaign must present a united front.

The advance man's responsibility to the candidate supersedes his responsibility to anyone or to any group. This includes the local campaign chairmen, any elected officials, important religious or ethnic leaders, or major financial supporters—*anyone*. Many campaigns will not use someone to advance a drill in his own area, because his local ties and friendships may be liabilities, rather than assets. The advance man gives the candidate undivided loyalty; the local advance man must understand and accept this condition. He must never forget that the local committee chairman or host will assert that the proposed schedule is in the candidate's interest, but they are preoccupied with their own status. They usually want more of the candidate's time than necessary, and they are unlikely to use the time effectively.

The advance man should always seek compromise rather than confrontation. He should try to effect a compromise acceptable to everyone, but on certain matters for which established campaign policy and standards provide no exceptions, the advance man must be firm. The advance man's compromise may be unacceptable to some persons involved in the drill, but it can *never* be unacceptable or inimical to the interests of the candidate.

The advance man never intrudes in a local or internal dispute unless doing so is absolutely essential to his mission. He cannot allow conflict and dissension to disrupt the unity and team work needed for a successful drill. However, he should not intervene to tell the local chairman or others who will introduce the candidate or who should sit at the head table. The best policy is to let the local chairman or committee make these decisions, unless the advance man is instructed to convey the campaign's preference. Although the advance man wants the best possible head table selection and the individual most liked and respected to introduce the candidate, he cannot do more than make suggestions, unless he is authorized otherwise; often, even suggestions can prove too controversial.

Relationship to Candidate. The advance man must be compatible with the candidate. This does not imply a personality match; indeed, the introverted candidate may require an extroverted advance man. Compatibility means the advance man is sensitive and responsive to the candidate's personal needs and that he never says or does anything to make the candidate feel uncomfortable. The advance man always projects stability and confidence. Unless he seems in control of the situation, the candidate will be nervous and apprehensive. The advance man, even in the midst of crisis, keeps his "cool."

Whether the advance man visits the site of the drill once, or several times, his sole concern is what is best for the candidate. He always looks for the most favorable ratio of the time invested by the candidate and the results obtained. To achieve any given objective, the advance man wants to minimize the increment of candidate's time; for any given increment of time, the advance man wants maximum results. When the advance man is with the candidate during the drill, he *enforces* the schedule, because he knows that even the most precise drill can be compromised at the last moment by carelessness. The advance man's enforcement of the drill is always subject to the authority and direction of someone accompanying the candidate. However, only one person on the candidate's traveling staff entourage should overrule the advance man; other staff members should work through this designated person, often termed the field or traveling tour director. This person is the ultimate enforcer of the schedule.

During the drill the advance man observes certain rules established by the tour director or chief advance man. These rules vary from campaign to campaign, and they are modified if there is more than one advance man, or if the number of traveling staff or security considerations present unique problems. The candidate understands, unless the rules are modified, that he follows the path of the advance man, who usually precedes the candidate by at least six feet. Alternatively, the candidate is escorted by the ranking staff member or another aide who, in turn, follows the advance man's lead. Whatever the procedure, it is known and understood by all involved *before* the drill begins. The candidate must grasp that the only way for the drill to go smoothly is to follow the advance man. He knows the exact schedule and how to keep to it; he is uniquely able to anticipate what lies ahead and to cope with any contingency. The advance man's judgment is rarely, if ever, in question; his dedication and loyalty to the candidate are *never* in question.

The advance man is always with or near the candidate during the drill unless he is advancing the next entry on the schedule. For example, while the candidate is "working" the reception, the advance man is insuring that everything is ready in the banquet room; while the candidate is eating, the advance man is monitoring the progress in serving the meal and again reviewing the sound and lighting arrangements for the program; while the candidate is speaking, the advance man is insuring that the driver and the car are in place and ready for the scheduled departure. The advance man leaves the immediate vicinity of the candidate only if:

1. The part of the drill in which the candidate is involved is proceeding smoothly and according to plan; for example, the candidate is circulating throughout the reception, he is eating his meal, or his speech is being received well.

2. The advance man notifies the field or traveling tour director, or other designated staff member where and how long he will be and when he will return.

3. The advance man returns well before the time for the candidate to move to the next point of the schedule, unless the advance man and designated staff member have agreed on an alternative plan; for example,

the advance man stays with the driver and car, and the designated staff member or another aide who knows the route moves the candidate from the banquet room to the departure point.[a]

The advance man does not talk to the candidate unless the candidate asks a question or the discussion is essential. Often, campaign policy is for the advance man to communicate with the candidate through the ranking staff person or other aide, who must judge whether the matter requires the candidate's time or attention. The advance man does not interrupt the candidate's conversation or thought to brief him on later activities, unless the matter is urgent; it rarely is, however, since most can be solved at a staff level. The advance man is supposed to keep the practical problems of campaigning from the candidate so he can concentrate solely on campaigning and the people he meets. When the advance man does talk to the candidate, he may be more respectful than in other conversation, but one characteristic describes the advance man's conversation with everyone. The advance man is calm. Internally, he may be worried, nervous, and upset about logistical problems and keeping the schedule on time, but he knows he can get the job done. He acts and talks in such a way that the candidate, and everyone else, shares this confidence.

Relationship to Media. The advance man is low profile. He gets the job done efficiently, methodically, and *quietly*. He does not seek credit or publicity. He wants the candidate to occupy center stage, perhaps while sharing the spotlight with the local chairman or hosts, but never with the advance man or other staff. The advance man wants to get publicity for the candidate and the activities and events that comprise the drill, but not publicity for himself or any controversy or disputes involved in preparations for the drill.

Before the advance man arrives on the scene, he explains to the local chairman that his visit is private. He avoids any encounters with the news media; if, despite all precautions, he meets an editor or reporter, he is cordial, but not loquacious. He indicates that he is an advance man preparing for the candidate's trip, and he arranges for the news director or an authorized local spokesperson to get in touch with the journalist. If the advance man is requested by the news director to deal with the news media, he acts within those limits. However, the advance man usually does not contact media directly but relies on the local chairman, publicity or public relations chairman, or local staff to arrange publicity. The advance man insures that someone has this responsibility, or he makes the assignment with the concurrence of the campaign news operation. He may supply

---

[a] When two (or more) advance men are used for a drill, one is senior. In a two-man advance, one is 5-10 feet ahead of the candidate, the other at the next point on the schedule or, in a major crowd situation, farther ahead in the route.

thorough media lists and form releases, but he usually does not call anyone or issue any releases.

Authority

Although the advance man is, in effect, a representative of the campaign scheduling operation, there are important differences between the advance man and tour director or scheduler. The scheduler is concerned with the entire campaign schedule, and the advance man is concerned just with his drill. The scheduler is based at the headquarters, and the advance man physically visits and inspects the site and times the candidate's anticipated movements. The advance man acquires a special "feel" for the drill because he personally visited the site and established rapport with everyone involved in the drill. Finally, the advance man will be present at the drill, while the scheduler will be in the campaign headquarters.[b]

The advance man's authority is not undercut by the candidate or campaign staff. If the dissatisfied local chairman calls the campaign headquarters, the caller is treated courteously and graciously, but not at the advance man's expense. After the call, the tour director or campaign manager finds out the facts from the advance man, who is usually right. The advance man then gets back to the caller, or either the tour director or campaign manager calls the local chairman and explains that the advance man will handle the problem. Ideally, any senior staff person contacted by a disgruntled chairman is already briefed on the situation; otherwise, he gets a report from the advance man before returning the call.

When an advance man is on the road preparing for the drill, he usually takes his direction from a single person—the tour director or chief advance man. Even the campaign manager or news director communicates with the advance man through his boss, unless agreed otherwise. Exceptions are often outlined in the campaign's advance manual; for example, the news director may work directly with the advance man in arranging certain media activities or in verifying the local committee's publicity plans.

During the drill, the advance man no longer takes his orders from the tour director, but from the field or traveling tour director or ranking staff person on the scene, unless another member of the traveling staff is designated as liaison with the advance man. In the major presidential campaign, the tour director has a counterpart who always travels with the candidate

[b] In some cases, the tour director may personally attend a drill to see things from the "outside." Similarly, the chief advance man will personally monitor some drills to avoid being insulated; also, he will probably supervise the advance team for the campaign's most important drills.

and who, during the drill, has authority over the advance man. Regardless of the arrangement, if the advance man is competent and has done his job, no one will question his cues or directions. Before contravening the advance man, the ranking staff member or designated traveling tour director will always ask the advance man for additional information; he usually knows something they do not. If there are any differences, they are *always* settled privately, never in front of the candidate, local chairmen or host, or reporters.

Even the most efficient campaign must deviate from the planned schedule when absolutely unpredictable opportunities or crises occur. For example, a major wire service story may cause reporters to track down the candidate for a reaction statement, and they may delay the schedule; alternatively, they may request a news conference or availability. Perhaps bad weather causes the commercial or campaign plane to be thirty minutes late. In either case, the schedule, no matter how much it emphasizes time cushions to permit some leeway, may require modification. The advance man knows the options and alternative plans; he does not make the decision, but only presents the alternatives and may make a recommendation. The field tour director or designated staff member decides what to do. If the news media must be called, or the next appointment cancelled, delayed, or shortened, the advance man executes the contingency plan.

Unless the candidate is accompanied by someone with superior judgment and clear decisiveness who can work with an energetic advance man who has mastered the drill, the campaign will be victimized by a rigid schedule unable to adapt to change. Someone must tell the candidate when to consider lengthening or shortening prepared remarks, when to include or drop certain issues or sections. Unless the candidate's aide knows what he is doing, the drill may go well, but it will be far from optimum. It will not exploit all of the unforeseen opportunities that presented themselves once the drill was underway.

Administering Advance

There are several levels of advance work, in addition to the improvised correspondence/telephone method. *Light* advance means that an advance man makes a single visit and runs through the drill; it assumes that the schedule is substantially set, and no problems are unanticipated. *Medium* advance involves some shaping of the schedule on the advance man's part; it suggests some problems and usually involves large public gatherings. It can involve two or even three visits to the site. *Heavy* advance requires at least two advance men and several trips; it usually includes arrangements for a large traveling entourage of staff and reporters, and greater attention to security problems. *Presidential* advance includes Secret Service arrangements. [c]

Regardless of the type of advance, or the structure or level of campaign, the theory of advance is unchanged. The advance man is the on-site representative of the campaign. He must understand the principles of scheduling thoroughly, especially their relationship to the criteria and standards of the specific campaign. Unless he understands the campaign's strategic priorities and the candidate's specific requirements for private time (Exhibit 10-3), the advance man cannot do his job. The administrator of advance (i.e., the tour director or chief advance man) must constantly review the advance man's proposed schedule to insure that any public activities are worthwhile expenditures of the candidate's time and do not preclude private time for rest, personal needs, briefings, speech preparation, telephone calls, and so forth.

Procedure

The major political campaign outlines its procedures in an *Advance Manual* given to each paid or volunteer advance man for his personal use. This manual, which applies the principles and techniques of advance work to the specific campaign, is the advance man's most valuable possession. It proceeds from theory to listing all the priorities, details, and methods for each type of drill, with sensitive discussion about the relationship between the campaign and the local committee, adjunct committees, the political party, and other campaigns. The manual includes the names, titles, and responsibilities of headquarters and traveling staff; it includes all relevant office and home telephone numbers, especially of local campaign and party chairmen. Although each campaign has its own standard operating plan (Exhibit 12-1), the rules of common sense always apply.

The advance man never meets with a committee or group before meeting privately with the local committee chairman or cochairmen. If this person is not the campaign's local political contact, he may meet privately with the key political contact first. The private meetings are more open and candid than the group meetings, which can be lengthy and unproductive. The advance man must project leadership and authority in the group meeting, but he cannot do so unless he first asserts himself in the private meeting. The private meeting gives the advance man the opportunity to

[c] Presidential advance requires one additional advance man to represent the Secret Service. Normally, the Secret Service advance man has veto power over any part of the drill, even if advocated by the regular advance man. Presidential candidates afforded Secret Service protection are entitled to fewer agents and precautions than the president, but the drill still is supposed to be approved by the Secret Service.

establish rapport with the chairman, gain his confidence, and, through him, communicate to the group. Whenever possible, the advance man, regardless of the prompting and prodding he must give to the local chairmen, tries to enhance the leadership credentials and position of the chairman. If this person is the local campaign leader, he needs the campaign's full support to mobilize others.

The best way to impress the local chairman and committee with his competence is for the advance man to understand the purpose of the drill. He must be briefed by the tour director or campaign manager regarding goals and priorities of the drill. He cannot set high goals for others with any credibility unless he inspires confidence. The advance man is off to a good start if he is well prepared (Exhibit 12-2).

Priorities

The purpose of having everyone involved in the drill meet together is so each person can see how he fits into the total drill; also, each person realizes that everyone else knows his assignment, so he better get the job done. The joint meeting should guarantee that there is no confusion and there is no danger that any person wastes time on a task assigned to someone else. Following the joint meeting, the advance man arranges to meet with each person privately to review the individual assignment. Whether the assignment involves publicity, decorations, or securing car drivers, each person is given a specific, detailed assignment with a clear deadline. If necessary, the advance man gives each key person a title (e.g., Publicity Chairman, Decorations Chairman, Transportation Chairman). Regardless of his title, each key person has a defined assignment, and the advance man notes that assignment, along with the person's name, complete address, and all relevant telephone numbers.

Although the advance man consults the Advance Manual for specific priorities required of each type of activity, he requires basic information for any drill (Figures 11-1 and 11-2 and Exhibit 11-4). The fundamental question the advance man asks before putting any entry on the schedule is, "Why?" The advance man can only defend his plan for the drill if he can explain the purpose of every activity or event. The drill, as a whole, may be a sound proposition, but if parts of it are weak, it can fall apart; hence, the advance man applies general priorities for any kind of drill (Exhibit 12-3).

Recruiting and Training

It is often argued that a campaign cannot afford an advance staff, but the real question is, can the campaign afford not to have an advance staff? The

Exhibit 12-1
Advance Man's Standard Operating Plan

1. In rare cases, the campaign assigns an advance man to visit the site of a proposed drill before accepting an invitation, then makes its decision; alternatively, it accepts an invitation subject to the advance man inspecting the facilities or moving to another location.

2. Generally, once an acceptance letter is mailed, an advance man is assigned to the drill. The tour director and chief advance man evaluate whether the drill requires more than one advance person and more than a single advance visit; the *heavy* drill usually involves a lengthy tour, intensive schedule, major public rally, or other complications.

3. The local chairman is notified of the advance man's appointment, and the advance man is given a copy of the drill file; from this point, the advance man receives copies of any additions to the file. After meeting with the chief advance man, the advance man decides when to schedule the first trip.

4. The advance man telephones the local chairman and indicates when he will arrive, the expected length of his stay, and what he hopes to accomplish. He asks the chairman to notify others of his arrival and tells the chairman who he will call himself. He indicates the type of information he will need on arrival.

    (a) If a commitment is accepted far in advance, the advance man's first trip may be weeks after the acceptance letter, unless the campaign fears that the conditions and guidelines of its acceptance letter should be supplemented by an advance man's visit, before any irrevocable plans or mistakes are made.

    (b) If there is a single visit, it is usually one to three weeks before the drill, most likely ten to fourteen days before the drill.

5. The advance man's first meeting, arranged earlier, is always with the key political contact, who is usually the local campaign chairman. If there is no single person in charge or if there is a conflict, the advance man, working with the tour director, agrees on a person to be in charge. In rare cases, the advance man becomes so disenchanted with the local chairman that he formally recommends to the chief advance man that the drill be *scrubbed*, unless someone else is put in charge.

6. After reviewing the tour director's draft schedule with the local chairman, who has his own ideas, the advance man formulates a synthesized draft; he explains that his recommendations must be approved by the tour director. Then the advance man meets with the local committee, gets its input, and revises the schedule accordingly (or later in private). The advance man and committee chairman agree on appointing specific chairmen for different tasks, and the assignments are given.

7. The advance man meets with each newly appointed chairman or key volunteer.

8. The advance man meets with the leader or coordinator of any group involved in the drill, or the host of any event in the drill, to review the schedule and problems.

9. Once again, the advance man reviews the schedule to find ways of condensing it that will allow the candidate to arrive later or leave earlier or ways of looking for more private time for the candidate, or a way for him to go to sleep earlier, or get up later. Once again, he seeks local input for filling in any open time.

10. During the dry run of the drill, under comparable traffic conditions, the advance man times each movement and notes possible complications. He examines all alternative routes, whether involving auto travel, or merely corridors or elevators within the hotel. He devises contingency routing plans to insure that he is acquainted with at least one alternative pattern for every movement.

11. Following the dry run, the advance man again modifies the plans and schedule for the drill. He meets with the local chairman before leaving town and again verifies that everyone has and understands his assignment.

12. Returning to the campaign headquarters, the advance man explains the drill to the chief advance man or tour director. He is able to answer any questions as he defends each entry in the exact itinerary he has prepared.
13. After providing any information requested, or changes are made, by the tour director, the advance man confers by telephone with the chairman.
14. During the advance man's first visit and the drill, he maintains regular telephone contact with the chairman to monitor progress.
15. The advance man arrives before the drill begins—one or two days, or a few hours, before the candidate's scheduled arrival. Everything is checked again. The advance man is on hand when the candidate arrives, guides the traveling party through the entire drill, maintains an on-time schedule, and anticipates problems and contingencies. The advance man sees the candidate off, and the drill ends.[a]

[a]Although the drill ends, the advance man's job does not. He must oversee the follow-up operation, especially thank you notes from the candidate.

Exhibit 12-2
Advance Man's Supplies

1. Campaign staff identification badge and lapel identification pin.
2. Advance Manual; notebooks, pens, pencils.
3. Advance supplies and forms (campaign luggage tags, motorcade windshield identification stickers, expense account forms, thank you note forms).
4. Money (campaign or personal credit cards, cash advance).
5. Sample campaign materials (photographs, biographies, information kits for media; modest quantity of all types of brochures, issue papers, bumperstrips, posters, buttons, and so forth).
6. Copy of drill file and supporting materials:
   (a) all correspondence, print invitations, advertising, newsclips, and so forth;
   (b) draft schedule formulated by tour director;
   (c) name, address, telephone numbers of local campaign chairman and key political contact (if different);
   (d) names, address, telephone numbers, and background information on (1) anyone presently involved in the drill; (2) anyone potentially involved in the drill; especially political party leaders, elected officials, supporters, major contributors, key volunteer leaders, adjunct committee leaders, leaders of relevant service groups, ethnic and religious organizations, community groups, unions, corporations, and so forth;
   (e) names, addresses, and telephone numbers of the relevant news media list;[a]
   (f) Notes on the candidate's schedule during the hours, day, or days immediately preceding and following the drill.

[a]This may include the news media for the surrounding areas or counties. Ideally, the compilation is on several duplicate computer printouts requested for the drill, and possibly sets of labels. If the advance visit is close to the drill date, many publicity opportunities may have already been passed up.

Exhibit 12-3
Advance Man's Priorities

1. Secure all necessary files, materials, supplies; get briefing on drill; understand purpose of drill before going on advance trip.
2. Make initial contact quickly; do not allow planned trip to be delayed; appoint chairmen to particular chores and give out assignments early.
3. Review every aspect of the drill in terms of the campaign criteria and standards; don't change criteria and standards for the drill, modify the drill instead.
4. Always make early reservations for airplane, hotel, and any public facilities or meeting halls required; make alternate travel arrangements and extra travel reservations.
5. Make an early estimate of any campaign materials (brochures, bumperstrips, posters, buttons, and so forth) required for the drill and confirm that they are shipped and received in time for the drill.
6. Determine the cost of the drill (travel, lodging, rental of facilities, decorations, reimbursement of volunteer expense, telephone, advertising, and so forth); review budget allocation with tour director; make sure local committee knows far in advance of any financial obligation, dollar or percentage, it has for the drill.
7. Make sure local chairman and campaign's news division are in contact regarding specific plans to publicize drill and handle media events and needs of traveling media.
8. Seek input from all local contacts; if time permits, acquire research from Chamber of Commerce, library, or other sources, for possible insertion in candidate's briefing.
9. Regardless of assurances by the local chairman or others that everything is fine, do not be talked out of a complete dry run; after timing all movements, *then* add time cushions; also, note all entrances, exits, alternate routes; verify precise addresses (including floor level and rooms) and telephone numbers; verify that telephone numbers apply during time of drill; note location of nearest telephone and restroom at every part of drill. Secure maps, floor plans, blueprints and similar materials.
10. Divide the drill into five portions and relate assignments to each: (a) the *arrival* and greeting of candidate, staff, media; (b) *transportation* of entire entourage throughout drill; confirmation of airplane or other transportation to and from area or location of drill; (c) *hotel/motel* accommodations overnight for entourage, including candidate, traveling staff, media, pilots, drivers; rest accommodations for entourage, if necessary; private "holding" room at each stop if candidate needs privacy; (d) *meetings and events* should be verified by checking personally with the individual responsible for each entry on the schedule; if necessary, appoint someone for each entry; (e) *departure* of candidate, staff, and media.[a]
11. Do not overlook the candidate's physical safety and security; establish liaison with police, especially if any escort or motorcade problems.
12. Review all plans for attendance and crowd turnout; give local chairman and others high, unattainable goals as incentive; explain how to increase attendance for every part of the drill.
13. Keep schedule rigorously on time.
14. Formulate the drill's schedule with some consideration for the candidate's schedule before and after the drill; for example, is he just completing an intense swing and then resting, or is it the beginning of several days of activity?
15. Throughout the pre-drill and drill period, compile an exhaustive list for thank you letters.

[a]One common denominator for the entire drill is keeping the entourage and luggage together. The advance man insures that luggage is never lost or misplaced and that it is always transferred on an orderly basis *before* any scheduled departure or is transferred between cars *during* an event. For the Level A campaign, a special chairman or volunteer may need to be appointed to supervise luggage transfer and handling and routing of each staff member or reporter's luggage to his hotel room.

Exhibit 12-4
Recruiting the Advance Man

1. The volunteer recruit should be able to contribute a significant amount of time:
   (a) He should be able to contribute time in minimum blocks of two days each, preferably three; these blocks are for advance trips and the actual drill.
   (b) He should be able to contribute several hours weekly for reviewing files, working on the schedule, meetings at the campaign headquarters, and telephone conversations between the advance trip and drill.
   (c) The time can be days off, sick leave, a leave of absence, vacation days, or a vacation period, but the campaign should know the days sufficiently in advance to schedule assignments for the advance man.
2. The volunteer recruit should have a record of accomplishment, preferably in a proprietorship or partnership, sales or marketing; however, anyone who is achievement and goal oriented can be a good recruit. He must be a hard worker.
3. The volunteer recruit should be physically fit, energetic, and young, preferably 20-40, ideally 25-35; the college student, if mature, can advance certain activities.
4. The advance man will come in contact with many political and community leaders; because he represents the candidate, he must make a good impression. He should make a good appearance, be courteous, polite, and attentive. He should be pleasant and friendly, and a good listener. He is tactful and diplomatic.
5. In addition to being presentable, the advance man should be aggressive, methodical, persistent, even pushy, when putting the drill together. He must be able to motivate others to work hard; hence, he must communicate well, with superior interpersonal skills. He must convey to others the importance of the drill and how important it is to the candidate. He is a perfectionist.
6. The advance man must be absolutely loyal and dedicated to the candidate; ideally, the individual is philosophically motivated and believes strongly in the candidate's cause. Also, he relates well personally to the candidate, who feels at ease in his presence.
7. Although he can be flexible on unimportant matters, the advance man is rigid and uncompromising on implementing campaign policy; he knows when to be firm.
8. The advance man thrives under pressure and is always calm; he is stable, confident, and in control at all times.
9. Although he welcomes detail work, the advance man can be creative and imaginative, and he is quickly able to evaluate available options and, if necessary, redefine or add to those options.
10. If the advance man is a volunteer, he is so dedicated, conscientious, and hard working, that he is the equal or superior of any paid advance man; if he is paid, he works such long hours and so intensely that he is underpaid.

cost of advance usually involves two components, salaries and expenses. The latter involves, travel, lodging, telephone, and other expenses related to the advance man's on-site inspection and subsequent communications. However, part of these expenses can be funded by the savings in scheduling expenses, since scheduling shifts part of its workload to the advance staff. Also, since the time of the paid scheduling staff has some worth, the calculation must consider the monetary worth of making better use of the scheduling staff's time.

Every campaign can recruit volunteers to serve as advance men. Assuming the right kind of person is recruited (Exhibit 12-4), the campaign can find a single, experienced advance man to hold an intensive, weekend seminar to train recruits. As a consultant, this person can help recruit and select candidates, conduct the seminar, and prepare the campaign's Advance Manual. As the campaign's full-time, paid tour director or chief advance man, this person can administer the advance operation. The objective is to have enough qualified volunteers so that every drill is advanced by at least one advance man. This means correlating each volunteer advance man's available time with the amount of advance work.

Recruiting advance men has other benefits. The list of applicants provides a supply of campaign drivers; any campaign always needs drivers for the candidate's car and for transporting staff, media personnel, and dignitaries or guests of the campaign. Novice recruits can get the feel of campaigning and advancing by driving the candidate or entourage or by being a junior or assistant advance man. This is especially true for young recruits who may lack the stature, self-confidence, or maturity to relate to older county chairmen, but they can provide valuable support for the senior advance man.

Follow-Up

As soon as the advance man is assigned a drill, he begins a special file for follow-up activities *after* the drill. The basic component of this file is a master list that inclue includes everyone who should receive a thank you note from the candidate. Every time the advance man talks to anyone on the telephone, holds a meeting, confers with a local leader, he updates his thank you list. If the advance man is thorough, he also supplements the list with anyone who is involved in any way with the drill, even the banquet manager, maitre d', hotel clerk, a cooperative airline manager, or police escort. The advance man also requests the local campaign chairman to compile a list to make sure that no one is missed.

Each campaign has its own thank you system. The candidate's aide, who is constantly with the candidate, prepares notes on who should receive a thank you letter, and what it should include. The advance man's report, coupled with the candidate's aide compilation, should cover everyone. The advance man begins compiling his list at the outset; in many campaigns, the list is submitted by the advance man *before* the drill. Then, if necessary, it is updated. Regardless of when it is due (but always within 48 hours of the drill), this project is not delegated by the advance man to a volunteer. The advance man may need the local committee chairman's help in getting names and addresses, but the advance man is responsible for the entire list. The candidate's aide may provide a few additional names or suggestions for personalizing the letters, but if the drill has an advance man, he provides the master list.

The list is typewritten or neatly printed and must include the person's full name, title, complete address, and the reason the individual should receive a thank you note from the candidate. The reason—the person's role or function in the drill—may be simply stated (e.g., "drove candidate from airport") or may be very specific (e.g., "picked up candidate at 7 a.m. in rain, did a great job in traffic . . ."). The campaign should provide a compilation form that includes space at the top for the day, date, and location of the drill, as well as a column for indicating what activity or event within the drill relates to each person. The form may also indicate whether the recipient should receive a general or VIP thank you note. The note will be either individually typewritten or on an automatic typewriter. Even the general thank you note will refer to the location and date; the VIP thank you note will always be more personal. The efficient campaign stresses the thank you operation and has one full-time staff person or a group of volunteers who prepare thank you letters daily and promptly after each drill. The superlative advance operation provides enough information for each prospective recipient of a thank you letter that each is personalized. In all cases, the advance man indicates the appropriate salutation (first name or other), and the letter is always over the candidate's signature.

Although the thank you project is the major follow-up activity, the advance man should also complete a form listing any special requests arising from the drill. The most common request is for a copy of a photograph taken with the candidate. It must be emphasized that arrangements for retaining or selecting a photographer, ordering prints, identifying individuals in each photograph, and mailing the photograph (autographed or otherwise), must be arranged *before* the drill. The advance man should also prepare to close out the file from the drill by preparing a short report explaining any deviations from the planned schedule and accounting for any delay of more than ten minutes. He should also include confidential recommendations for any future drills in the area or involving the same people. Finally, he should make arrangements, unless the news director has already done so, for a report of broadcast coverage and any print media clippings of the drill to be sent immediately to the news director.

The last part of closing out the file is very important to any advance man, especially the volunteer. He must use specially provided expense account forms to list and explain his expenses for the drill and submit originals of receipts, stubs, credit card slips, or invoices; he can retain copies of these, or the campaign will make copies and mail them to him.

13 Advancing the Drill

The successful drill has two seemingly paradoxical characteristics. First, it is carefully planned and scheduled; every route, movement, and detail is reviewed in advance through on-site inspection. Second, the drill, no matter how meticulously coordinated and timed its planned movements are, is adaptable; it can be changed on short notice. The advance man is aware of all possible options relevant to any portion of the drill; he knows what meetings or activities can be added or scrubbed from the schedule, alternative routes, earlier or later flights, and so forth. He knows the implications if the candidate spends less or more time than expected at a particular activity, and he has a contingency plan if more time "opens up" at any portion of the drill.

Since we do not live in a perfectly predictable world, even with the most skilled advance men, the schedule must be constructed to permit quick response to changing circumstances. Last minute modification can be due to late arrival from the previous drill, or the need to arrive earlier than planned at the next drill. Despite the advance man's effort to consider every possibility, it is possible for the schedule to run late precisely because an activity is much more successful than even the most optimistic forecast. Assuming the advance man and ranking staff member conclude that the candidate should spend more time at an event, this decision necessarily requires many other decisions, unless the delay can be absorbed in one or more time cushions. Should the candidate arrive late for the next event? How late? What, if anything, should be done to placate or entertain the waiting crowd? Can and should the transportation time be cut? How? Should the advance man move ahead to the next stop to modify the event? Should the next activity be scrubbed altogether? If the candidate arrives late at the next event, should he leave late, in order to spend the previously planned time? Or should he adhere to the planned departure time and cut short his visit? Or should he compromise and leave later than planned, but not spend as much time there as previously scheduled?

The advance man knows that several factors insure an adaptable schedule. First, he must have previously reviewed all options and then maintained a mental or written list, including options considered but not included in the final schedule; in the fast moving campaign, the advance man will not have time during the drill to research alternatives or options. Second, he must have a contingency plan for each option. Third, the internal schedule must have the names and telephone numbers of everyone involved in the drill; these telephone numbers should not be limited to home or office, but must be operational during the time of the drill (i.e., for the site of the activity or event). The advance man may need to inform the contact of a schedule change, get additional information to make a decision, or make a special request. Fourth, the schedule must have built in time cushions, not so the schedule is loose and has dead time, but to prevent a *chain reaction*. The novice drill is scheduled so tightly that if the candidate arrives late for one event, he arrives late at every subsequent event, because there is no "catch up" time.[a]

In some cases, the campaign is so fast moving that even slight changes require telephoning many contacts on the schedule. Whenever any significant change is made, the advance man or a traveling staff member (reflecting policy or the immediate situation) must telephone the campaign headquarters. Based on the campaign's standard operating plan, a secretary in the tour office may be designated to make all necessary telephone calls and thus shift the burden from the harried advance man.

Preparations and Debriefing

The overzealous advance man can let his loyalty and dedication *interfere* with his job. The principle that the schedule is built around the candidate, rather than the candidate accommodating himself to the schedule, is followed rigorously *unless it compromises the candidate's self-interest*. It is correct to apply this principle in dealing with the local campaign chairman; however, the principle must be qualified when dealing directly with individuals who are politically lukewarm toward the candidate, neutral, uncommitted, or even apathetic. The tour director and advance man always ask themselves, "Are we (the candidate and campaign) doing a favor for this person or host group by appearing or speaking, or is the host doing us a favor by letting the candidate visit the reception, sit at the head table, speak to the dinner, tour the factory, meet the newspaper editors, and so on?"

When the campaign accepts or solicits an invitation from a nonpolitical or nonpartisan group, it may be on *their* terms. The advance man does the best he can, but he may conclude, or be so directed by the tour director at the outset, that persistent negotiation may jeopardize the event. The candidate can be the loser if the advance man's victories are at the expense of good will or possible support, or if the invitation is modified in a way unacceptable to the candidate or withdrawn altogether.

Briefing

The best advanced drill is worthless unless the candidate is prepared. The

---

[a] The chain reaction is accelerated and aggravated if transportation movements (driving time or flying by private plane) are underestimated.

candidate must know the schedule, especially *what is expected of him*. If he is to be escorted through a reception to shake hands, the schedule should be unambiguous and use the words "work the reception," "hand shaker," or whatever code words are specified by the campaign's Advance Manual. The candidate should never guess what he will do, whether he will speak or for how long, and who will escort him through a crowd. Spontaneity can be delightfully productive, but should not be at the cost of the candidate's performance.

Each campaign has its own procedures governing how much material to include in the schedule and how much in an attached briefing. Attached material is always neatly typewritten in an easy-to-read format and is always in chronological form (the order of the schedule), although there may be an introductory or overview section to the briefing. Whether by all capital letters, underlining, or other method, the briefing must distinguish between important and supplementary information, especially if it is lengthy. Since the quality of the briefing depends on material provided through the cooperative efforts of the tour or scheduling office, and various campaign divisions, especially news, political organization, research, and speechwriting, someone, often the candidate's aide or in the smaller campaign his secretary at the headquarters, must collate and edit the material.

The advance man must allow time in the schedule for the candidate to review briefing materials. In the fast moving campaign, the candidate is briefed orally throughout the day, so the candidate is prepared just before each part of a drill; thus, his mind is clear, he can focus on the immediate activity and ask the most relevant questions. He will not get confused or forget the material. Every advance man has nightmares of the candidate telling a large banquet audience in Rochester, "It's great to be here in Buffalo." The oral briefing, like the written briefing, is selective, but probably includes certain standard information (Exhibit 13-1). In order to avoid giving the candidate too much material, many campaigns do not give the candidate the internal (or *detail*) schedule, because it has so much technical and logistical information. Instead, he has the index cards mentioned earlier, plus the written and oral briefing elaborating on each event.

Debriefing

The advance man's report summarizing the drill only concerns the candidate indirectly. As part of the advance man's follow-up activities, this report's main emphasis is accounting for any discrepancies from the planned drill and providing resource material for the thank you operation. The advance man should comment candidly, in the report and orally, on any problems in the campaign's scheduling and advance operation. He should recommend any changes in transportation or lodging arrangements, espe-

Exhibit 13-1
Briefing the Candidate

1. *Schedule*: what is happening; when; who is involved.
2. *Purpose*: why was each activity scheduled; history of invitation (i.e., how candidate came to be there).
3. *Attendance*: number expected at each event; price of ticket; how were tickets sold.
4. *Performance*: what is specifically expected of the candidate; who will be on hand to help him (local chairman, escort at reception, staff members, assigned advance man).
5. *Speech or remarks*: how long will the candidate speak; whether prepared text or extemporaneous or impromptu speaking; what will he say; type of audience.
   (a) *Technical aspects*: whether there will be a podium, microphone, lighting to read the text or notes; whether indoor or outdoor; whether notes are appropriate (e.g., they are often awkward in speaking without a podium or to a small reception).
   (b) *Content*: acknowledgment of person introducing candidate, possible comments on other parts of program; local examples of statistics to illustrate statewide or national issues; personal anecdotes concerning political leaders present at gathering, and other material, synthesized from information *below*, and put in introductory portion of remarks or, where appropriate, in body; ideal briefing includes some local humor and indicates pronounciation of important names of people or places.
6. *Event and program*: name and background of person introducing candidate, as well as others on program, head table, escorting candidate, meeting candidate, or other VIPs; copy of letter of invitation and campaign response, copies of printed invitation, newsclips, advertising for event; history and purpose of sponsoring organization and specific event; if regular, or annual event, information on past speakers.
7. *Area*: information from Census Bureau, Chamber of Commerce, library, and other sources to provide economic and social statistics; also, political statistics, voter history, voter registration, survey research, demographic profile; list, background, and voting records of elected officials; news and editorial clippings and research information on issues of local concern.
8. *People*: profile of people involved in drill or expected to be present, including those mentioned above, plus community leaders, political activists, key volunteers who helped put the drill together, and others the candidate will meet.
9. *Media*: a complete report on the types of media, individual reporters, and so forth.[a]
10. *Prior Visits*: recapitulation of dates, places visited during prior visit(s), with emphasis on names and background of individuals candidate met previously.

Note: Any briefing has four purposes: (1) inspires a more confident, relaxed candidate; (2) allows the candidate to cite local information or seem better informed during media interviews; (3) helps the candidate to communicate more effectively in personal conversation with the local chairman, supporters, or reception guests by appearing knowledgeable and empathetic; (4) provides material for inclusion in the candidate's remarks or speech.

[a]For discussion of the media briefing and of specific media events, see Part II.

cially as they relate to the candidate, traveling staff, or media. He should suggest any improvements for future drills of the same type.

Because the advance man worked so closely with the local chairmen, other supporters, and hosts for particular events, he can often secure valuable feedback, positive or negative, to improve the candidate's performance. Either the candidate's aide, or the advance man if he has the time (he usually doesn't), monitors the candidate's speech or remarks. The staff person given this responsibility carefully notes the length of the candidate's introduction, as well as the starting and ending times of his speech, so it can be timed precisely. He notes the number of times, if any, the speech is interrupted by applause and by laughter (presumably at jokes). He notes which specific sections or lines evoke applause or laughter and which lines receive more applause or laughter than others. He watches audience reaction to gauge attentiveness and boredom and looks for any change in mood during different parts of the speech.

After any speech or remarks, the candidate's aide (rarely, the advance man) may be called upon by the candidate to indicate how long he spoke, whether it should have been longer or shorter, and to provide a report on audience reaction. Although the candidate's standard speech varies only slightly—portions are added or deleted for each different audience or the introductory material is adjusted to acknowledge whoever introduces the candidate, VIPs at the head table or in the audience, and material about the group or event—the basic text can be changed. Not only can issues be added or dropped to suit a specific audience, but the campaign's high command or the candidate himself may decide, based on the debriefing, that certain lines, jokes, anecdotes, stories, words, sections, or issues should be deleted or added, cut or enlarged. The monitoring of the candidate's speech should also watch his timing of lines, voice inflection, pauses, hand gestures, and so forth.

Transportation and Lodging

The advance man arranges and reserves transportation and lodging early, because reservations can always be cancelled. When using commercial transportation, especially airlines, he always makes additional reservations to allow for extra staff or reporters; he also makes alternate reservations, in case of a schedule change, and these are often held until the last minute. The advance man works with the tour director to insure written confirmation of all transportation and lodging arrangements and purchase of tickets. The candidate and traveling entourage are never involved in purchasing tickets, checking in or out of hotels, or paying bills. The advance man is responsible for such arrangements; if there were no advance man, this task is the scheduler's responsibility.

Transportation

One rule governing transportation of the candidate is inviolate. The contact person at the point of departure and the contact person at the point of arrival must always be able to contact each other. While this sounds deceptively simple, it requires, in addition to each contact's telephone numbers, those numbers that are relevant during the time period of the drill (e.g., an airport terminal, or the last stop before departing, or first stop after arriving). This system often requires knowing where the contact person or driver will be immediately before he is scheduled to drive the candidate to an airport or event, or after he is scheduled to pick up the candidate. This rule is inviolate because if there is any change in the schedule, the appropriate contact person must be notified immediately. In addition, if the candidate leaves the departure point late, either the contact person at the departure point or the advance man *must* notify the contact person at the next arrival point.

Generally, the communication system is either from the advance man at one drill to the advance man at the next drill; however, the advance man may be in touch with the contact person at an event that is part of the same drill. An alternative method is, time permitting, routing the message through the campaign headquarters tour or scheduling office. Although the elaborate campaign has telephones and walkie talkies, even the modest campaign must maintain constant communications between the traveling candidate and the home base—that is, campaign headquarters should always know where the candidate can be reached. In the fast-moving campaign, it is frequently necessary to get in touch with the candidate or a traveling staff member or to leave a message. This is especially true for media activities, particularly reaction statements.

Automobile. Each campaign has its own standards (outlined in its Advance Manual) for automobile transportation. However, even the candidate for local office should have a staff or volunteer driver who knows the route and can worry about driving while the candidate works; for the Level C campaign, this person may double as the candidate's all-around aide. The advance man enforces certain basic guidelines (Exhibit 13-2) applicable to almost any campaign. The Level A campaign requires a motorcade for any movement, because the traveling staff and contingents are so large. The local campaign uses a motorcade for a parade or car caravan. In any case, the motorcade requires more rigorous advance (Exhibit 13-3).

Airplane. The campaign uses either commercial or private aircraft. If commercial aircraft is used, the advance man should utilize the tour director's contacts in the airline's public or customer relations office; alternatively, the government relations department or congressional desk can be used. If a campaign uses private aircraft, it must select the type of plane most conducive for its candidate's travel. Some planes may be impractical because they are too large for small airports; this means the campaign may lose time by having to use a larger airport farther away from the destination.

Exhibit 13-2
Guidelines for Automobile Transportation

1. Arrangements must be made for an automobile and driver for the candidate. If the candidate does not need privacy to work or chat with staff and there are only one or two reporters (small campaign), there will only be one auto. However, there is usually a need for at least one more auto and driver to accommodate staff, media, and VIPs comfortably. In any case, there should be the required number of autos (and assigned drivers) for each leg of the drill.

2. The automobile should be an American-made, four-door, standard-size sedan, preferably not ostentatious. It should have five or six seats.

3. Each driver should be interviewed in advance; he should know the schedule and the route. He should be presentable, attentive, and able to take directions. He should be briefed to drive as rapidly as is consistent with speed laws and safety. His job is to drive, and he should allow the candidate and passengers privacy to chat or work. He *always* has the keys to his car.

4. The schedule must include, after each driver's name, his telephone numbers (home and office) in parentheses and a separate notation if another telephone number will be relevant before the drill.

5. Each car must have an assigned driver and roster of passengers (by name); this is especially true of the candidate's car: If the candidate will be interviewed by a reporter, the news director is always on the passenger roster. The roster is likely to include the local political chairman. If any roster puts reporters with a driver or local chairman or supporters, they should be briefed not to engage in controversial conversation with the media; preferably, reporters should be isolated, and they should not be put in a car with local VIPs.

6. The advance man must weigh the need for a police escort against its disadvantages. It may be difficult to secure, it may cause resentment—among those who regard it as a waste of taxpayer funds or those who resent the superior treatment given the candidate. Never use an escort unless necessary or dictated by security conditions. The unmarked car is usually preferable to the marked. If a blinking light is sufficient, never use a siren. Avoid motorcycle escorts unless essential or dictated by security. Always brief the police drivers before the drill to avoid misunderstanding.[a]

7. Even for a single car, arrangements must be made for rapid, unblocked automobile passage into and out of events (i.e., the precise entrance must be known in advance); there must be provision for easy access, special parking.

8. Each driver *must* be ready for immediate, on-time departure. This means he must have the auto in place (unblocked) and ready to move well before scheduled departure. He does not accompany the candidate and staff to the car, as long as someone else (the advance man) can guide them; he is already there waiting.

9. If any luggage must be transferred from one car to another, this must be done during the event. The driver never takes time to transfer luggage while the candidate is waiting.

10. Each route must be charted and mapped out in advance, with the optimum route carefully chosen, but alternate routes considered and ready for contingency. The actual route is driven and timed under comparable traffic conditions. There is never any last minute road construction, because the route is checked again before driving. The driver must have a map (as well as an oral briefing); if more than one auto, additional drivers must receive same material and instructions, in case of separation.

Note: Where applicable, the larger campaign should extrapolate motorcade instructions (see Exhibit 13-3).

[a]The police escort should not be used unless the driver of each campaign car is briefed. Drivers should know the anticipated speed; even when there is only one police auto and the single campaign auto, if there are flashing red lights or the siren, the autos must stay close together, and the drivers must be especially alert for a short stop. The second driver should keep his emergency lights blinking and stay on the escort car's tail.

Exhibit 13-3
Guidelines for Motorcades

1. Any motorcade must be sufficient to move the candidate, traveling staff, traveling media, and VIPs. The motorcade must consider any additional needs for luggage, campaign materials, or television equipment.

2. Automobiles should meet requirements for campaign driving (i.e., four-door, American-made sedans, clean); they should be prechecked to be in good running condition, especially battery, oil, water, and have full gas tanks. Cars should be new or late model, if possible, but never brand new (at least 1,000 miles).

3. Drivers should be well briefed, reliable volunteers, or, preferably, paid or volunteer, off-duty or retired policemen. Any driver must be able to negotiate traffic and stay in motorcade formation.

4. The motorcade ideally is assembled 45 minutes ahead of time; alternatively, 30 minutes. The longer the motorcade, the greater the need for advance assembly. It must arrive a minimum of 30 minutes before the candidate's flight time, or 30 minutes before departure from hotel or other location for airport.

5. Each driver must stay with his car; the keys must be left in the car at all times. The keys must include the trunk key.

6. The transportation or motorcade chairman appointed by the advance man must remain with the motorcade at all times. He is the advance man's contact.

7. If a motorcade involves multiple stops, it is *essential* that specific and adequate parking areas be reserved. The motorcade always "docks" in the identical order in which it will depart. If this is not the case, the drivers reposition the motorcade in correct order during the commitment. They *never* waste time putting the cars in order while the candidate, staff, media, and VIPs are kept waiting. Repositioning the motorcade, if necessary, is the first order of business after passengers leave for the commitment.

8. Special attention should be given to traffic problems in and out of stopping off points. Police escorts, roped off traffic lanes, or running escorts may be required to assure quick entrance and exit. When the motorcade does dock, its passengers should have easy access to the hotel, stadium, outdoor speaking area, airplane, and so forth.

9. The purpose of any police escort can be to keep the motorcade intact, increase speed, or both. Generally, the driving time of the motorcade is computed to be slower than normal driving time; faster, if the escort is used to avoid red lights and traffic; slower, if no escort, or the motorcade gets separated. There should be no separation; if there is, the entire motorcade should not be delayed. Each driver should have his own map, schedule, and route instructions.

10. For the large motorcade engaged in multiple stops, specific meal arrangements are made for drivers as a group. They either eat a boxed lunch in the car, or, in an extended commitment, they eat together, at a banquet table or restaurant. They do not eat separately or at different facilities. They are always accessible.

11. The usual order for the motorcade is as follows: *Auto A: Advance Auto* (advance man and traveling tour director); *Auto B: Candidate's Auto* (candidate, spouse, local committee chairman, possibly staff member); *Auto C: Press Auto* (news director and reporters); *Auto D: Staff or VIP Auto* as needed.

12. The Level A campaign supplements this motorcade by having two press autos behind the candidate's automobile. The first is a convertible for still and film photographers, the second for reporters. In a presidential campaign, this second car usually includes the pool reporters, especially the AP and UPI reporters. The press car is sometimes a station wagon, although station wagons are usually added to the end of the motorcade to accommodate luggage or television equipment. In the presidential campaign, a bus may be used for reporters.[a]

13. If there is a police escort, it always includes one police car at the front and another at the rear of the motorcade to keep it intact. Motorcycle escorts are usually alongside. All cars use lights during the daytime; if approved by the police and thought necessary, flashing emergency lights are used. Each driver must stay directly on the tail of the car in front.

14. For the major motorcade, there are *at least* three points connected by walkie-talkie communication: (1) the advance man and traveling tour director in Auto A; (2) the candidate's aide in Auto B; (3) the news director in Auto C. Keep in mind that Auto C may not be the third auto if additional cars—convertibles or station wagons—or a press bus is used.

15. If the motorcade is part of a parade or car caravan, the motorcade is preceded by a sound truck, but *never* directly in front of Auto A. It is at least 1,000 feet in front; however, for the presidential campaign and large motorcade, it may be 10-15 minutes ahead of the motorcade. The sound system is always checked out beforehand, and its speakers usually point forward.

16. In the parade or car caravan, it is permissible to use banners on the sides of cars and bumper strips on the front and rear; also, cartops can be put on top. However, the candidate's car must be somehow distinguished and more decorated than others. Obviously, the convertible is conducive to crowds.

17. Whether a regular motorcade or parade or car caravan, each car always has a campaign identification sign or sticker on the lower right hand corner of the windshield that says: Auto A—Number 1; Auto B—Number 2; and so forth. The car in which the candidate is a passenger also says *Candidate's Car*. Any car for only staff says *Staff Car*. The press car always says *Press* or *News Media*.

18. Every motorcade should always have at least one reserve car and driver, preferably two.

19. The campaign never embarks on a publicized, crowd-oriented motorcade unless it can draw a crowd. If the route is longer, it is better to concentrate the parade, crowd-oriented portion of the motorcade, on a populated area; this area must be absolutely saturated with flyers to announce the motorcade.

20. If the motorcade involves several stops at outdoor rallies, headquarters openings, parking lot or shopping center rallies, and so forth, the advance man or contact at each event must be in touch with the motorcade to know the exact time of arrival. The candidate should arrive on time, from the point of view of the planned schedule, but his publicly scheduled arrival should always be at least 15 minutes, often 20-30, before he actually arrives. This is to guarantee a large crowd; this is especially important if his stopover is a few minutes, and he can miss many people altogether.

21. No campaign should pursue the complex drill of a parade/car caravan, with multiple stopover points for quick rallies, unless it has skilled advance men and plenty of volunteers to generate the crowd.[b]

Note: Guidelines must be changed for any campaign involving Secret Service advance.

[a]For any presidential candidate, the candidate's car is always followed directly by the Secret Service car.

[b]See the section in this chapter summarizing rally advance.

Whether the campaign is using a commercial or private aircraft,[b] certain basic guidelines apply (Exhibit 13-4).

It is important to have the airport greeting properly arranged. If someone is held in high esteem by the candidate and that person wants to be present, the advance man can speak to the tour director. However, the priority is having the correct number of cars and drivers to handle the candidate, staff, media, and luggage. A second priority may be having someone on hand to ride with the candidate to brief him; or if authorized by the tour director and news director, an important reporter can ride in the car and interview the candidate. What should generally be avoided is the large airport welcoming committee that takes campaign volunteers away from their work.

The only rationale for a large airport greeting is for media attention. The burden is on those who advocate such a greeting because it is a massive undertaking involving airport officials, police, traffic problems, and the diversion of valuable campaign staff and volunteer workers. Since media is the rationale, the project should not even be considered unless there is a near perfect chance of turning out a large crowd. The brief program casts doubt on pursuing all of the work (Exhibit 13-5), unless (a) the coverage is substantial, and (b) there is no easier way to generate similar coverage.

Lodging

Hotel lodging requirements vary greatly among campaigns, but the same guidelines that govern transportation apply here. Reservations should be made early, and the location should be the most convenient one available. In some cases, a hotel or motel adjacent to the airport is selected because the candidate flies in very late at night or is scheduled for an early morning departure. It is always wise to make more reservations than needed, especially for unanticipated traveling staff or media; however, unneeded reservations should be cancelled. Although the traveling reporters either have the rooms billed to their media outlets or pay the bills themselves and are later reimbursed by their outlets, reservations made by the campaign insure that there will be no shortage of rooms. Even if the candidate is not staying overnight but merely is attending a banquet at a hotel, the advance man always secures a "holding room" for privacy, meetings, telephone calls, or working on the speech, especially if unexpected time opens up. Even the modest campaign can apply many of the guidelines for lodging (Exhibit 13-6).

---

[b] Besides safety, the basic problem with helicopter transportation is accommodating traveling staff and reporters. For reasons of space, helicopters will not be discussed. If a private airplane is used, the campaign usually bills each media outlet an amount equivalent to first-class airfare for the route; in some cases, the campaign can successfully adopt a policy of billing at 150 percent of first-class airfare.

Exhibit 13-4
Guidelines for Airplane Travel

1. The campaign always chooses the airport carefully; it considers its distance from the ground destination, traffic conditions, time of day, accessibility, and ability to handle the campaign plane (if not using commercial aircraft). Scheduling must also consider whether the candidate will transfer to another airplane flight or helicopter; also, if the last point on the drill is closer to another airport, the private plane can be moved to take off from the second airport.

2. For commercial or private aircraft, the schedule always lists the full and complete name of the airport, and the precise location of the terminal, gate, or private airfield.

3. The schedule lists all relevant telephone numbers: anyone who will meet the plane, including drivers, and anyone who will see the candidate off at the last stop, including drivers. The contact people at both ends have all telephone numbers. The telephone numbers of the airport, airfield, airline, message desk, or private charter company are also listed; if private aircraft is used, the pilot's telephone numbers are listed.

4. There must be a contingency plan for delayed landing or alternate flights. This plan relies on communication between contact people at both ends of the plane trip; for private aircraft, it relies also on air-to-ground communication.

5. Drivers always get the candidate and staff to the airport in time for the flight, and drivers assigned to pick up the candidate and entourage are always at the airport at least 30 minutes ahead of time. Commercial airplanes present special problems for auto parking; hence, the advance man secures a special parking area or arranges for airport police to drive the candidate from the plane directly to the pick-up point. If it is necessary for drivers to park in a commercial lot, they are always prepared to depart, on notification, from the lot to the front of the terminal, so the candidate can depart immediately.

6. For commercial flights, the campaign works with each airline's public relations staff to secure VIP treatment for the candidate and his entourage, including private lounge facilities, message service, quick entry and exit from the airplane, reserved seats, expeditious luggage handling (including permission to bring aboard luggage normally checked). Tickets are always purchased in advance.

7. For a private plane, the tour office and advance man check the hours of the airfield, especially whether there are night lights; it also considers its facilities and length of runway. If the private plane will use a public airport, the tour director considers take-off or landing delays necessitated by commercial traffic.

8. For any air travel, the tour office considers weather problems (e.g., morning fog) and, if commercial travel, the airline's on-time record for the route. Its decision regarding a late night or early morning flight may be affected by this information.

9. For any private plane, the schedule must include type of plane, description and coloring, identification number and markings, name of pilot, copilot, number of passenger seats, list of passengers, luggage capacity, cruising speed, air miles for each leg of route, departure and arrival times, and expected flying time.

10. Campaign policy should favor twin engine planes, pilot and copilot, and use of established, fully paved airfields.

Analyzing the Drill

Each type of drill has its own requirements, but the advance man must ask certain basic questions of any drill. What is the purpose of each activity and will it be accomplished? How much of the candidate's time is requested; can the time be cut? How many people will be present, and what supports this estimate? Will the candidate arrive at the height of activity; will the

Exhibit 13-5
Planning Airport Greetings

1. The greeting should have at least one band, either paid professional or recruited free from a local high school. If more time is anticipated to warm up the crowd, two bands can be recruited.

2. The advance man requires one person to oversee the event. In addition to the Airport Arrival Chairman, the advance man must recruit a Transportation Chairman (who handles the cars, motorcade, luggage), and an Entertainment Chairman (who handles the bands, cheerleaders, noise makers). In addition, he may need a Decorations Chairman, Physical Facilities Chairman (to work with airport personnel and set up any area for the news media). The major campaign will use at least one specialist for any airport rally.[a]

3. Attendance requires extensive mailings to every available list of supporters, volunteers, political party activists, and so forth, especially to youth organizations. If the candidate is popular, the advance man should seek community and civic group support and invite schools to send student delegations or even let school out earlier; the mayor and elected officials should be invited. Business firms, labor unions, Lions, Kiwanis, and service groups, especially the Boy Scouts and Girl Scouts, should all be represented. If possible, enlist the youth groups to serve as ushers, honor guards, or in some similar capacity.

4. No airport rally can be successful without a major telephone campaign involving thousands of telephone calls. These calls are placed the day before and day of arrival. However, if volunteer manpower permits, lists can be called throughout the week. It is often better to call a good prospect twice than to call two names from the telephone book.

5. There should be a temporary platform only if the candidate intends to speak; this is especially true if there are no other scheduled activities in the area, or the airport rally is part of a series of rallies the day before election. Whether the candidate speaks or not, the advance man should always schedule ample time for handshakes. The microphone should be cordless; the sound system checked out to see that it reaches the entire crowd (for audience reaction).

6. There should be plenty of large, colorful placards for television visuals.

7. Any area that the candidate will "work" as a hand shaker, or any area that may be filmed by the media, must be densely packed with people. The best method is to control access by limiting it to one area until that area is totally packed; then going into a second area, and after that, a third area. Veteran advance man say the crowd should be *forced* into being at least ten deep for visual effect. If still or television photographers have an elevated platform or can use a roof, the visual effect can be especially favorable.[b]

8. Permitting supporters to break down barriers, fences, or slip through police "spontaneously" is extremely effective, but can present major security problems.

9. The arrival is choreographed so that the plane lands adjacent to the crowd; the candidate steps out first; the advance man signals when the media is in position to cover any further activities (e.g., hand shake tour along fence or roped area).[c]

10. The speaking area is usually between the plane and crowd. The motorcade waits at least 200 feet away to pull into position for departure when signaled.

Note: This is an abbreviated summary. It assumes (1) a statewide campaign, (2) no press plane in addition to the campaign plane, (3) no security problems or Secret Service involvement.

[a]Any major rally requires a "rally man."

[b]The absolute number is unimportant if the turnout is considered heavy for the area or the crowd is pushed together in a small area for effect.

[c]The preprogram entertainment period occurs during the crowd arrival; by the time the plane actually lands (later than the handbills indicated), the crowd is at its peak.

hosts be ready for his arrival? Can the activity be improved by altering its format?

Although some parts of a drill are clearly more important than others, each entry on the schedule is, from the standpoint of the advance man, a major activity. Every schedule entry must have a contact person who is in charge, no matter how minor or brief the entry. Whenever the candidate arrives anywhere, the schedule always shows the name of the contact person designated to meet the candidate ("Met by: . . ."), followed by relevant telephone numbers. The advance man insures that each entry is "covered" by appointing someone responsible for that part of the schedule. Each volunteer must concentrate on his assignment; it is the advance man's job to integrate each schedule entry or part of the drill into a unified whole.

Every drill requires movement on the part of the candidate. The advance man examines all alternative movements before deciding on the optimum. He uses blueprints, diagrams, floor plans, and any similar materials he can secure from the hotel or public facility. Just as he relies on a map for auto or motorcade movements, he secures or prepares a layout for any pedestrian movements. He surveys all available entrances and exits, corridors, stairways, escalators, and elevators. Generally, his objective is rapid entrance and exit for the candidate. This requires dividing seemingly simple movements into smaller components. For example, one person is moving the candidate from the ballroom after the speech, while the advance man or someone designated is opening a path and leading the way; perhaps another person is holding an elevator, while the volunteer drivers have pulled their car into position directly in front of the exit selected by the advance man.

The advance man's contingency plan always allows for time unexpectedly opening up in the schedule. Regardless of the type of event, the advance man always has a "holding room" in reserve, in case the candidate needs to confer with staff, make a telephone call, work on his remarks, or engage in a media interview. Even if there are only a few extra minutes, the harried candidate may just need the time alone—away from the crowd. Above all, the advance man's exit plan insures that the candidate can leave any event quickly by avoiding crowds; the exit and precise route are selected in advance; a path through the crowd is cleared if necessary, and the car or motorcade are positioned near the relevant exit, with cars in an unblocked position and drivers ready.

Receptions and Dinners

There are many kinds of receptions, but the common denominator is always the social interaction between candidate or guests. This is true

Exhibit 13-6
Guidelines for Lodging

1. Reservations should be made early and confirmed in writing for a suite for the candidate; rooms for each of the core staff; three rooms for unanticipated staff or VIPs; an appropriate number of rooms for expected traveling media.[a]

2. The reservation should specify, and the advance man should confirm, that staff rooms are adjacent to the candidate's suite, in a prescribed order (outlined in the advance manual); ideally, the traveling media should be on another floor. The candidate's suite should be far from the elevator; by definition, it includes a parlor; however, if the advance man foresees problems in being able to terminate any private meetings planned for the candidate's suite, a staff member's room, or another parlor, may be used, so the candidate can depart for his suite to end the meeting.

3. The hotel selected should give fast laundry and valet service and late-night room service; at the minimum, the dining room should open early and close late. The advance man should check the possibility of arranging special service; also, whenever possible, room service is ordered far in advance and reconfirmed (e.g., arrangements for the candidate's early morning breakfast meeting in his suite are made the evening before). The Level A campaign may have a staff lounge (located far from the candidate's suite); the advance man can arrange for a continental breakfast for staff.

4. Just before the drill, the advance man confirms and corrects the guest list—the candidate, possibly spouse, candidate's aide, and various other traveling staff, VIPs who may be along just for this trip, and the traveling media. He submits a typed list to the hotel. By the time he meets the candidate and traveling entourage, he has an envelope for each person (including media) with their keys. Staff members also receive a copy of the full roster of room assignments (although Level A campaigns may not list the candidate's room).

5. The advance man (or his appointed hotel chairman) preregisters each member of the entourage and gets each key, then puts it in the envelope with the person's name on the outside. At this time, billing instructions are again reviewed (a letter of authorization should have been sent from the campaign); also, each reporter's room is billed to his media outlet.[b]

6. Before the drill, the advance man again reviews his (or the campaign's) written letter or memorandum that notes the candidate's room number will not be given to anyone, and no calls will be connected to the candidate's room. Instead, all personal or telephone inquiries at the front desk will be referred to a designated staff member and room.

7. The schedule must show the hotel's complete name and address; the headquarters must have a copy of room assignments. The hotel switchboard should be 24-hour; preferably, each room should have its own direct dial telephone.

whether the reception is a single activity, or part of a banquet, headquarters opening, or other event. The traditional, formal reception, called the "handshaker," is rarely used outside of Level A campaigns (Exhibit 13-7). The most common political receptions do not have receiving lines, but involve circulating the candidate. The advance man never schedules the candidate to be present during an entire reception, but always for the last half or third and rarely for more than thirty minutes, often twenty. If the candidate will only visit an area once and the reception is well attended, the tour director might approve forty-five minutes, but this would be the exceptional case. The advance man absolutely insists that the entire recep-

8. The room for the candidate and each staff member should have the latest editions of the city's daily newspaper, including early morning delivery of the next day's newspaper; also, the candidate's suite should have his favorite beverage available.

9. Unless agreed otherwise, the advance man should provide for wake-up calls to the candidate's suite and certain staff members; he should also have an alarm clock to wake up earlier and insure that wake-up calls occur.

10. There should be no confusion or mistakes in routing each person's luggage from the plane or car to the hotel room; staff luggage is always marked with campaign luggage identification, including the person's name; the campaign can also provide similar news media stickers. If the entourage goes directly from the plane to an activity, the luggage is simultaneously routed to each person's room. The volunteers prepare an inventory of luggage, with approximate size or color, to avoid error. The same systematic approach applies to departure, including early morning departure. If there are activities scheduled before departure, the entourage usually goes from the activities to the airport; the luggage is already loaded. The advance man arranges a system to get each individual's room key, and everyone is checked out automatically. To repeat, luggage is always loaded into automobiles in advance of departure. After departure, someone (previously assigned by the advance man) checks each room for items left behind.

Note: Sometimes the Level A campaign plans a hotel arrival greeting for the candidate (see Exhibit 13-5 and 13-10).

[a]The core staff defines those staff members who always travel with the candidate. The Level A campaign has prescribed alternative floor plans, based on whether the candidate occupies a corner or central hallway suite and whether the spouse and additional staff besides core staff members are in the entourage. If there are enough staff rooms, an entire corridor or section of hallway is secured.

[b]In *any* political campaign, the candidate and entourage are always preregistered. If there is no advance man, then the local chairman or driver preregisters the candidate and staff, secures the keys, inspects the rooms, and when the candidate is picked up at the airport, brings him directly to the suite. Similarly, the candidate and entourage never check out of the hotel; the advance man or someone else is designated to handle check out, billing, and return of keys. Ideally, suite and room bills are mailed, based on prior billing instructions.

tion not be scheduled for a two- or three-hour time period, but preferably for one hour, perhaps a half hour. Otherwise, the candidate misses too many people, no matter when he arrives.

It is the advance man's responsibility to schedule the candidate's visit to the reception in such a way that he is exposed to the peak crowd and "works" the reception in such a way that he shakes the most hands. In addition to standard guidelines for any reception, the advance man must insure that the reception preceding a banquet does not delay the meal and therefore the entire program (Exhibit 13-8). One problem encountered by the advance man may be that the printed and mailed invitiations list the

Exhibit 13-7
Guidelines for Handshaker Receptions

1. The candidate is either on a platform or in a roped off area; if a platform, its height is based on crowd size, at least 3 feet high, but about 6 feet for a crowd of 1,000 or more.

2. The microphone and sound system should be checked if the candidate will speak; however, the microphone should not be visible or near the candidate, but only put in place if needed. It should be a stand-up microphone.

3. Directly in front of the candidate should be a secure area reserved for still or television picture taking and for any campaign photographers. For the fast-moving reception, the campaign requires two or three photographers to alternate taking pictures, so there is no delay; also, there must be a clerical operation to get each person's name so the pictures can be sent to the right person.

4. The advance man should use runways and, if necessary, roped-off walking corridors; the corridor or aisle should be narrow, about 3 feet wide, to encourage a single-file line and prevent groups from congregating just before or just after shaking hands with the candidate. If a person's name is needed to identify his or her official campaign photo with the candidate, this operation follows, never precedes, the picture taking; also, the clerical area used for this process has enough space so a group does not hold up others from leaving the candidate's area.

5. Any bar should be at the opposite end of the room or outdoor area. If there is a band or entertainment, it should be far away.

6. The area behind the candidate should have the official campaign backdrop with curtain material about 15 feet high.

7. Any area involving stairs should have a railing, and a staff member or volunteer is designated to guide and assist guests.

8. The advance man must have an appropriate entrance, exit, and path so the candidate can enter and leave the reception quickly (i.e., without crowd interference).

reception or banquet at unrealistic times or lists the reception as a two-hour affair. The advance man must negotiate a solution with the tour director, who should have approved the final copy for the invitations.

When the advance man first visits an area, he looks for reception opportunities—that is, a chance for the candidate to make an appearance, meet people, get publicity, but not necessarily attend the banquet. Such a visit is called a "drop by" and usually does not exceed thirty minutes and is probably about twenty minutes. An even briefer visit is called a "brief drop by." These visits require advance work to get an invitation, arrange escorts, and, on rare occasions, an opportunity for the candidate to speak (rarely more than five minutes).

Media

This subject has been covered in detail earlier in the book. In addition to obvious priorities, such as advance speech texts, the advance man should work wth the news director to prepare information packets tailored to the drill. These not only include the schedule news release, but basic political, social, and economic data about the area visited, including past electoral results. If properly coordinated, this same envelope includes the reporter's room key and other important information, including the traveling press aide's room number. The advance man is responsible for the care and feeding of the traveling press; this includes both room reservations and arranging for a press section or press table at every activity.[c]

The Level A campaign has specific requirements for a working press room. This room requires an adequate supply of typewriters, predominantly manual, plenty of paper, pencils, and at least one long working table. The presidential campaign advance man usually provides for at least three television sets, telephone lines, a special Western Union hook up, and adequate refreshments (coffee, soft drinks, beer, sandwiches). This press room is accessible only to accredited reporters with campaign-issued identification. Although the Level B campaign may have lesser requirements, it still should provide for typewriters, telephones, and especially for food, if the reporter will not have time to eat.

The news conference for a presidential candidate enforces limited access strictly. There is a tendency, however, to secure too large a room or, even worse, set up too many chairs. The advance man should review the number of chairs immediately before the news conference to preclude an unsatisfactory television visual. If the room is large (often desirable from a temperature standpoint), the news conference should occupy a corner. The temperature should be no more than 60 degrees, preferably 50-55 degrees to allow for the full effects of television lighting. The presidential advance system also uses a "bridge" microphone—that is, one microphone that connects to all television or radio stations. This prevents interference and makes for a better visual. The candidate uses a three-foot-high riser, and a television platform is placed about 25 feet away. The Level B news conference uses a one-foot-high platform, about 5 by 8 feet, preferably carpeted; or no platform.

Whether or not the campaign uses an official backdrop for the news conference, the area behind the candidate should feature a thick, velour-type, dark colored (preferably blue, never black or white) fabric; it should not be the same color as the candidate's suit. To provide a full television picture, the backdrop should be at least 15 feet high and 15 feet wide. If VIP guests will be present, the advance man should provide chairs for them towards the rear of the room; almost always, the candidate is alone, in front of a podium with microphone. A table is sometimes used to permit radio reporters to place their microphones on the table.

---

[c] Each campaign has its own media accreditation system (presidential requires Secret Service liaison) detailed in the Advance Manual. Also, the local information packets can include a list and map showing nearby restaurants, bars, and their hours.

Exhibit 13-8
Guidelines for Receptions (and Banquets)

1. The advance man must convince the local chairman or host that the success of the reception is not based on the amount of time spent by the candidate, but *how* the time is spent.

2. From the moment the candidate enters to the time of departure, he must circulate continuously, shaking hands and meeting people.

3. The advance man must select two people, preferably the local chairman and the host, who will accompany the candidate during the reception. They must be briefed to (a) stay with the candidate at all times, never leaving his side; (b) move him steadily and prevent any one person from monopolizing his time. One escort is usually insufficient; two are best; three are the limit. The escorts should be prominent and must know most of the guests.

4. Unless agreed otherwise in advance, the reception is assumed open to the news media; hence, anything said is on the record, including the candidate's private comments to guests if overheard by an adjacent reporter. If press will be present, hosts and candidate must be briefed.

5. It is best to avoid picture taking at the reception but to have a separate room in which all photos are taken consecutively, without any delay. If a campaign photographer is at the reception, he takes directions from one person and no one else; the photographer does not order the candidate around. If a separate room is used, the advance man must assign someone to compile a list of guests for picture taking, and they must be ready and on hand.

6. If the reception is held at a private home, the advance man must check parking problems, whether the bar and food will be adequate, and so forth.

7. If the candidate will or may speak, the microphone and sound system must be checked before the reception, and anyone introducing the candidate must be briefed. If the candidate does speak, it should never be in the first half of the reception, but just after the midway point or later, if appropriate (e.g., just before leaving). However, he must be introduced in time to speak and still leave at the scheduled time; this usually means an additional cushion of five minutes after the remarks, to allow for thanking the host, final handshakes, and so forth.

8. If the reception is followed by a banquet at which the candidate will be speaking, the advance man must arrange to end the reception in time to transfer guests to the meal function. This means that the bar must be closed fifteen minutes before the time the reception is to end; lights should flash on and off; if necessary, chimes can sound or hostesses can circulate and invite guests into the ballroom. The goal is to have the reception room empty five minutes before the reception is to end (and dinner to begin).

9. If the ballroom is not adjacent to the reception room, the advance man must estimate how long it will take for that size crowd to clear the reception and move to the ballroom. This calculation will affect what means are used to end the reception.

10. The schedule is also affected by arrangements for collecting tickets. Guests should not have to wait in long lines, and there should be provision for last-minute ticket sales; these activities should be concurrent with, not following, the reception.

11. The banquet room, like the room chosen for the reception, must be just the right size or slightly too small, but never too large (i.e., there must always be a capacity crowd for the sake of appearance). If necessary, there should be increased space between banquet tables, or seating for eight instead of ten per table.

12. A formal entrance for the head table is impressive, but can be time consuming. It should not be done unless it can be executed well *and* guests can be moved very quickly from the reception to banquet room, since the head table cannot be introduced to an empty or half empty room.[a]

13. Ideally, the first course of the meal is a cold item (e.g., salad) and is already on the table (but placed there immediately prior to the dinner's scheduled start); if there is an invocation, the clergyman must be on hand and ready.

14. The advance man must review with the head waiter or maitre d' plans to serve the dinner; if a buffet, the major problem is queues, number of servers, and so forth. If a traditional banquet, he must make and keep a commitment to the maitre d' that the dinner will start on time, then get a return commitment on when serving will be completed.

15. Normally, the advance man arranges for the waiters to depart after dropping off dessert and coffee; dessert and coffee dishes are cleared after the banquet has concluded. In any case, there should be no waiters serving during the candidate's speech or, ideally, during any part of the program (although parts may be expendable).

16. Liquor and wine are not served; if they are, this should not be allowed to interfere with the promised serving time for meal.

17. The advance man must cut the program down to its essentials; if it is still too long, the dull, routine portions (e.g., introductions of head table, volunteer workers, party leaders) should begin during the actual serving of the meal. This method can save as much as sixty minutes if the local chairman or master of ceremonies has planned a lengthy program of multiple introductions and short talks; if these are relegated to the time the meal is served, no time is lost. However, it is preferable to cut the program, rather than allocate part of it to the meal.

18. The master of ceremonies must have the program planned carefully, he must know exactly what to do, and each participant must have a precise and brief time limit; if necessary, the advance man should speak with each person who has any part in the program. It is often helpful for the advance man to remind the master of ceremonies a few minutes before he is supposed to begin the program.

19. If the advance man has done his job, the candidate will depart on time because the reception room was cleared completely five minutes before it was scheduled to end, dinner guests were already seated at the time the dinner was scheduled to begin, serving was prompt, and the program was brief, started on time, and had no surprises.

20. The advance man must provide all of the standard briefing materials, especially relating to receptions or banquets; the briefing should emphasize—if need be, diagram—the head table, with comments on each person, and whether the candidate should acknowledge anyone, and so forth; also, the person introducing the candidate must be briefed.[b]

21. The advance man is responsible for lighting, sound, decorations, and attendance; the fourth item may be a given, but the first three items more easily lend themselves to advance work. The sound system is always checked again just before the banquet; the advance man must always have a communications system arranged with the engineer to raise or lower the sound level when and, if need be, during the candidate's talk. The advance man always checks the temperature of the room and arranges for it to be cool enough to accommodate a large crowd.[c]

22. If the candidate attended the reception for a reasonable amount of time, the advance man's schedule provides for a quick exit, often through a side or rear door. After an evening banquet, the candidate must get to sleep for the next drill.

Note: See the prior discussions on fund-raising events and forum (banquet) events, as well as sections on servicing the media.

[a]Whether or not the head table is introduced in a formal procession, or during the program, there must be an agreed-upon assembly point; a head table chairman or coordinator must gather all participants at this point on time. The head table seating arrangement must reflect etiquette and protocol; someone experienced in head table organization should be in charge. Protocol also applies to the introduction of each head table guest. Whether introduced by the master of ceremonies at the podium or (preferably) by an off-stage (i.e., unseen) announcer, guests are introduced in order of farthest seat first. The introduction always has title first (e.g., "the senior Senator from the State of California, the Honorable Alan Cranston"). Introduc-

Exhibit 13-8 (cont.)

tions are coordinated with spotlighting; head table guests always remain standing when they arrive at their chair. The announcer has a set of index cards with large type and phonetic spellings; at his side is someone with another set of cards who can verify that each card is for the appropriate person. The fail-safe method is for each guest to also have a card and give this card to the unseen announcer just before he is to be announced. The last card includes an ink entry "last card." The honored guest is usually introduced last.

[b]See Exhibits 10-1, 11-4, and 13-1 and Figures 11-1 and 11-2. Also, the advance man usually puts one extra seat at each end of the head table for contingency planning; then, minutes before the dinner, if the seats are not needed, they are removed and the place settings spaced apart, since two settings are removed. Similarly, the head table must be checked just before the banquet to remove or substitute settings for any last minute absentees. Obviously, the candidate's briefing must be updated, usually orally. Sloppy work here results in more than an uninformed candidate; he could refer in his speech to a head table guest who is not present, or forget to acknowledge someone who should have been mentioned.

[c]The sound level is checked by the advance man (or someone else) listening from the rear of the banquet facility; ideally, sound problems are resolved in the program before the candidate begins speaking, although sound level is always adjusted again, if necessary, for the candidate's speech. There should never be more than a moment's delay in making any sound adjustment during the speech. Also, the advance man should insure against distracting noises from other sound systems, Muzak systems, a nearby bar or other facility, or from the kitchen; as pointed out, the waiters should not be working during the candidate's speech.

Crowd Turnout

From the standpoint of providing excitement and stirring enthusiasm to impress reporters and provide a good visual, there must always be a "full house." The advance man always gets a room that is barely adequate—that is, slightly too small for the anticipated crowd. If an outdoor area is planned, it must somehow be roped off in such a way as to exaggerate the size of the crowd. Similarly, the advance man provides for an insufficient number of chairs so that some people will stand or chairs will have to be secured at the last minute. In this way, the press will report a "standing-room-only crowd," or "the turnout was much larger than expected, and volunteers were pressed into service to set up more folding chairs." Whether by means of switching banquet tables of ten to eight or giving free tickets out at the last minute to deserving volunteers, every activity has a *capacity* crowd. It must be emphasized that chairs in front rows or at front tables must be 100 percent occupied for appearance, especially for television cameras. In addition, the advance man usually arranges for younger people and the members of the candidate's youth group to occupy sections that may be photographed or filmed. If last-minute intelligence just before an event indicates an attendance problem, tables or chairs are removed or partitions are inserted.

The advance man always gives local supporters an impossible attendance goal; this goal is translated into specific quotas for geographic areas and chairmen. If they indicate a goal, he insists on itemized proof that it is attainable. He looks for examples of past successes involving the particular local chairman or committee and evaluates the ability of the activists to "deliver" the crowd. The advance man never authorizes any hall or out-door area unless it can be filled to capacity; it is better to set a more modest goal that can be achieved than to fail in the ambitious goal. In other words, 550 people showing up at an auditorium that holds 500 (50 have to stand) is better than 700 showing up in an auditorium that holds 1,000.

The basic crowd-building techniques are mail, telephone, hand delivery, and advertising. Mail should usually be first class, and the lists must be high quality and up to date. The names must be from the campaign or cooperative groups, and they should be supporters or interested in the candidate. The telephone campaign assumes similar standards for the calling lists. Hand delivery includes door-to-door canvassing in neighborhoods and commercial areas—that is, distributing one flyer per house in residential areas and delivering groups of flyers to commercial establishments. Youthful volunteers can hand out flyers in cafeterias, supermarkets, and shopping centers. However, this should only be done with approval; otherwise, volunteers should use parking lots, especially putting flyers on car windshields. Advertising involves posters, newspapers, and radio.

Regardless of the methods employed, the campaign must contact far more people than are required for a capacity crowd. To fill an auditorium that holds 1,000, the campaign may have to have a mailing of 10,000 or 20,000, make 2,000+ telephone calls, and distribute at least 5,000 flyers the day of the meeting. It may also need to charter buses to bring in groups of political supporters from outlying areas. Other techniques include lining up community groups (to participate in some phase of the program), bands, entertainment, and celebrity figures as well as giving away novelties or contest prizes. The advance man cannot overlook the need for the news director and local publicity chairman to coordinate efforts to secure as much pre-event publicity as possible. However, a well attended event can still be played down in the media if a news release or campaign volunteer leader was quoted as predicting a larger turnout than expected. Generally, the campaign does not make crowd predictions.

Mailings and Telephone Campaigns. The advance man must review the quantity and quality of lists used. Events with a paid admission, such as banquets, require quality invitations and are normally mailed thirty days in advance of the event, or earlier. Public meetings or rallies require later mailings, but the labels must be accessible or prepared *in advance* of the mailing date. Properly printed invitations or flyers are useless if they are stored in the campaign headquarters for lack of mailing lists or labels. Free events that have entertainment or do not require a major time commitment from anyone attending can use invitations mailed about a week or even several days prior. However, when dealing with youth groups whose members have transportation problems, or if the event, meeting, or rally is not centrally located or far from the area represented by much of the mailing list, an earlier mailing is required.

The capacity crowd will never be achieved by mail alone. However, a telephone campaign is a major undertaking. Ideally, volunteers should call from a central location so they can be supervised. This can be the campaign or political party headquarters or space donated by an insurance or stock brokerage firm or other commercial operation. The telephoning operation can be costly if banks of telephones must be installed in the headquarters. Another problem is the time element: calls should usually be made no more than a week before the event, the last few days is preferable. This time problem means that a large number of telephones and volunteers is required.

Although volunteers telephoning from their home are superior to nothing, productivity is drastically reduced. It may even be worthwhile arranging auto transportation or chartered buses to centralize all callers. In any case, they require a written and oral briefing. Each worker should have a prompter sheet with the message and should be discouraged from undue conversation. The approach must be quantitative; each caller has a quota of calls, per hour and per day. Whether the local candidate is planning a public meeting or rally for 200, or the statewide candidate a meeting for 400 or 500, there is no substitute for a concerted telephone campaign. Any Level A campaign planning a mass attendance event—airport greeting, hotel rally, large public meeting—requires the type of telephone operation usually reserved either for presidential candidates or for statewide candidates planning one of the campaign's most impressive, capacity-crowd events (Exhibit 13-9).

Advertising. If a candidate is visiting an area only once during the campaign, newspaper ads and radio ads (drive time) can be helpful. Weekly newspaper ads are often relevant, but they require a longer lead time. Any newspaper ad, like the radio ad, should be placed very near the date of activity (assuming admission is free). All advertising should be presentable, but *simple*; it is designed to tell the facts at lowest cost possible. Newspaper ads should be small, but preferably three column width, and well positioned. Radio ads should be short, never over thirty seconds, and preferably ten. The skilled advance man persuades local contributors to underwrite the cost of all crowd-building advertising.

Other advertising methods include distributing posters to be put up in public places, on telephone poles, and on trees (with approval) and using sound trucks, airplanes for skywriting, blimps, or even theater marquees.

Exhibit 13-9
Guidelines for Telephone Campaigns

1. Every telephone campaign is tedious work; but it must be done, with a goal of contacting some multiple of the capacity crowd number.

2. Ideally, this boilerroom operation should have telephones installed that have nonconsecutive, unlisted telephone numbers, to prevent incoming calls from tying up the lines. These telephones should never have the number listed on the inset.

3. Enough telephones should be installed in time for the final push—the week before the event—particularly for constant use of the telephones during the last four days.

4. The text for the telephone message should be taped to the desk. The same message should also be printed in large block letters on a wall sign.

5. The message should be no more than thirty seconds, and the caller should aim to complete each call in less than a minute. A typical message might be: "This is Mary Jones of the San Diego County Smith for Senate Committee. John Smith will be speaking Thursday night at 8:30 in the new convention center, at Main and Eighth streets. The program starts at 7:30, with plenty of free entertainment, including . . . . There is no admission charge, lots of free parking, and you're invited. Hope you can come."

6. The telephone operation should be continuous, even twelve hours per day, although there should be different shift supervisors who oversee operations and monitor progress. If a volunteer works intensively, with a goal of one call per minute, the volunteer should work no more than three hours.

7. The telephone operation must have a goal (e.g., 50,000 calls, 100,000 calls); the goal should be broken down on a daily and hourly basis, and each shift should have a quota. Different volunteer groups or shifts should compete for the highest number of calls.

8. The calling list should cover all supporters and political party activists; however, the list should be so large that it tries to cover as many voters registered in the candidate's political party as possible, subject to geographical constraint.

9. There should be light refreshments for the volunteers, and a good work atmosphere; sound absorbing material or devices for each telephone are helpful.

10. There should be no media coverage of the telephone operation.

Note: Although these procedures are for a Level A campaign, it is imperative that any public campaign event, even for the local campaign, rely on some kind of telephone operation, even if only volunteers calling from their individual homes.

A cheaper advertising method is printing or mimeographing large quantities of handbills. However, this method is only as good as its distribution system. Generally, a minimum of ten times as many handbills as the crowd objective should be distributed, preferably twenty times as many. This means that a goal of 5,000 people requires 50,000 or 100,000 handbills. The lesser figure is acceptable only if other crowd-raising methods are being employed.

Handbills are distributed in two ways. First, the campaign must use large numbers of volunteers, especially young people. Although large shopping areas are preferable, door-to-door distribution is better than nothing. This system must be tightly controlled by distribution captains who *verify* that the handbills and flyers are actually distributed. The second method involves persuading others to distribute the flyers. Besides putting flyers on windshields, in door handles, or in people's shopping bags, the volunteers ask newspaper boys to deliver them with newspapers, supermarket managers to let cashiers or box boys insert a flyer in each grocery market, and any public facility to keep a stock in a reception area or for distribution within the facility. This includes dormitories, sororities, hotels, student unions, service club meeting halls, and large office buildings.

Of course, before all of these crowd-building techniques are employed, someone must decide if it is worth all the money and time. Unlike traditional campaigns, the contemporary campaign does not have to sponsor mass public meetings to get publicity. There are *easier* ways to create visuals. In addition, people are simply more apathetic than in past years, and they don't want to be given flyers or handbills. Supermarket managers and others don't want to cooperate in distribution. The exception is if the candidate is a very popular incumbent; however, in that case, he will probably win the election anyway.

Rally

The Level A campaign does not plan a rally without a specialist who works alongside the advance man. The *rally man* is responsible for crowd raising and most of the specifics of what is called the preprogram—that is, the entertainment and festivities scheduled in advance of the candidate's appearance. In contrast, the advance man's responsibilities are limited to the schedule, transportation, lodging, luggage, physical movement of the candidate, and the basic program (section involving the candidate). Each campaign's Advance Manual further delineates each person's functions; unless specified otherwise, the advance man usually selects the hall or outdoor area and supervises mailings, telephone operations, and advertising. The rally man, usually responsible for the handbills passed out the day before or day of the rally, is sometimes given additional crowd-raising responsibilities normally given the advance man.

Although the intricacies of a major campaign rally are beyond the scope of this book, some fundamental guidelines can be extrapolated to apply to less ambitious efforts or even banquet events (Exhibit 13-10). These details are discussed far more extensively in each presidential campaign's *Rally Manual*.[d]

---

[d] The *Rally Manual* explains the campaign's rally policy and the responsibilities of the rally man, including the campaign's standard operating plan for organizing and promoting rallies. In addition to any chairmen or committees appointed by the advance man (e.g., publicity, invitations, transportation, lodging), the rally man will need committees or task forces on entertainment, promotion, and decorations, as well as another committee for balloons and confetti. The manual should provide detailed instructions on use of balloons, confetti, decorations, signs, banners, bunting, and volunteer groups. The rally man makes no contacts without checking with the advance man; also, both must review the entire physical layout, with emphasis on the candidate's route and movements.

Exhibit 13-10
Selected Rally Guidelines

1. Regardless of how effective the advance man and rally man are in getting word of the rally to the masses, most of the audience will already be committed to the candidate. Therefore, the rally has two purposes. First, it must excite the crowd and make volunteers even more enthusiastic so they will work harder for the candidate. Second, it must provide an excellent visual for television coverage.

2. The total workload must be divided into components—entertainment, decorations, balloons, bands, handbills, posters, signs and banners, and so forth—and a key volunteer appointed to be responsible for each component. The rally man and anyone else in charge must do more than supervise in order to motivate volunteers.

3. Major rallies require huge backdrops, either in blue or red, white, and blue; cloth bunting, not crepe paper, should be used. The area behind the candidate should be secured to prevent anyone from walking through a picture. There should also be space for back lighting. Television-oriented rallies require a television specialist to assure proper back light (usually 4-5 feet in back and shining down from above to reduce shadows and to light shoulders and hair). Lighting should be 3200 Kelvin color temperature lights; there should be proper quartz lighting in front of the candidate.

4. The news media should have an adequate, secure area, with provision for a television platform, usually 3 to 3½ feet high, provided by the station. The public address system should provide a bridge into which all television and radio can connect for sound (to avoid multiple microphones at the podium).

5. In working with any sound engineer or when retaining a company, especially for major public meetings or political rallies, always check for references and how long the firm has been in business, with particular emphasis on the personnel assigned to the rally. There must be more than one person handling sound for the major rally, a backup system, and provisions for changing the audio level during the event.

6. The microphone should be directional (to avoid any background noise); even so, there should be no speakers behind the candidate or microphone. The height of the microphone must always be at the candidate's optimum, or adjusted for him before he begins speaking.

7. The sound engineer must make certain the amplifying system is of sufficient wattage (usually 100 watts in a single system or several systems added together; however, the large gathering or an outdoor event will require much more wattage). There should be alternate inputs from the microphone to the amplifying system, in case of failure.

8. Besides the microphone and amplification system, the sound operation has a third element, the speakers. Speakers do *not* face the candidate. The proper place for speakers, at virtually any event, is in some kind of elevated position (often overhanging) in front of the candidate and facing forward. There is usually one speaker at each side of the candidate—but they are usually not close to the candidate—and they are quite far apart, at practically opposite ends of the room, stage or area. If these speakers are inadequate, additional speakers are placed into the crowd (e.g., at the midway point of the auditorium or outdoor gathering); however, these speakers *must* face away from the candidate. Generally, avoid any speaker that *faces* in any direction other than that of the candidate when he looks straight ahead.

9. Major sound problems relate either to the microphone, amplification system, or speakers. The microphone problem is easy to solve: it should be directional, placed at the proper height for the candidate, securely fastened, and the candidate should not speak too close into it or touch it. The amplification system should use major equipment (Altec, Collins, McIntoch, RCA, and so forth); it should be compatible with a low impedance type (50/250 ohms) microphone. There *must* be provision in any gathering to adjust amplification, preferably from some control point away from the candidate. During the talk, the advance man, rally man, or other designated staff member always circulates near the rear of the hall or outdoor area to see whether amplification is adequate and uses prearranged signals

Exhibit 13-10 (cont.)

or a communications system to alert the sound engineer. As for the speakers, two important points are that they are always in front of the candidate and always face forward (not backwards or sideways); the general guideline is six paging horn type speakers for the first 40,000 square feet, and one for each additional 10,000 square feet.

10. Sound systems are always checked before the rally or any speaking commitment, including a final check just before the candidate goes on. The check also includes inspection of microphone lines and other cables, which should be placed beyond reach; similarly, speakers should be beyond reach. Although most major hotels have good sound systems, nothing must be taken for granted; there must be a trial run that includes the facility's sound engineer, who must be on duty during the event.

11. Balloons, especially those printed with the candidate's message, can add excitement to the rally. Do not use balloons unless enough are used to make a solid impression (at least 250); if the rally exceeds 2,000 people, try for 400-500 balloons; the goal might be for the number of balloons to equal 10 percent of the crowd.

12. Balloons require helium tanks; always buy extra helium in case of miscalculation. Check with local vendors to determine amount needed (varies from about fifty 40-inch balloons per 250 cubic foot tank to 400 11-inch balloons for the same size tank). Valve adapters with squeeze or pressure triggers are preferable to the slower faucet handles; always have extra valve adapters. There must be some kind of distribution system for balloons and confetti.[a]

13. Any large political campaign meeting should use the candidate's female supporters, either in custom costumes, or variations of red, white, and blue, with distinctive hats. Teenagers and older women can be separated into different groups with varied names and specific functions at the event (ushers, escorts for the candidate, ticket takers, and so forth).

14. Unless the candidate is on stage waiting to be introduced (not the case with an active preprogram of entertainment, bands, cheerleading), he enters on established cue, either from directly behind the stage (through a curtain) or a walk-on from either side of the stage. In either case, television cameras are alerted to the area and timing of walk on. The most effective walk-on is the long entrance from the opposite end of the auditorium or outdoor area. This should only be done as part of a plan, rather than necessity arising from poor planning. It requires a narrow, secure aisle and an enthusiastic, dense crowd to create the most effective visual. Also, the candidate's advance man or traveling tour director should not be immediately in front of him to obscure photographs and films of him. The band, cheerleaders, balloon drop and confetti managers, and so forth are all alerted just before the candidate's entrance to achieve optimum coordination.

Note: Because space limitations prevent more detailed discussion, this very limited sampling of rally guidelines has been included to show applicability to banquets and other campaign events, including "mini rallies" that use placards, balloons, confetti, sound trucks, bands, female supporters in colorful costumes, and other attention-getting devices for walking tours or to support the candidate's appearance before a group or conference.

[a]Balloons can be attached to chairs, pillars, railings, almost anything. Clusters can be taped to walls, or affixed together as "balloon trees" and anchored. If balloons are used near bunting, the bunting should be extra large. The rally man is proficient at balloon drops, which use nets to release balloons and confetti from above, and balloon releases, which use boxes to release balloons and confetti from below. Balloons and confetti are always released on cue (preceding any authentic spontaneity) and in a limited area selected to involve the candidate and crowd in photographs and television filming.

Index

Index

108; opening of, 95-96; opportunistic, 88; participants in, 97; planned, 88; preparation and briefing for, 89-92, 105-106; procedure and protocol at, 95-101; questions and answers in, 54-55, 90-92; rationale for, 88-89, 104-105, 122-123; scheduling of, 99-101, 107-108; statement for, 89-92; tips for, 102; visual, 87, 102-109, 122

News director (media director, press secretary, spokesperson), 50-51, 113; and bias, 52-53; guidelines for, 51-52, 54-55; in levels of campaigning, 7, 9-10; and media personnel, 53-61; policy of, 50-62; scheduling and, 181, 218. *See also* News conference; News function, administering; News release; Servicing news media

News function, administering, 113-137; audio-video delivery systems, 134-135; delivery systems, 128-137; election night, 126-128; hand delivery, 135-136; introductory or editorial board meeting, 115-117; liaison, 117-122; liaison with adjunct committees, 121; liaison with candidate, 118; liaison with local committees, 121-122; liaison with other divisions, 120-121; liaison with research, 119-120; liaison with scheduling, 118-119; mailings, 132-133; media and mailing lists, 128-130; media information kit, 130-131; meeting media, 114-117; monitoring media coverage, 125-126, 127(exhibit); reaction statement, 137; structure and tasks, 113-128; television and radio appearances, 125-126, 127 (exhibit) traveling media, 136-137; wire and news services, 117. *See also* Servicing news media

News media (journalists, reporters), 53-61; advance man and, 229-230, 256-257; bias of, 52-53; versus campaign, 51-53; daily newspapers, 24-25, 56-57; magazines, 30-31, 60-61; meetings with, 114-117; policy toward, 50-53; radio stations, 27-29, 58-59; servicing of, 39-62; television stations, 29-30; weekly newspapers, 24-25, 56-57. *See also* Media; News conference; News release; Servicing news media

Newspapers, daily, 25-27, 57-58, 61, 65-66, 140-142

Newspapers, weekly, 24-25, 67, 140-142

News peg, 90

News release, 63-86; advisory or background, 66-67; contact person for, 68-70; dated, 65-66, 133; dateline for, 70-72; delivery systems for, 128-137; format and style of, 63-75; hand delivery of, 135-136; headline for, 70-72; instructions for, 65-66; instructions, additional, for, 67; instructions, special, for, 67; inverted pyramid in, 75; lead for, 74-75; mailing of, 132-133; opportunistic, 76-77; planned, 76-77; preparation of, 70-75; queries on, 69-70; for radio stations, 58-59, 63; sample, 71; schedule, 65; stationery for, 64-65; structure and appearance of, 64-70; style of, 73-75; telephone queries on, 68-70; text of, 72-73; timed, 66; types of, 75-86; for weekly newspapers, 56-57

News releases, types of: advisory, 110; campaign materials, 81-82; events, 77-80; form, 82; futures (hold) file for, 75-76; incumbent, 80; issues, 78; negative, 80-81; news conference, 93; opportunistic, 76-77; other, 80-82; photo caption, 81; planned, 76-77; reaction, 80; schedule, 65, 82-86; speeches, 77-78; support, 78-80

News services, 26, 61, 99, 117

Off-the-record statement, 62

On-the-record statement, 61-62, 116

Orchestration of news media strategy, 39-44; major stories for, 43-44; pacing of, 40-42; phases of, 42-43; with surrogates, 44

Outdoor advertising, 34-36

Pacing of news media strategy, 40-42

Persuasion strategy, 169, 170, 171-172

Phases of news media strategy, 42-43

Photo caption (release), 81

Press release. *See* News release

Press secretary. *See* News director

Printed matter, 32-33

Print media. *See* Magazines; Newspapers, daily; Newspapers, weekly

Private time (scheduling), 197, 198

Questions and answers, 51, 54-55, 88, 90-92, 101-102, 103

Radio (stations): advertising on, 142-143; appearances on, 125-126; audio releases and systems for, 63, 67, 69, 115, 134-135; ethnic, 32; news and advertising on, 27-29; personnel at, 58-59

About the Author

Arnold Steinberg has been active in politics, public affairs, and journalism since 1963. He has been a volunteer, staff member, and consultant in organizational politics and political campaigns throughout the nation, and is the author of *Political Campaign Management: A Systems Approach*. Once described by the *Los Angeles Times* as a political press relations "wunderkind," Mr. Steinberg has conducted seminars in press relations, advertising, scheduling, advance work, demographics, survey research, political strategy, and overall campaign management. He has served on the board of several foundations and directed the Charles Edison Memorial Youth Fund's Journalism Conferences. His articles have appeared in *The Alternative, Dialogue* (U.S. Information Agency international magazine), *Human Events, Indianapolis News, Insight and Outlook, National Review, The New Guard, Santa Ana Register, Twin Circle*, and the *UCLA Daily Bruin*. He has also contributed articles to the *Los Angeles Herald Examiner, Newsweek* and the *Washington Post*. A former political aide to Sen. James L. Buckley (Cons.-R., N.Y.), 1971-1973, Mr. Steinberg attended U.C.L.A. before receiving the B.A. in public affairs and economics from The George Washington University and the M.B.A. from Pepperdine University. Mr. Steinberg is also an honor graduate of the Defense Information School.